THE MOTHER VINE

THE MOTHER VINE

How I Healed My Heart With Ayahuasca

SHANNON NERING

SHE WRITES PRESS

Published in 2026 by
She Writes Press, an imprint of The Stable Book Group

32 Court Street, Suite 2109
Brooklyn, NY 11201
https://shewritespress.com
Library of Congress Control Number: 2025920902
ISBN: 979-8-89636-124-4
eISBN: 979-8-89636-125-1

Interior Designer: Andrea Reider

Printed in the United States

Names and identifying characteristics have been changed to protect the privacy of certain individuals.

Dedication

For my mother, whose grace shaped my path,
and my father, whose sudden departure carved my depth.
This book is made of both your love.

Author's Note & Disclaimer

This is a work of nonfiction, a memoir drawn from my lived experiences, shaped by memory, emotion, and time. The events described are true to the best of my recollection. While some names and identifying details have been changed to respect privacy, the heart of each story remains intact.

Where necessary, I have reconstructed dialogue and taken limited creative license to convey emotional truth and narrative flow. In a few instances, timelines may be adjusted or characters may reflect a composite of individuals. These decisions were made to serve clarity—not to distort or dramatize the essence of what occurred.

Nothing essential has been altered. The core events, especially those central to my transformation, have been presented as faithfully as memory and documentation allow.

This book is offered in the spirit of honesty, healing, and service.

In Regard to Plant Medicine

This book contains descriptions of my personal experiences with ayahuasca and other sacred plant medicines. These accounts are offered as part of my healing journey—not as medical advice or universal recommendation.

Plant medicine is not for everyone. It requires deep discernment, physical and psychological preparation, and above all, the right set and setting. I am not advocating the casual or recreational use of any entheogenic substance. These are powerful, ancient medicines that must be approached with humility, clear intention, and guidance from qualified, ethical facilitators.

It is important to distinguish ayahuasca from what many in the West would call a hallucinogen. Ayahuasca is not used to "get high." To do so would be a misunderstanding—even a desecration—of its sacred role in healing, spiritual alignment, and ancestral wisdom. It is an *entheogen*, meaning "generating the divine within." When used properly, it is not escapism—it is revelation.

Regarding what some say are so-called "demons" that can appear in plant medicine ceremonies: what I've come to understand is that the shadows we meet are our own unprocessed pain, ancestral imprints or distorted energies we've carried unknowingly. Ayahuasca is not summoning darkness—it's illuminating it. And when held in a safe and reverent space, what rises can be transmuted.

What I share here is not a prescription but a path that helped me remember who I am. If it inspires curiosity, let it also inspire responsibility. And always, seek truth over trend, healing over spectacle, and the wisdom of the plants over the ego of the seeker.

With love,
Shannon

PART 1

CHAPTER 1

What do you do when your crazy-busy supposedly perfect life isn't enough because it's too much?

a) Quit your TV career of twenty years.
b) Move to a remote island in the Pacific.
c) Take an ayahuasca plant medicine journey.
d) All of the above.

CHAPTER 1.1

Ayahuasca Journey

September 2021

Ayahuasca is the name of a spirit who resides in the ayahuasca vine. The Indigenous ayahuasqueros of the Peruvian Amazon call her Abuela Ayahuasca. She is said to be a sentient mother spirit of nature who provides teaching, guidance, and healing to people who ingest this archaic plant mixture.[1]

His hair was trimmed short around a face as dimpled and round as the moon. Tiny sweat beads collected on his forehead. Every few seconds he'd swipe at it as though swatting a fly. To no avail, the dewy jungle air just kept swirling through the tent, encasing all in her reach.

I should've been used to it. Humidity. Heat. Being moist in all the places. Instead, as I sat before this mystical little man, my lungs felt like two wet sponges trapped in my chest. Each breath laden with copious water molecules, pollens, and God only knew what else, as though rain might materialize without a cloud in sight, right there, over my head, like Bad Luck

---

[1] *Grandmother Ayahuasca* by Christian Funder © 2021. Reprinted by permission of Inner Traditions International and Bear & Company. www.Innertraditions.com

Schleprock. Which made me think of my childhood glued to a TV set watching Saturday morning cartoons, which made me think of my kids glued to a different kind of screen, one with a mindless video game unfolding, first-person shooter style, probably right this very minute.

"Focus," I instructed my brain, wondering if the medicine man could read my mind. He was a world-renowned shaman, perched in front of me like a Buddha statue.

Who'da thunk, this guy and me? I mused.

His legs were folded neatly beneath him, knees nearly touching mine, as though we were old pals chitchatting on an oversize sheepskin rug. Only we sat muted by the sounds of a nearby brook that bubbled and gurgled over rocks and root. A few months prior, it had been a mighty river when the island was hit with a tropical monsoon.

This was a sacred spot tucked off the coast of one of the oldest islands in the Hawaiian archipelago, under the flank of a lone ridge of mountains. The center peak had a dark triangular face shaped like a gorilla. It cast a long shadow over the valley, as the sun blazed its final golden rays on this late September day.

The shaman didn't speak any English, which had me wondering what would be lost in translation. There was so much he needed to know if I was to come out the other side healed. I tried to play it cool, but it felt like my first day of school. Moreover, my spine hated this position, crisscross applesauce. I shifted quietly side to side in an attempt to straighten my scoliosis curve, bowed from a vicious trampoline accident too many years ago.

This was serious business, an ayahuasca retreat. Anything could happen. I'd heard of journeys to other dimensions, visits from interstellar beings . . . Instead of preparing my thoughts to explain my intention and myriad little problems, I wondered whether I'd make it out alive.

"So, Shannon, what are you here to fix?" Steven, the shaman's apprentice, asked in good, clear English.

Um, everything? I thought but did not say out loud, like I could sum up all the broken pieces of five decades on the planet in a minute or two.

Steven was a larger-than-life, forty-something Luke Skywalker type, steeped in the ways of the ayahuascero jedis. As a plant medicine facilitator, his job was to translate and guide us through the evening, along with his partner Sarah and a crew of three middle-aged men with kind smiles. Steven didn't so much have a kind smile. He was all business with his white linens, considerable height, and Dave Navarro swagger.

Will he cuddle me if I barf? Gah, he makes me nervous.

"Tell us why you're here." Steven leaned in. "What's troubling you?"

"Um—"

Poof! I suddenly had nothing. *Where'd it go? My problems? I mean, two working arms, two legs, a house, a family, I'm fortunate, right?*

Around me were people with real trauma, abused, molested, perhaps beaten by supposed loved ones or mired in heavy-duty addictions. What business did I have with a Peruvian maestro of the Shipibo tribe? I had my health, a good critical-thinking brain, a good husband, two healthy boys, an adorable dog, raised by sane parents in a once sane Canada.

The shaman hunched and gripped his ankles, rocking back and forth slowly, looking at me, then Steven, then his feet, then me, then Steven, and his feet again.

He's onto me. I inhaled deeply, sinking into that familiar feeling of not belonging. *No really, I've got tons to fix. Tons!*

In a hushed tone, I began, "Well, I'm impatient. Super speedy. I have chronic back pain, sometimes limping when it flares. Lately, I'm unsure about everything, live here, live there—I don't know where I should be, or what I should do. I feel a little lost."

Good luck unpacking that one, boys, I said to myself, replaying my last four years spinning about career-less, country-less, direction-less for the first time in my life.

"Old stuff too, like the accident when I was ten. I wasn't supported. None of us were. We never talked about it. Not my mom, my brothers, my sisters, no one. No therapy. Not sure I ever healed—" *Seriously, not over that yet?*

The shaman nodded as Steven translated. I continued.

"I broke my back when I was eighteen. It was terrifying. But I powered through. Like I do. No time to feel sorry. Then I mangled my foot a few years later. Now I have a lot of pain on my right side. It never goes away." I frowned as I listened to Steven translate, thinking they must be dying of boredom, or skipping over bits, or talking about what they had for lunch.

Step it up, woman! You were a TV producer for God's sake, give them a story!

"My family, my boys, they fight. We were better for a time, but once again we need work. There's too much yelling, especially me and my eldest. I don't know what I'm doing wrong? And the sibling rivalry, fistfights, on the floor, then Josh and I step in to fix it and we fight, *then* it gets ugly. Tempers run on my husband's side and my dad's side. My European ancestors had a tough go. Maybe I was a slave in a former life?" I smirked.

Where in hell am I going with this?

"No Egyptian princess for me. Will we see that tonight—past lives? I'm not sure what I believe. Reincarnation? Heaven? It kind of scares me. I was raised Christian. I believe in God.

I just don't *know* God." I frowned. "But I'm all about justice, helping the little guy. I can barely kill a cockroach. My great-grandpa's last name meant king in Hungarian—" It all rolled out in a jumble of nerves, giggles, and self-consciousness. "My mom thinks we might be from royalty; she's proud that way." *Jesus, Shannon!*

Steven continued in Spanish, undeterred.

I took a deep breath, attempting to slow down. "A few years ago, I left my career of twenty-five years. Now, I'm rudderless." I smiled sadly. "I just want to heal—to find my true purpose. I'm middle-aged now. Yuck, that word. Do I get a second chance? . . .Yeah, that's it."

The shaman didn't move. He was silent.

Is he bored? Duh, yes. My problems are dumb.

Steven grabbed the jar on the tray beside us and poured the cocoa-brown elixir into a shot glass like it was liquid gold. It may well have been. One night at a plant medicine retreat cost $350.

Come on, is that enough? I thought, abruptly changing gears. *I'm here to finally try this bizarre hallucinogenic tea. More, please.* God help me if I didn't get my money's worth. *Oh yeah, money stuff, I should have mentioned that too—*

As though reading my thoughts, Steven tipped the jar a second time for another splash of the brown goo, then held the glass before me, his elbow resting on his knees as he peered through enviably thick black lashes.

Am I special? God, how I wanted them to like me. *I know, we all are. But maybe I really am? Will the ayahuasca show me that? Never mind, I'll find out soon enough.*

With a serious smile, I placed my hands in namaskar and nodded like I was some prize yogini from Katmandu. "Cheers." I tipped the cup to my mouth.

It tasted like barbeque sauce, dirt, burnt coffee, and something else, vomit. I prayed I wouldn't puke then tiptoed on the grass back to my lone mat alongside the other lone mats that housed bodies of all shapes, ages, and afflictions, under this one great big open-air tent.

Officially, I was an ayahuasca tea virgin. Though I had tried a heart-opening plant empathogen once, and mushrooms mixed with a small amount of ayahuasca in a pretty little chocolate another time, it was profound but not scary. I was told both those experiences were a walk in the park next to this. This would be like climbing Everest. Powerful and life-altering, she was the mother of entheogens, traditionally brewed by the Shipibo tribe of the Amazon as they'd done it for a thousand years or more. I told myself I was ready—

Let's break old Shannon and her stupid patterns! I'm a grown woman now, fifty years old. Time to get real. Time for a rebirth.

That's it. That's what I wanted. That and maybe God?

No, for sure, God.

CHAPTER 1.2

Rainbows

September 2017 - 4 years earlier

Up. Down. Arrived. Three words that had come to sum up my life. The creed of the adventurer. The warrior who answers the call. The super mom who does it all. Not a bad thing, I supposed, my Tilt-a-Whirl life. Better than a boring old Ferris wheel.

"Mom," Tyde said, rubbing his sweet blue twelve-year-old eyes as the plane's wheels hit the runway with a jolt, "will we like it?"

"Of course," I replied with too much flare, making up for something I did not yet know. "Look at us—as of this moment, we live in Hawaii. Who gets this?"

My mother always said mediocrity was a curse. God forbid I ended up ordinary, doing ordinary things. Not sure moving overseas counted, but it certainly felt unordinary. And it went with my *try anything once* mantra. Given I'd just spent the last twelve years in the same place, it was time for something new, something big.

"Mom, this better be the last airport today." Tyde placed his hand on mine as we taxied toward the terminal at Lihue International, arriving to a place as extraordinary as the end of a rainbow, the most northern and oldest of the Hawaiian island chain, Kauai.

Harsh pot-lights glared through the cabin. Except for the yellow runway lamps, it was pitch-black outside. We'd been traveling since sunrise all the way from Canada. I squished my nose against the thick oval window to push past my reflection. Raindrops drizzled like tiny glass beads as the wind blew them sideways instead of down.

My stomach gurgled, reminding me that somewhere in the bottom of my purse sat two partially eaten, mostly flattened, cheddar-bacon egg bites I'd purchased from SFO at noon. It was now nine o'clock. I always ate all my food. I was a completer. I liked new things and I finished old things. But, for the last few weeks, nothing felt finished and very little was going down: not food, not drink, not the packing, the culling, the boxes, the containers, the customs brokers, the loose ends, or the goodbyes—especially not the goodbyes.

I exhaled with force and rubbed Tyde's fluffy blond head. "Yup, sweetie, we're here."

"Our fourth airport," he said with an edge, lugging his backpack to his lap and collecting his things from the seat back pocket, always organized. "Vancouver," he began, counting on his fingers the cities we'd just been, "San Francisco, Honolulu, and Kauai."

"Sorry for the milk run." I squeezed his hand, wondering why Josh and I could never spring for a direct flight.

Josh was fast asleep with his mouth agape like a wild animal. His five-o'clock shadow so overdue, it was practically a carpet over his handsome features. Nine-year-old Canyen drooped like a rag doll across his lap, lips pressed together like billowy pink pillows. So precious these boys, these faces. I rubbed Canyen's silky cheeks, wanting to make sure he was real, that this was really happening.

"Come on, sleepyhead, we're here, our new *home*."

Canyen moaned while Josh lifted an arm to wipe the drool.

How I loved our meager unit, so vulnerable in the quiet, braving our way into the unknown.

"Aloooooooha!" boomed over the airplane speakers. "Welcome to—"

"*Fantasy Island*," I finished, picturing Tattoo running up the bell tower with his finger in the air, *Da plane, da plane!*

Every Saturday of my childhood, I'd stay up late to watch the spooky TV fantasy series. No clue that I'd one day live on the mystical isle that made Mr. Roarke and Tattoo famous. Hawaiian kahunas claimed that somewhere on this primordial lava rock was a portal where souls entered our earthly plane. On the other end was a gateway to the afterlife, where souls departed into the light, or dark, I supposed, depending on their choices.

Meanwhile, this would be the third time my soul had entered Kauai. Fourth, if I counted the time I arrived for an afternoon. Each time a tourist, except today. Today was not a vacation. Today was momentous. The air shared that sentiment: clouds cloaked a sullen gray, airport lights stout with the glint of a copper moon.

"Fantasies rarely play out as you or I might expect," I heard Mr. Roarke announce to his guests from 1979, "but they always play out exactly as they should."

A shiver streaked down my vertebrae as I wondered what strange twist my fantasy might entail. *Will I become a mermaid? Will we be hunted by billionaires? Get swallowed by a whale? Tossed into molten lava? Will we traverse time?*

It had all been so big. Herculean. Down the coast, across the border, over the sea, from the mountains of western Canada to the center of the Pacific and the most isolated archipelago on the planet. First, a sudden announcement, then an abrupt departure from everyone and thing I held most dear: my mom, siblings, friends, my career, my home, and a seemingly perfect life checking off boxes. Josh and I uprooting all that we'd spent fifteen years of marriage building. Poof! Gone the moment we loaded that plane.

In exchange: a simpler, more peaceful existence. And weirdly—for me—a new career, a more fulfilling one, as a holistic nutritionist in paradise. Yup, just like that, from big-city career girl to country farm girl, I planned to magically acquire a booming health consultancy in a tropical outback, a land where sane people go to suntan and drink piña coladas.

"Mom, can you carry this?" Canyen handed me his backpack heavy with toys, snacks, pajamas, and underwear, everything he needed for twenty-four hours of travel and sleep. I lobbed it over my purse that had already sliced a thin groove in my shoulder, then yanked at my carry-on as it rolled unhappily on the jet bridge, daring to split at the seams.

Large gray moths greeted us, fluttering through the breezy open corridors of Kauai's lone airport, while the clay-colored tile floor unfolded beneath us like the hallways of a medieval temple. No one spoke. There was only the sound of runners squelching against stone and music streaming dewily through the speakers from a bygone era, the Iz and Don Ho.

Whoever said we couldn't time travel? We had raced in a jumbo jet at the speed of sound over an ocean to land in a place as foreign as the moon. That's what my first trip felt like, at age fourteen, all the way to Waikiki with my family, my first time on a plane. When we disembarked, I stood in shock: the flowers, the air, the sky, precocious life budding at every turn, through a crack in the cement, up a wall, on a rock. We were still on the tarmac! And the smell! I was hit with a plume of gardenia so potent, so silky, it was like being swaddled in cashmere, like Heaven and Earth had a baby and her name was Hawaii. The best part? I felt ever so strangely at home. But, Kauai, here, this time, now . . .

"You good?" Josh looked at me encouragingly as we crossed the doors into baggage claim.

"Yeah." I gave him a smile, hoping he might not notice the hollow behind it. "Just tired."

Before that trip to Oahu in grade 9, I'd never really traveled outside my home province, except a ridiculously long road trip to Tijuana with my mom and dad and siblings. How my parents thought that was a good idea? Five weeks sleeping and cooking in a Chevy Super Van with four kids age five to twelve—rest stops, campouts, visits to every national park and natural wonder, and Vegas to cap it off—was crazy making.

Never again, my parents swore. After that debacle, travel was relegated to a nearby camping spot or a visit to Edmonton to see relatives. It was then I knew that television had to satisfy my wanderlust. That big gray mystery box in the middle of the living room was my part-time babysitter and comfort.

A typical Saturday night, I'd go to Grandma and Grandpa's house. They were like a second set of parents; by the back alley, they lived practically next door. Grandma would cook my favorite dinner: spaghetti with cheese, onions, and tomatoes, then brownies or no-bake cactus cookies. I'd lick the bowl, ice the brownies, then sneak as many as possible throughout the night. Meanwhile my belly grew round and I pretended not to care. Mom would've sent me to fat camp, but Saturday night meant she and Dad were out playing in their band, so I pigged out. By eight o'clock, Grandpa would settle into his big green mohair chair to watch *Hockey Night in Canada*; two hours later, I'd give him the heave-ho just in time for *The Love Boat* and *Fantasy Island.* Nothing would stand between me and my favorite night of television.

This ritual set the stage for my career. When I grew up, I was going to be Wonder Woman or Diane Sawyer, or one of Charlie's Angels. My mom, on the other hand, never watched TV. She worked: teaching school, directing musicals, lessons on top of more lessons, playing the piano ad infinitum, plus weekends on the town with her band and a hall of adoring strangers. Hence my obsession: Marcia Brady got me.

"Where'd Canyen go?" I spun around to Josh while swiping the stray hairs that had blown onto my freshly applied lip balm and sweaty cheeks, now juggling the food bag, two more carry-ons, Josh's water bottle, everything of Canyen's, and a pile of Vancouver rain jackets.

"Don't know." Josh whipped another bag off the carousel like it was a ball of fluff.

What is he, Thor?

"This air is so invigorating!" Josh stood, puffing his chest.

"I can see that," I said, mustering enthusiasm. *Amazing, my crotch has a sweat ring.*

Sixteen years of marriage and, for better or worse, Josh still surprised me. How on earth was he still moving like that? He'd loaded almost our entire forty-foot shipping container in two days and was still at it, still hoofing like a farm-grade oxen. Work was our life and life our work, and it was a scarily familiar place. Kauai promised less of that incalculable spin. Maybe we'd break the pattern of who knows how many generations of workaholics.

"Mom," Canyen's voice mewed like a kitten. He was folding paper airplanes on the dusty floor. "I'm here."

"I'm hungry!" Tyde pleaded, rubbing his stomach. "Can I get a hamburger with bacon?" Twelve years old and sprouting like a tall blond weed.

"Me too!" Canyen's eyes widened.

"We'll see." I kneeled beside Canyen, who, unlike Tyde, didn't seem to grow or change.

Canyen was our Benjamin Button. Though he wasn't anywhere near bald, with wavy brownish-blond locks that curled around his chin and made strangers ask, "Is he a girl?" My reaction was usually a horrified, "I would not dress a girl like that!" Canyen was most often disheveled in sweats with his T-shirt stretched out at the neckline from sucking on it or pulling it over his face, sleeves coated in whatever he'd had for lunch.

"Watch this." Canyen ran his fingers along the center crease, then sent an origami aircraft for the rafters. The four of us watched it swoop and alley-oop, then fall to hit the old man in the flowered shirt. The man laughed, unfettered, and handed it back to Canyen.

"Sweetie, wait until we get outside." I placed an arm around him. "People spend good money on these tourist pamphlets, not for you to fold them into the Nakamura Lock."

"You remember that one?" Tyde asked. "That was my favorite."

"I do," I said, recalling the hundreds of times I'd folded airplanes on the carpet of my boys' bedroom that housed all the things they loved, including a mini bouldering wall that Josh had installed and giant colorful blocks that made for cheerful days of tumbling hijinks and way too many good times to count.

"You okay, Mommy?" Canyen looked up at me with sincere hazel eyes framed by the most perfect set of brows. "You look sad."

One moment, in fact, just yesterday, my boys had been playing with friends in the only home they'd ever known. The next, life as they knew it had vanished, for seemingly no good reason, at least not to a child. They'd no clue the feat their dad and I had just pulled off. They'd no clue what we'd just left behind or what we were arriving to. They'd no clue life would never be the same. And instead of getting the chance to grow out of it, they'd been yanked. Which made me question—*Do they understand that we're not going back, that we've moved? And did we do it for them or did we do it for us, and why?*

"I'm good." I shook my head as though erasing the thought, then began anxiously counting the bags Josh had piled beside him from the roller belt. "Eight, nine . . ."

Twelve. We needed twelve in all or I'd burst a pipe, or an artery, or my cranium. Those twelve suitcases housed all our most precious things: the title to our new property, a stovetop espresso maker, Uno cards, my favorite summer clothing, my greens powder and vitamins, tax files and important paperwork, my most special jewelry (including an ornate pink sapphire ring from Josh's mother), my laptop that contained every document written since Gutenberg (and not backed up since then either), homemade marmalade fresh from a neighbor, and a photo album from our goodbye party loaded with memories of our Canadian seaside community and friends. I cared more about this particular suitcase than our entire forty-foot shipping container full of everything else, parked somewhere in the Port of Seattle at that moment.

A message dinged from my phone as we stood silent in the chalky mist of Lihue's pocket-sized airport waiting for our ride. It was one of my besties. She left the longest texts ever:

> *Hey Beauty, hope you had a safe flight. We miss you guys already. This will crack you up. I drove to your house tonight by accident to pick up Finn, thinking he was at your house with Canyen. I sat there waiting ten minutes until I realized—YOU'RE GONE! Your whole frickin family! I'm going to start crying all over again. I can't believe you guys moved! I don't think Finn or I will ever get over your boys not living up the street anymore. I'm a blubbering mess. What will we do without you? Love you, dear friend. Call me once you're settled. XOXO*

Tears welled up in my eyes like an over-poured glass of water bursting from the rim. No turning back now. My old life, and the people I had held so dear, had just exited out of that crazy Kauai portal with the rest of the transitioning souls.

CHAPTER 1.3

1969–1979

"Look, Jim, a mermaid," my mom said, turning to my dad with a broad smile.

It was my very first bath since the womb.

"Jesus, she's a fish!" Dad wiped a splash from his cheek.

From the day I slid out of my mother, almost onto the floor of a taxicab, she saw it: raw pink flesh swimming in a puddle of amniotic fluid—*Hello, world!*—nearly ecstatic, half human, half fish.

So, it made sense that I joyfully thrashed and cooed and dunked my head in the water as though there was no other place for me to be: below the surface, deep where things are still, safe in a fluid cocoon. My three older siblings weren't so much like that, preferring terra firma.

It was weird to be a water girl growing up in the arid prairie of Southern Alberta, surrounded by mustard and golden wheat fields, grassland as far as the eye could see. Tall blades marching to the horizon, softening, curving, rising, and falling like waves on the wind. Everywhere prickly cacti would spring from mounds of dry earth in the hills behind our home. My brother Troy and I would dart around the spiky land mines in a chase, then stop to bravely pry small berries from the thorns.

But I was inexplicably drawn to water. Mom expected I'd be an Olympic swimmer. I only wanted to be a mermaid. By age ten, I was a legend at the local pool, setting a record eight-in-a-row forward somersaults without a breath, bathing suit firmly up butt crack. Nose plugs had proven revolutionary, and with it, my underwater acrobatics game skyrocketed to the next level.

I'd dive and spin through the legs of friends as they formed an upside-down row of V's. Thrusting my limbs like one long fin, eyes open and stinging from chlorine. *Should mermaids feel their eyeballs burn, blood vessels swollen red like a sea monster?* Then emerge triumphant, gasping and giggling at the sight of my best friend's sun-kissed face, proud of our prowess.

At age three and a half, Mom said I scared the hell out of her by clamoring up the steps of the high-diving board. "Twenty feet up in the air, Shanni, I swear, on a skinny plank. A toddler! What three-year-old does that?"

She'd clap with eyes wide, treading that line between encouragement and hands-off parenting typical of the seventies. I'm not sure Mom had ever been to the pool prior to that singular crowning moment. She let me be me: free-range in the hills and neighborhood in my rainbow-striped swimsuit, running through sprinklers, sucking Kool-Aid popsicles with lips a neon purple.

Summers took the cake: kick the can until midnight, sweet peas from the garden, sleepovers at grandma and grandpa's—a quick dash down the alley. Evenings so tranquil I'd doze to the purr of grasshoppers while my cat Tip-Dip burrowed in a ball under my arm. These moments were so dang beautiful they almost hurt.

Mom and Dad were busy-busy and out weekend nights with their band. Mom played the piano like a butterfly, like it was her sole purpose on earth, to share that talent. Dad was her drummer. The shush of the metal fan-brush hitting the skins was my favorite of sounds. Both my parents worked harder than any I knew, jobs on top of jobs. Mom with her teaching and piano, Dad a millwright foreman who owned a gravel truck to add to my grandpa's small fleet. Mom said Grandpa built half the roads in Southern Alberta. She'd tear up just thinking about it; I was never sure why.

Work was always a theme in my family. I played along, staging lemonade stands, acting president of my disco roller-skating club, as I twirled with girlfriends in my too-tight pink rhinestone-studded shorts.

Some days, Dad arrived home from work and Mom couldn't take it anymore. With four kids seven years apart, she refereed every permutation of conflict: oldest vs. youngest (me); brother vs. brother; brother vs. sister; three against one, two against one, and on and on to infinity.

"Jim, get these kids out of here," she'd plead. "Take them! Please!"

No matter how tired Dad was, he'd load us into his orange-striped Chevy van and drive us to Kin Coulee to play on the swings, then Dairy Queen for soft serve. The ice cream would drip faster than I could lick, my fingers sticky no matter how hard I tried to stay clean. Some days just Dad and I would go for a ride on his motorbike. I'd wrap my arms around his waist and snuggle into his back with my purple sparkly helmet glinting in the sun.

Saturdays, Dad would take me to set up their band's equipment at the Legion. He'd crack a sweat hauling in the heavy speakers, then holler to the bartender, "Shirley Temples for this one!" I'd spin the barstools like I owned the joint, popping maraschino cherries like Tic Tacs, anticipating the crunchy blast of sweet red syrup. It was beyond me how this divine little ball once grew on a tree. *Deeelicious!* How could

Dad have resisted such things? He sipped ginger ale in a tumbler, just ice.

My siblings said I was spoiled. Cruising the neighborhood on my sister's ten-speed with hardly a care, blissfully unaware of mortgages, cancer, recessions, the price of oil. The thought that bad things happened, that life would not always be *this good*, never occurred to me . . .

A late summer Sunday, the air so hot it shimmered, Mom and Dad marshaled us into my grandma's garden for a raspberry-picking marathon. This was totally out of character. Even Robin, my seventeen-year-old boy-crazy sister, deigned to join us. Teasing all the way, we poked and prodded each other with berry-stained hands. Hours passed without a single row amongst us siblings. The sun crossed the sky as we filled buckets and stomachs, then made the short walk home.

That night, I slept at my grandma's with a friend. But strangely, I was jumpy.

Once, twice, three times, I sprinted the short path between my house and Grandma's to kiss Dad goodnight and say goodbye for his week long stint at work. I even begged him not to go. This was unlike me. I always understood my parents had to work because that's how things go: work hard and work harder, that was their example. So why bother stopping them?

By the third trip back, Dad might have been annoyed (Mom sure was), but I couldn't help myself. "Love you, Dad. Please don't go. Stay home. We can play and pick more berries . . ."

Dad stroked my hair as I smooshed my face into his thick chestnut curls and neck stubble, still basking in the warmth of our afternoon in the berry patch. Despite my efforts, in a few hours, Dad would be off in the middle of the night for his weekly drive north.

The light of the long summer day gave way to a peaceful prairie evening. Crickets hummed. Frogs croaked. The neighbor's dog barked. A train rumbled down the tracks high in the hills behind our home. I waited for the squeal of metal wheels against the track and the low broad pitch of the horn as the train receded into the distance like a gravel-toned lullaby, then drifted off to sleep. This was my perfect world. It would only last the night.

CHAPTER 2

What do you do when your world flips in an instant?

a) Bargain with God. There must be some way to turn back time.
b) Get mad. God's not listening. Unleash your fury then crawl into a hole.
c) Life's rough. Hold on tight and chin up. Bury your feelings (that always ends well).
d) Cry. What else can you do but blubber away and surrender to the sad?

CHAPTER 2.1

Ayahuasca Journey
September 2021

Those seeking to escape from suffering hasten right toward their own misery. And with the very desire for happiness, out of delusion they destroy their own well-being as if it was their enemy.[2]

It was eight o'clock. It occurred to me how strange the whole scene was. Thirty or so fractured souls lying quietly in the dark, under a white vinyl pole-tent, on a bed of St. Augustine grass, set on a very large volcanic rock in the middle of the Pacific.

"Tell me how to be," I whispered into the moist tropical air. "Tell me how to serve. Be gentle, Mother Vine. Or do you prefer Grandmother? Abuela? Connect me to Spirit. Guide me to my purpose during these tumultuous times on earth . . ."

Over and over, I repeated my intention, speaking to the plant, imagining a pearly pink light filling me from above like a waterfall, as someone suggested I do.

Ten minutes in. Nothing. Total stillness.

Twenty minutes. Still silent.

Then, beat by beat, the room began to come alive.

---

[2] Santideva, *Bodhicharyavatara.*

First Jenny. Retching across from me and crying. She was close to my age. I'd no clue her story. Pretty. Smart. Hip. Maybe even famous, an athlete of some sort. Retching. Then sobbing. I sent her love because I felt I had the capacity to do so.

Then, the two guys beside me. Partners. Old men. Gay before gay was cool. Retching. The way only men could. Guttural, deep, straight from the core of the earth. I sent them love too.

Then me. It took an hour and—*whoop!*

First, my stomach. Nausea. Heartburn. Acid reflux. Then prickles. Like when your foot falls asleep. Then nausea again. Then lightning-like zaps as the vine weaved its way into my every crevasse: intestine, head, teeth, elbows, fingers. I felt her bouncing about—*Please, no games. Show me the way, but no tricks. Be kind.*

And so, for a time, it was expansive and light. There were colors, kaleidoscopic and beautiful, pulsing in sharp angles and boxy patterns. It was easy . . . ish.

No problem. I won't puke. I got this.

Then—a burp. A wave of nausea.

Oh no. Not puke!

It went away. Replaced by a yawn. Another deep yawn. Then exhales and sighs. Voluminous sighs. Necessary sighs. Then heaviness. I couldn't move. I was frozen.

Slowly, I'm fragile. I didn't know it, but now I do. I'm weak. I pretend I'm strong and they think I'm strong, but I'm not. It's a show. Shit.

Silly me. I hadn't *got this.* SHE was just getting started.

CHAPTER 2.2

Twinkle, Twinkle

September 2017

After forty-five minutes of highway, we pulled up to our fancy new palm tree–lined driveway. I felt a wave of relief. The farm was undeniably well-kept.

From the corner of my eye, I caught a red-and-yellow heliconia flower hanging dutifully in the garden like a chandelier, flanked by giant leaves appropriately named elephant ears. I smiled. We had arrived to a warm, wet Eden.

"Move it, Mom and Dad!"

The kids blew past us like wild boars, on to claim their bedrooms. One would get the loft at the peak of the house with bookshelves, a built-in two-person desk that the original owner built for himself, slanted ceilings, and a large crawl space for storage or to hide or make a fort. The other would get the second master suite beside ours, with its own bathroom and sliding door to the garden. I suspected we were in for a fight for the latter—what I wouldn't have done for a room like that as a kid.

Rain overflowed from the eaves like miniature waterfalls. I silently thanked God for our large carport, protecting us from the elements, seemingly as robust here as they were in our rainforest home of Vancouver.

"I can't believe it," I whispered to Josh, standing at the threshold of our new home like newlyweds, like it was the first day of the rest of our lives.

"I know." Josh bent his knees and cupped his arms like he might swoop me up.

I smacked his shoulder. "You'll hurt your back."

"You're right," he grunted.

The lump in the back of my throat pulsed to remind me that this—like so many good things since I could remember—would be bittersweet.

"After you." Josh pressed his hand to the small of my back as we entered the door of our new life.

If there was one thing I knew, it was this: We were moving to a completely dialed-in house with soaring ceilings, beautiful beams, and plantation-style furniture made of koa wood and monkeypod. We had thick poster beds and pretty wicker armchairs that conveyed with the sale of the house. There were three brass palm tree chandeliers dripping with crystal pedals, originating from the Coco Palms Resort where *Blue Hawaii* was filmed and muckety-mucks chased starlets, years before Hurricane Iniki shredded it to bits. Local lore had it that our dining room chandelier hung in the Palace Room where Elvis had slept. On top of this, there was a shiny black grand piano, and despite an entire decade or two ignoring the instrument I'd spent a childhood honing, I couldn't wait to play it.

Outside, the farm was manicured and the trees cared for. Weeders, pickers, and trimmers had all been through. We couldn't afford to keep them, but we were off to a good start. The previous owners would, naturally, leave the house spotless. Toilets would be sparkling and beds would be made. Josh had hired painters to give the interior a coat of fresh white paint and promised me they'd finished the job and had moved to the exterior. Overall, things would be pretty perfect.

"What—the—fu—" I cupped my face.

The house was completely disassembled with drop cloths everywhere. The walls were half crisp white, half mirky beige, with furniture haphazardly pulled from the walls. The hall to the two bedrooms had been barricaded with ladders and pails. The painters were not done—*as Josh had promised*—they weren't even mostly done! Beds were covered with pictures and shelves and screws and nails, while dressers and closet doors sat jammed into doorways and against the beds. Stuff was everywhere. On top of it being hot and muggy from the rain, the house felt like a deserted movie set.

Josh strolled through, unfazed and happy to be here. *How could this be?* The kids zigzagged into nooks and crannies like they were zipping through a fun house at the Midway. Meanwhile, the two veins in the center of my forehead throbbed into an alien V.

Rancid olive oil? Brown gook dripping down cupboards? Rotting potatoes in the crisper? What's going on here? Frantically, I opened and closed dirty cupboards, ready to cry. Stuff was everywhere. The house packed to the gills with shit.

I just cleaned three fridges! I threw away ten boxes of half-empty jars and bags of past-fresh goods! I gave away a frozen quarter cow, a turkey, and a minibar! It took me a month to clean out my kitchen in Lions Bay. Now this?

This place needed a thorough culling. I'd just spent twelve weeks culling all of my things: collections of a lifetime, an entire 2,800-square-foot house full of kids' stuff, sports equipment, camera gear, clothes for every age and stage—and junk, loads of junk. But nice things, too, like heirloom dish sets, collector knickknacks, furniture, hand-me-downs from grandmas on both sides, my entire life and other people's lives too. And now I was in charge of culling a complete stranger's life.

Meanwhile, Josh was whistling Dixie. "Amazing, hey?"

"Um . . ." I pursed my lips, scratching the back of my mouth frantically with my tongue.

Something—paint fumes, mold, fungus—had the capillaries in my eyes watering and my throat swelling wildly. I was halfway to an allergy attack. I sniffled and gurgled and rubbed my temples, wondering why I couldn't be one of those drinky-drunk moms who got sloshed on airplanes. *Another margarita, please! Let's party! Nothing bothers me!*

"Didn't you say the painters were done?"

My whole life, I could handle anything: bucketloads, truckloads, container ships of stress. *Bring it on!* I'd been to Hell and back when I was ten, then for a good part of a decade or two fending for myself with a mother (albeit beautiful and amazing) caught up in her own whirlwind. Whether it was my sports, my schooling, my career, a move to New York, Vancouver, or LA, I figured it out myself. Me against the world, bundled with stress, novelty stress, chronic stress, nonstop stress. And I did it. I managed. I even flourished.

Until now. Decades later, something was cracking and that *thing* was me.

"Shan, what can we do?" Josh looked pained. Like I sucked. Like I was the worst wife ever. "It is what it is." His eyebrows pinched together an apology. "Look around, this place is amazing."

I sighed like a horse, lips rattling, and looked around in defeat. "It was supposed to be a clean slate, a reset, a new life!"

Josh dropped his head.

"They left us Spam!"

"I'm sorry."

"We need a do-over! You, me, the boys, no disruptions, no distractions. Instead—"

I splayed my arm through the air like Vanna White on *Wheel of Fortune*, the audience screaming out vowels.

"Weeks of work!" I huffed. "Then our container will arrive with all our *actual* crap. The stuff we didn't cull. Where will it go?"

The producer in me couldn't stand it. Every job, every show, if something went wrong, I'd solve it on the spot, not a second to spare. You could count on me. But I was out of solves. I was tired, bedraggled, and cooked. I started to cry. No tears, just shakes and gasps, a shoulder-quaking ugly cry.

Waah, poor me, I get to move to a messy house with too much stuff in Hawaii. Poor baby.

It wasn't just the state of our new home. It was fifteen years of up, down, and sideways as mother, wife, career girl, in the role of a lifetime where nearly nothing was easy. No one tells you that being married and raising children will be the hardest thing you ever do. It's a sidebar: *What's the big deal? A few boxes of diapers, some wipes—you're still you.*

For years, Josh and I couldn't afford our mortgage, or the bills, or the time to connect or even pretend *we got this* when we so clearly didn't. Knee-deep in drywall dust and a runaway train of a renovation, young kids, crying kids, au pairs, nannies, contract jobs, precarious jobs, out-of-town jobs, canceled jobs, and bills, so many bills. Meanwhile, we marveled at friends and neighbors who had it all figured out: Christmas at the cabin, summers in Europe, weekends in Whistler, fancy dinners downtown, hotels and galas and designer cars to match designer lives.

Is that why we left? We couldn't keep up?

"I'm sorry, hon." Josh grabbed my hand.

I need to cry. I want to cry. I'm so freaking tired. I want to blubber until my ribs hurt and my jaw aches and my nose drips with snot. But I didn't want the kids to see me or Josh to feel sorry for me because I knew that was crazy. I wasn't the type of person anyone should feel sorry for, not anymore. Plus, I didn't want a hug. Crying almost always guaranteed a hug. No thank you. I wanted sleep. I wanted hibernation.

"I thought I told you about the painters," Josh said, leaning in to hug me.

"It's okay," I said softly. Maybe I did want a hug.

"This has been—"

"Brutal," I sighed, then that same muscle in my throat that made me cry pressed out a laugh like a hole punch. "I'm a mess."

"Let's get some air." Josh opened the sliding doors and windows while I made strange squeaking sounds, pinching my nostrils for relief. "Recycled air is murder. We just did three airplanes and a moving marathon . . ."

I should have been grateful. Josh had done so much to make it all happen. He'd done a fine job, brilliant, actually. Big deal, painters in the house, a few more cupboards to clean and boxes to pack.

"Thank you," I muttered sheepishly. "Let's get some sleep. It's already one o'clock."

Josh moved the gunk off the bed, while I found a pile of sheets in a closet and got to work fitting linens to settle the kids, and maybe attempt a little shut-eye for ourselves. When—

"I'm the teenager!" Tyde belted. "I get the loft!"

"No, you're not. Stupid! You're twelve."

"Don't call me stupid, dumbass! I'm the oldest. I get first choice."

"You always get first. I get the loft," Canyen belted back. "Why do you always get your way?"

"You're a loser."

"No, you're a loser."

"F--- you."

"Mom, Tyde said the f-word!"

Josh looked at me. "Did he say frick or fuck?"

"No clue." I stared back, frozen in place.

No, me! No, you! F you! No, you!

"Boys!" I yelled as calmly as possible, despite my left eyeball twitching. "The main floor bedroom has its own bathroom, and a sliding door to the Jacuzzi. Canyen, it's the best room and you'll be beside me and Dad."

Slam—Body check—Smack!

Canyen hit the floor with a thud. I could've sworn I heard teeth on tile, a crash test dummy against a cement wall.

"Boys! Stop!"

I ran to check for blood, but Canyen was already off the floor swinging—*Rocky vs. Ali!* And like the King of Sting, Tyde's bark, and bite, and height, and breadth, was so much bigger that Canyen would lose. So began a swift meltdown into depths I had never before witnessed from my youngest. Nine years old and scared, so scared.

"Why did you do this to me?" Canyen sobbed, curling into a fetus on our new oversized couch. "Mom, why did you take me away from my friends, from Lions Bay? I hate it here. How could you do this? I hate it so much. I want to go home!"

He didn't just cry; he bawled, bellowed, and wailed. In no time, his whole face was blazing red and his T-shirt was soaked. Worst of all, there was nothing I could do. Because at that moment, in that space, I wanted to cry and click my ruby slippers home too.

The kids finally fell asleep, nestled into pillows and sheets left over from the previous owners with their foreign smells and detergents. I glanced around in disbelief.

"No champagne?" I said to no one as I took a glass of tepid tap water, wishing I had a Brita filter nearby. "Simple life. Ha!" I was officially talking to myself. "Who needs champagne? I need a spa and a decluttering wizard!"

I leaned over the counter and sipped my water, waiting for the hit of chlorine.

Hm. It tasted fresh, like a waterfall. Then I thought of something I'd read from a natural health magazine: In a few weeks, upon moving to a new place, your body, 70 percent water, will take on the water of the local watershed with its minerals and salts and fantastically shaped snowflake molecules. The immediate land, water, and earth becomes a part of you, fusing with your essence.

"Amazing," I said to myself, welcoming the sweet water entering my cells, as though it might actually fill the sorry spaces.

The air began to move, slipping over my skin like a glove. Then came the scent of mock orange wafting toward me. My lungs expanded to absorb its honeyed plumes.

Where's Josh to experience this?

Nature was so alive here. Pulsing, circling, entering me as though to remind me that beyond the drama, beyond a painfully stressful move, beyond the years of grinding to make ends meet, that maybe, just maybe, this place could be magic, just like my first trip to Oahu had been so many years ago.

"Josh?" I called.

"Over here," he said from outside.

I paused, not wanting to release the feeling of splendor, the first of its kind in months. Our move had been littered with setbacks, colossal expenses, unexpected challenges, garage sales and vehicle sales and giveaways galore, temper tantrums from kids *and* adults that tested us to our gristly cores, right down to saying goodbye to my beloved dog Patty, the family pet of fifteen years, handed off to my sister, who at this moment wasn't speaking to us.

Humans. Conflict. Dysfunction. Up. Down. Arrived.

"Coming," I called.

As I stepped onto the lanai, wicker furniture was splayed about in a labyrinth, as though to test me once again: *Can you ever be happy? Will you ever relax? Or will you just keep getting annoyed at every little thing?* I took a breath, then wound my way through the too many chunks of furniture toward Josh, standing at the edge of the grass with his chin tilted to the sky.

"Wow," I said, breathing in the rain that dripped from the funnel leaves onto the grass.

Whatever I had just been feeling vanished with the sound of frogs croaking in the brush, while the breeze, so full of wet, felt like I was taking a bath while standing, fully clothed, and it wasn't annoying—it was delightful. There were no buildings with twenty-four-seven fluorescent lights blazing through the night. The neighbors had slipped into their ritual slumber. There wasn't a streetlamp or car for miles, just billowy clouds that opened like a curtain to reveal a distant dance of constellations just for us.

Twinkling lights blanketed the blue-black-silver heavens in a way that was not possible if there had been a city nearby. It was the sky of seafaring Polynesians, stars as far as the eye could see and a yellow crescent moon bright as a spotlight. I felt as Mark Twain had once said, *No other land could so longingly and beseechingly haunt me . . .*

Perhaps Josh and I were experiencing it just as the ancient Hawaiians had, as they dozed in the open air, alongside primitive huts, kneeling to mystery gods while palm trees bowed overhead.

"Do you see this?" Josh pointed to the trees that spanned the orchard in a silhouette, looking like paper cutouts in a puppet show castelet. "It's ours now."

"Amazing." I exhaled fully.

"I'm sensing a *but*—"

I craned my head to look behind me, past the wicker, past the sliding doors where several misplaced bits of furniture sat with crumpled drop cloths and forgotten pictures that didn't belong to us.

"We left *everything* we know."

I thought back to the book club I started eight years ago, initially tentative friendships that stitched together through time. One mom who'd turned down my invite lamented she'd committed social suicide. *Yup, you missed out.* Once a month, for a few hours, a dozen moms would gather in a trust circle where nearly all was divulged. We had ski trips, cookie exchanges, Sunday brunches, and shopping weekends in Seattle. Sure, there were catty moments, alongside divorces, delusions, departures, and disease, but through it all we were friends. We had a code, our own little mama village.

"I don't know anyone," I said to Josh's profile, his gaze fixed to the land. "I just left all my people, my home, my land."

"Shan, I couldn't do the grind any longer. Winters of endless rain." Josh grabbed my hand and pulled it into his. "Then both my parents dead, just like that . . ."

He stopped to swallow. In fourteen years of marriage, I'd seen him cry once.

"I was never home." Josh dabbed the corner of his eye.

It was true. Since moving from LA to Lions Bay/Vancouver, when Tyde was just nine months old, Josh had been on hundreds of flights for work as a director of photography, lugging as many as ten Pelican cases at a time through customs and airports, pulled into secondary for hours as though he were smuggling drugs, day after day with a fifty-pound camera on and off his shoulder countless times, right eye socket squinting and pressed to the viewfinder, directors blasting in his earbuds, shoots in rain and snow in the middle of nowhere, garbage food lunches at Denny's because that's all there was, hotels with bedbugs, back and forth to LA . . .

"We earned this, Shan." Josh gulped back a sadness that I'd not yet seen in him, even when his parents died. Anger, I'd seen. Frustration, I'd seen. Resentment, there'd been loads. But sorrow? Never.

I wrapped my arm around him: no fat, a sculpted surfer's body. Surprising, because in the past twelve years he hadn't had time for his beloved sport, let alone a gym.

"It's so lovely," I said, nuzzling into him, taking in the scene as though we were young again. Newlyweds. A time of no expectations, before the stakes were so high. Before mortgages and childcare, dead parents and life insurance. Before a complex life had become the be-all and end-all.

Josh turned to me, the stars so bright I caught the aqua blue of his eyes in a flash. "We're free."

CHAPTER 2.3

August 1979

It was a toasty summer evening in the Alberta prairies. Rose-colored clouds lined in shimmering gold rings floated by while a green corn moon ripened like a birthday balloon in the sky. Earlier I'd been berry-picking in my grandma's garden with my parents and siblings, a rarity to have us all together laughing playfully. It had been my perfect summer day, minus the part about my dad having to leave for work early in the morning.

My friend Rhonda and I were in the midst of a two-day, nearly-end-of-summer sleepover. It was late and we'd just finished watching *The Shaggy D.A.* on Disney, taking our final slugs of Grandma's yummy Coke-and-cream fluffos for dessert. We couldn't decide what to do next.

Given our only viewing options were the pastel-suited, soft-talking *Lawrence Welk* (the only show Grandma allowed herself to watch), or the ragamuffin *Beachcombers*, which Grandpa had already tucked into, TV was out. So, off we went to the guest room to hide under the sheets with a flashlight and make up ghost stories, then plan the next day at the neighborhood swimming pool.

Rhonda and I hadn't always been so cozy. When I was five, we were playing school with her younger sister. I couldn't see what Rhonda was writing on the blackboard—and assumed spelling words (my favorite thing after drawing)—when Rhonda looked over her shoulder with a devilish grin.

What's she up to? I thought.

Ominously, she slid her body away from the chalkboard to leave me confronted with my greatest fear . . . a witch!

Sure, it was just a drawing, and not even a detailed drawing, but it was wicked. She had a broom and a wart as big as her nose! Plus, it wasn't just the picture, it was what my imagination was doing with it!

Rhonda cackled, while her sister, younger than me, gurgled in laughter. Not me. I screeched like an alley cat, jumped to my feet, ran for the door, and sprinted home, tears pouring off my face, frightened out of my wits.

For weeks, possibly months, the two of them taunted me: *Crybaby, crybaby.* But I couldn't help my brain. I really did believe that witch would spring to life, swoop me up, and fly me to the Black Forest to toss me in her oven to cook forever. Every time I closed my eyes for sleep, I saw that drawing. But that was many years ago and I was over that now (*ish*).

It seemed Rhonda and I had only just finished our bedtime stories and nodded off to sleep when I heard a shriek. A morning sunbeam pushed through a crack in the curtain of Grandma's guest room. White light spilled across the bed. I tried to make sense of the noise.

Again, a shout. A bellow.

Did Grandma just scream?

Every part of me flooded with fear. Shadows swooped madly in my periphery—

What is it? A witch? A dragon? A chalkboard sprung to life?

My heart was in my throat. Something awful had happened. *Am I too late?*

I flung off the blankets. Hit the floor. Raced down the hallway. Around the corner. And there they were—

Grandma, weeping, her body braced against the doorframe.

Grandpa, mute, his eyes like saucers.

Mom, ashen, ghostlike, still as a statue on the other side of my favorite screen-to-summertime doorway, a plaid work jacket thrown hastily over her nightie.

"Who died?" I yelled.

Grandma wept. Tears blanketed my face.

"Who died!"

Ten years old and the only one with words. Frantic, I rattled off the names of my siblings. "Troy? Robin? Marc?"

No one answered.

"Is it Marc?" I cried, knowing it had to be him—he was always getting in trouble. "No! Not Marc! Is he dead?"

"Shanni." Grandma shuddered, her words tangled in her sobs. "It's your dad." She held her special hanky up to her nose. "This morning, in his van."

Dad. The only man killed in a forty-vehicle crash on a highway thick with summer fog.

Marc. My fifteen-year-old brother, struck with anguish, dove into Mom's car and peeled out of the driveway, hell-bent on getting to the crash site. *If he could just drive fast enough, he might get there in time to save Dad.*

Grandpa. On the phone to Rhonda's father, a detective and family friend, who called the RCMP and told them to set up a roadblock. "Be gentle, he's only fifteen. But stop the kid before he gets to the carnage."

Mom. Earlier that morning, before my dad began the last day of his life, he took the laundry from the dryer and folded it into perfect neat stacks. My mother began the lament that would echo through our lives: "If only he hadn't folded the laundry, he'd have been through that stretch of highway before the accident."

If only.

Me. It never occurred to me it would be my father, my dad, who just the night before I'd begged not to go to work, not to make the early morning five-hour drive, to stay at home and live in my tiny bubble of a world and pick raspberries by the bucketful.

Every inch of me twisted and coiled, then splintered into a pile on the floor. Grandma's once safe linoleum was now a pool of sorrow, while my mermaid dreams of *a life so sweet it hurt* scattered into a million pieces across the heavens and the hells, never to be found again.

CHAPTER 3

What's the best way to pack up your life and start over in paradise?

a) Sell everything. Hop on the next flight to Hawaii. Rent a camper van with fold-out beds. Park on the beach. Pray the cops don't drag you in.
b) Ask your boss to relocate you to Honolulu (*da big city*). Have boss lady foot the bill. Bury your head in work (as we do). It'll be like you never moved at all.
c) List pros and cons of moving on an Excel spreadsheet. Agonize over every gritty detail. Be sure to remove all spontaneity. Then decide to stay put. It's too painful. Plus, those lists never work.
d) Plan a six-month sabbatical in Costa Rica to chill and do nothing. Then ditch that plan after a two-week trip to Kauai where you lose your mind and put a hasty deposit on a plucky little pineapple plantation. *Alooooooha!*

CHAPTER 3.1

Ayahuasca Journey
September 2021

Ayahuasca tea is prepared from a combination of two plants: the vine of Banisteriopsis caapi/ayahuasca, and the vision-inducing leaves of Psychotria viridis/chacruna. When brewed together they bring out in each other a chemical harmony capable of changing their users at an anatomic level . . . rebuilding damaged serotonin receptors in the brain, resulting in stronger mental health.[3]

Around me there were murmurs, some sobbing quietly into their pillows, some barfing, many silent, a few perfectly still.

That was me for the first while. Motionless. Locked to a kaleidoscope of shapes and colors in my brain. Also locked to my mat, curled up like a pill bug, my armor a thin yellow sheet I'd taken from the linen closet a few hours earlier.

Mustard yellow would be the perfect color for the night. It was ugly and I didn't care if it got dirty. I'd no clue how I acquired the twin sheet set or when it landed in my house. Which was why I chose it. It didn't matter. Unlike the other

---

[3] "Ayahuasca Benefits: How It Can Heal You," A Spiritual Hand, https://www.aspiritualhand.com/ayahuasca-benefits/.

women at the ceremony, who had created a proper shrine of their mat-space with nice things. One had a large metal cross with gemstones, another had amethyst and rose quartz crystals and floral essences in various bottles and sprays, and the woman across from me had a macramé blanket covered in pretty purple yarn flowers.

Me? A puke bucket (which we all had), a bottle of water, and a tiny tube of rose oil that I tucked into my tissue box. No special jewelry. No altar items. No semi-precious stones.

Ever the pragmatist, I wore a dumpy pair of sweatpants with a swirly blue-and-white cloud pattern, a T-shirt and a Billabong sweatshirt in case I got cold, comfortable underwear (of course), black in case I pooped myself. Which I did not plan to do, but an acquaintance told me that she never puked during her many ceremonies, she only ever pooped, and one time in her pants. Learned her lesson quick. She also told me to wear white because *it represents the light.*

Suddenly, all of this mattered. I wished my sheet set was white and my clothes were white and that I was wearing my favorite necklace from Josh that said LOVE on it, and my wedding ring, and maybe had a Bible—*Yes, I would need that, Him, Her, er, God.*

It made me wish I was one of those people who used their best things instead of hoarding them away for a special occasion. If this wasn't special, what was? This triggered a revulsion toward myself I hadn't experienced before. A lifetime of mistakes rippled through my mind, pouring forth like a geyser. Somewhere deep from the Pacific trenches, past the Hydra, past the den of the Kraken and the goblin sharks, was this girl who could be so dumb and so cruel. *Good God—she was me!*

I thought I might puke. I didn't want to puke. *Please, no puke.* I began to squirm and twist about, my arms reaching then folding, legs stretching then curling, like a worm wriggling through the soil, lost outside its home, drying out on the pavement.

Amazonian tribes were onto something. There's a reason we did this in a jungle, an inch of foam separating us from the skin of the planet and her gritty life-giving hummus. I was connecting to her, Mother Nature, in a way I'd never felt before. Helpless to the carnage from the humans around me. Wracked with parasites nibbling my every groove.

Out of nowhere, Steven appeared at the front of my mat, hands folded in prayer, looking ominous. He began to hum quietly. With the blanket tight in my grip, I wrapped my head to hide. *Is this just for me? What is this? I don't trust him.*

Then unwrapped my head to crane toward the sound—

Maybe it will help. My body wound into a fetal coil, I'd no clue the words or what he was singing. Perhaps a native Indian chant, or the *icaros*, medicine songs used precisely for ceremonies such as this.

His clothes began to take on the rainbow hexagonal patterns that were swirling through my mind at greater and greater speeds. It was too much. I closed my eyes again. This only moved the patterns to the backs of my eyelids. So, I opened them again. Then closed. Then opened. Nowhere to hide. She was inside me now, in my blood, my bones, my brain.

My body contorted. Something needed to move—

I'm going to puke!

I grabbed my bucket and dropped my head, ready to catch whatever would come.

Nothing came.

Instead, I yawned, mouth wide, like a lion lying in the savanna, like I might suck in the entire tent, then lay back carefully.

Crisis averted. I think.

The patterns slowed, became less frenetic, less scrambled, as though responding to the steady beat of Steven's chanting. Another yawn. I sighed, grateful for a reprieve. . . I knew it wouldn't last.

CHAPTER 3.2

Pineapple Palace
September 2017

"Where am I?" I whispered to myself, muddled, like someone put my brain in the oven and baked it overnight. "Where in the *hell* am I?"

My first thought, on my first morning, in my new home.

Truly, I had no clue where I was. Late last night, I hit the pillow and fell unconscious. Didn't even get up to pee. Dead for six hours.

"Josh!" I slapped my hand on the mattress beside me, and then shook my head from side to side, smacking my forehead the way people whacked the old tube TVs to get a signal, bunny ears wobbling on top. "Josh?"

In my periphery were two caramel-colored bedposts, two white muntin windows with bamboo shades partially drawn, a sturdy wooden ladder up to a small private loft with a skylight, a number of random pieces of furniture from some other part of the house, and no Josh.

"Josh?" I called out, waiting for my brain to wire itself for the day.

This isn't Lions Bay.

I'm in Kauai.

At my new home.

New home?

Shit, we moved!

The series of events that led us here flooded my brain like a hailstorm: *five hundred boxes, everything we own, loaded up and driven away on a semi-trailer to a giant container ship in Seattle, soon to cross US customs in a corrugated steel container the size of a mobile home, to land here on Kauai's only port, Napa-wili-something-or-other, then hopefully this house—*

Dear God, what have we done? Until now it was just a dream. And now, suddenly it's happened. I'm here. It's done. The four of us gone, just like that, disappeared into thin air yesterday at 6 a.m., off to bake on a volcanic rock in the middle of the Pacific.

"Josh!" I called again.

He was gone. Already up without me. Our first morning on the farm. *Dammit!*

And just like that, on cue, monkey brain kicked in:

Danger! Danger! Listen lady, there's trouble in paradise. Someone could die! Canyen screaming on the couch, "Take me home!" The house bedraggled. Tortuous goodbyes to friends and family. Leaving the dog in your sister's car—who does that? OMG! This is so your life! How about that doozy argument with Josh the day before you left? Baggage. Guilt. Remorse. You brought it all with you Samsonite, Eddie Bauer, Louis Vuitton (actually, not that, you wish).

Up. Down. Arrived.

Time to get up! the sun announced by way of harsh white beams poking like tree branches through the window, hitting me square in the eyeballs. I pulled the sheet over my head and curled into a ball, not wanting to get up, *never* wanting to get up.

Stress didn't just disappear. It needed somewhere to go, like a treadmill or a punching bag or a bottle of vodka. It felt glacial. Giant sacks of flour glued to my limbs. I wasn't ready, not for sunlight, not for this move, not for my shadow side kicking my ass with hard truths.

What are we doing here? Actually? I don't belong! Maybe I liked Vancouver's ridiculously bleak, soggy, gray winters. They gave me an excuse to sulk. And there was always something to sulk about.

Slowly, the bedroom began to swell from its seventy-two-degree nightly reprieve to jungle hot. I had my eye firmly on the air-conditioning unit gleaming above the window like an ice cream cone. Then I thought of what Josh had said a few days earlier: "Electricity in Hawaii is quadruple that of the mainland."

AC's out.

"Water is super pricey. We're screwed in a drought."

Water's out.

"Property taxes are ridiculous. But it's Hawaii, I'd be happy in a beach shack."

Then you'd be happy alone.

"Groceries are double that on the mainland. Everything is imported over thousands of miles of ocean. Good news is, it's the most temperate climate with the world's best surf. Nothing between us and the mainland but raw ocean swell."

It all rolled off his lips a little too smoothly. Canada was my country. Was Hawaii his?

"Jesus, woman, enough," I said, coaxing myself out of bed. "You're in frickin' paradise!" Then stared into the bathroom mirror. "You're good. This is good. It's an adventure."

Through the window, I spotted Josh zigzagging through the trees, sizing up the orchard with an ear-to-ear grin. He pulled a big round yellow fruit the size of his head off a branch and held it up with pride. It was humungous. A giggle worked its way up as I ran my fingers through my hair to untangle the knots.

As quietly as I could muster, I tiptoed past the kids snoozing on the couch. They looked like little drunkards after an eighteen-hour binge of airplane cookies and apple juice, despite the organic almonds, veggie crackers, and grass-fed cheddar that sat untouched in my carry-on. Such gentle faces as they slept: perfect mouths, long lashes, silky hair, so close to the angels, not yet wholly of this earth. I stopped to take them in, knowing it wouldn't last, it simply couldn't—*the days are long, but the years are short*—then worked my way to the lanai for a view.

Holy moly!

It was a Willy Wonka Wonderland of nature's candy. I had only seen the land when the orchard was dormant. Nothing had been fruiting, nine months ago, when I flew over to make the final call on this massive life change. But today, avocados, lemons, and tangelos dripped from branch after branch. The star fruit tree was so laden with its crop that its largest artery had broken, and in the small shaft of bark that remained, there was enough nourishment for nearly two hundred fruit to thrive. A weeping willow of juicy cylinders that, when cut, were the shape of little yellow stars, bursting with vitamin-rich sweetness.

In no time, the kids followed in a flurry. At every turn, there was something to discover.

"Look, three macadamia nut trees!"

"Look, a tractor with a bush hog!"

"Have you seen the size of these avocados?"

"Kumquats? I didn't know we had kumquats!"

"There's a lotus pond!"

We plucked and ate and ate some more until our bellies swelled like a monsoon river and there was nothing to do but lie on the grass and stare at the sky.

Ahh, this is why we're here.

Puffy white clouds danced over our heads. Canyen forgot about his late-night tirade, skipping through the yard, chasing lizards, climbing trees, and spraying his brother with the hose.

"Mom," he yelled, holding his shirt bottom rolled up and overflowing with lemons. "Can we make lemonade?"

"Of course!" I bit into a kumquat, skin, seeds, and all, absorbing the bittersweetness of this unusual miniature citrus. "We need to add honey or it'll be tart."

"Yay!" He dropped the lemons on the lanai, then scrambled back for more.

"Mom, Dad, we have a hot tub!" Tyde called from behind a bush glutted with birds-of-paradise, poking their goofy orange heads from the green. "You never told me!"

Josh came careening through the trees riding the lawn mower, grass flying from the blades. The kids clambered for a try. When it was my turn, I zipped up and down the knoll and through the fruit trees with the kids scampering alongside wanting another go. Josh was in his element; the only thing missing was a chunk of straw in his teeth.

Within the hour, the boys had stocked the honor stand with fruit for drive-by business. Like something you'd see in Bali, it stood tall at the end of our driveway complete with bamboo siding, shelves, a proper roof, and screened half doors to keep out the birds. We told the kids that if they kept it stocked with fruit, they could collect the money in the lockbox: *Three limes for a dollar, a hand of bananas for four . . .*

Pineapples were too expensive to leave in the stand. At twenty dollars for the large ones, we weren't taking any chances; selling them would require a table on the side of the road. They were the famous Kauai Sugarloaf variety, white in color, low acid, edible core, super sweet, and consistently delicious. Each pineapple took over a year to grow, planted by hand, weeded several times with great care so as not to get skewered by the sword-shaped leaves with sharp needle tips.

The chaos of last night's arrival seemed far behind us. It gave me a surge of energy such that by ten o'clock, I was already unloading our five giant suitcases. It would be weeks before our container would arrive with the rest of our things. I tried not to think about the myriad boxes we had just packed in Canada, and how I would need to handle every last item, in every last box, and find a meaningful place for it. For now, I was smack-dab in the present.

It was ninety degrees every day for weeks. We'd been told it was unusually hot—a drought. Sunscreen was required on noses and shoulders just to step out the door. Toasty tropical rain sprinkled almost every night, making for incredible humidity during the day. As far as the orchard was concerned, it was a near perfect cycle of showers at night and sunshine by day.

City Shannon was gradually morphing into barefoot country Shannon. The girl who ran yellow lights, raced to jobs and appointments, gritted her teeth while waiting at school pickup, and struggled to get a deep breath when tucking herself too late into bed had begun a very slow drift to the ground.

Every second day or so we'd make a point of getting to the beach to squish our toes in the sand, then dunk and dive into shore breaks, while Josh taught the boys the basics of bodysurfing. A critical skill given the thousands upon thousands of miles of ocean that moated our new home. One wave flung me like a torpedo skipping across the water then catapulting me onto the sand, scraping my chin and thighs so hard I could barely get up. The kids grabbed their bellies in laughter as I spat sand from my teeth, feeling a ridiculous five years old again.

I had yet to surf. A sport I'd craved since my childhood, when I splashed and thrashed in that overly chlorinated, water-filled cement rectangle four blocks from my home. Swim meets weren't my thing, lifeguarding a snore, synchronized swimming too weird. No, I craved the unpredictability of the ocean, the moment-to-moment challenge of do or die, well, maybe not *die*, but a good humbling. Surfing required true devotion (especially at my age), a total willingness to release and let nature reign. My training would be brutal and I wasn't yet ready to get walloped, so I delayed my apprenticeship and stuck to rope swings with the kids.

Once home from our salty sea dips, we'd load into the hot tub. Josh would grab a gluten-free beer, I'd pour a chardonnay, and the kids would play with the controls. Never still. Bubbles, no bubbles, waterfall, no waterfall, purple, red, green, a light show every night.

Mostly, we'd ask them to shut it off or calm down so we could gaze quietly at the sky, only to be interrupted seconds later by their asking for a sip of beer, or to dunk the bottle or my cup or my face or Josh's feet. Usually ending up with glass in their hands, flipping, filling, dumping, and Josh and I on edge. This only served to remind us that, despite a move to paradise, the mainland rat-race decompression might have to wait for the college years.

Post soak, we'd shower under the stars, suits on, fighting over shampoo, getting sand out of nooks and crannies while the kids rolled around, dripping wet on skateboards, attempting ollies and kick-flips and smashing their shins. The four of us spent every night together: movies, card games, Nerf wars.

At bedtime, Tyde and Canyen would fall asleep on our speckled-brown shag carpet with their pillows, duvets, and a stuffy nestled under their arm. They said our room was comfier than their rooms, but Josh and I knew they were craving safety. After all, it was a strange new world and our only friends were the wild chickens who slept in our lychee tree at night.

Until our container arrived, it felt like a vacation, even though we'd recently begun the routine of school. We ate out often (cringing at ninety-dollar tabs for take-out burritos loaded with cheap white rice), shirked workouts and schedules, bought a guidebook to explore Kauai, plus a Hawaiian song-book and two ukuleles. We had a garage sale, went to tourist shops, and even took a dodgy bike ride to the beach with a neighbor where we cut through farms, flew down a skinny winding road littered with fallen lilikoi and dead chickens squished by heavy-duty pickups, to land at a beautiful bay sur-rounded by stilted luxury beach shacks and canals. A place like that on the mainland would have been a zoo, a sea of tourists and beach umbrellas, chemical sunscreen fashioning a film on the water like an oil spill. Here? Not a chance. It was practically empty.

We learned how Mr. Facebook came to be our neighbor, and how he cheated the locals to get himself a chunk of cherry coastline that Hawaiians had fished and farmed for hundreds of years, and could no longer do thanks to him. We saw his guards patrol the quiet countryside and the incongruence of employing private security on this homey garden isle.

It was odd. Exciting. An adventure. Best of all, I found myself slowly unwinding from a nearly three-decade-long stress tornado that I hadn't realized I was in. I did things I couldn't do back home, like run through sprinklers and make giant batches of guacamole that vanished in an instant.

Josh and I even found time for each other. In three weeks, we'd had more dates than we'd had in years, off to see our painter moonlighting as a jazz pianist at Sam's or The St. Regis.

The band would sit with us during breaks and I'd beam like I belonged here.

There were no bears, no lions, no scary spiders or scorpions that I knew of, just beauty. Like the great sea turtles that floated in the rocky pools at Queen's Bath, air-breathing reptiles, sages of the sea, mythical mothers looking out for us humanoid earth creatures.

Nearly everywhere, the honey scent of nature unfolded through emerald valleys while the big blue Pacific spread to infinity around us. Pretty birds sang intricate ballads, often two notes at once, then flitted limb to limb in the trees like feathered blossoms. Tiny ants danced as they crawled up my arms looking for crumbs or sugar. It reminded me of the eyelash kisses I'd flutter on my boys' cheeks before tucking them in not so long ago. Even the grasshoppers, with their bulbous eyes and neon green antennae, added whimsy as they defied gravity, upside-down, stuck to the glass of the window, ten o'clock at night, sending Tyde into fits of laughter, while Canyen chased salamanders up the walls to snatch in his fingers and place back outside.

It occurred to me that maybe nothing bad ever happened in a place like this. A place with a fantastical supply of fresh fruit, salt water, sunshine, and the freedom to roam, for my children to be children, untethered by the pretense of the big city with its designer cars, private schools, and status friendships. That was distraction. We wanted less of that and more real life in a place where there were few other options.

CHAPTER 3.3

January 1987

It was the second time I'd ever flown on an airplane. Seventeen years old and flitting off like a grown up, alone to a place I'd never been before: a luxury villa in paradise.

The house would be sitting empty on an emerald-green cliff, above thousands of miles of deep blue ocean, breathing its dewy jungle breath in anticipation of me, the lucky Snow Princess. My new title, I'd just decided, while soaring 38,000 feet in the air.

Randy had said the place was stunning. There would be a maid named Rosa, fresh mangoes dripping from the trees, and a writer's desk with a view to the sea so I could conjure next steps for my fabulously complicated young life.

This was the promise made to me on a blustery night in December, in a bar in downtown Calgary, from a stranger. A man in a navy-blue suit with bleach blond hair, an unusual winter tan (in freezing cold Alberta), driving a white Mercedes convertible with California plates, who wouldn't leave me alone. Who told me I *floored* him while cozying up to me, surrounded by bar stars and wallflowers.

Floored? I'd never heard that word before. Wasn't even sure what it meant. But it had to be good. Good enough to want to hear my story. Good enough to take me to the fanciest restaurant in the city. Good enough to offer me his vacation home in Kauai.

"You're too talented to waste away here in the Great White North," Randy whispered in my ear as we sat with our knees tangled at a corner table in the bar. "You need to find your purpose. You need time alone to write and dig deep."

He'd read my mind. *You're so right, Mr. LA Songwriter Randy Whateveryourlastname. I do need to find my purpose. And I need to do it in a plush tropical villa if it's ever going to work!*

It didn't occur to my seventeen-year-old, not yet fully formed prefrontal cortex to ask this stranger, *Why me?* We barely knew each other. *What's the catch?* There had to be a catch.

I was an about-to-be university dropout in a singles bar, wearing a tight black leather skirt, a boxy white art nouveau sweater with chunky shoulder pads, glittery pink lipstick, and Cleopatra eyeliner, vogueing underage and chugging vodka sodas with my girls, thinking myself quite the woman, full of that devil-may-care freshness that only the young (or very drunk) could pull off.

How my mom allowed me on this flight of fancy was beyond everyone I knew. Even my older sister couldn't believe it, and she'd run away from home at least twice.

"Shanni, you can't go. You're seventeen, for God's sake!" Then she'd look to my mom. "Are you serious with this?"

My mom's boyfriend also had a strong opinion for a guy who'd only been in the picture a few months. This I admired. Seven years with no dad made me appreciate a fatherly type.

"Marguerite, you're allowing this?" he said, elbows planted on the pile of newspapers that plastered my mom's large oak table every morning. "She can't go alone to a foreign country to some guy's *villa*. He's thirty. She's not even eighteen!"

I'll be eighteen in a month. And it's not a foreign country! I didn't have to say.

It was totally unnecessary. My mom had already said yes. Pretty much, Mom let me do whatever I wanted. The good news was that I never wanted to do anything too crazy. I was adventurous, perhaps (no, definitely) a little loud at times, but also, according to her, a reliable young woman with a proper head on her shoulders who got the job done. And yeah, I liked to party. Big whoop.

At age seventeen, I had already completed my first semester of Frozen U in the snowy steppes of Calgary. Parking at the Stampeder's football stadium then walking the twenty-minute slog to campus in my white-leather, silver-studded cowboy boots was like crossing Antarctica in kitten heels. Uggs had not yet been invented, so I slipped and slid my way to class freezing my butt cheeks off. To make matters worse, I had a barely C average thanks to my habit of cramming all-nighters and falling asleep just a few pages in. My perpetually busy mother hardly noticed.

University was too much for me. It was big, twenty-five thousand students big, with classrooms the size of concert halls. It was cold, minus-twenty-five-degrees snot-freezing-to-nostrils cold; and it was lame, as in my closest friends went to chef school, tech school, or no school. Gap years were not quite a thing. There was no Lonely Planet guide to finding myself or getting a clue. European trips were for the über-bold or super-spoiled. I had no workout partner, no study buddy, no clubs to join, and most importantly, no one to go to the campus pub with where good times streamed out like party confetti every time I walked by.

Then came Randy, out of the blue and so out of place that I thought him a mirage.

My friends asked, "Why are you talking to that Oompa-Loompa with the white hair? What's with the suit? How old is he? Is he rich? Do you even like him?"

"Like?" I pondered. "Hmm."

I wasn't attracted to him. I was intrigued. Randy was unlike anyone I had ever met: a songwriter from LA, a big shot home for the holidays and hanging out in Calgary's only chichi nightclub, The Banke, membership required. Plus, his hair wasn't white; it was blond, sort of. And no, I was not down with the sugar daddy thing. I'd been modeled such fervent independence from my widowed mother that gold-digging would've required a lobotomy. As a true Gen Xer, soon-to-be nineties woman, I would make my own money, thank you very much.

The lure had to be curiosity, with a dash of opportunity, or a stitch of divine intervention, that had me considering such an offer. *Why has God placed this man before me? Do I quit school to go find myself in paradise? Is it better to regret what I do, or what I don't do?*

It was a fairy tale. First the Dom Perignon in the private booth, two bottles on ice, enough for my friends. Then a waltz, his left hand fitted neatly on my hip, twirling me around like a ballerina. Then the ride home in his James Bond roadster with the heated white leather seats and spiffy red trim. Then the silver snowflakes that fluttered like diamonds as we watched them melt on the windshield, idling in front of my house for hours while he spoke in platitudes. And finally, the incredible stillness of the brisk winter night, just us and the orange glow of the lamppost glistening in the crescent, while inside me hope and curiosity bubbled.

"When opportunity knocks," my mom always said, "answer, and quick. It rarely knocks again."

It would have been an insult to the high heavens to not take a stab at this freshly cracked door to paradise. So, mid-January, I packed my bags, canceled my winter semester at university, and caught the next flight to the Hawaiian archipelago by myself.

The plane touched down in Lihue. The only other exotic place I'd ever been was Waikiki, so I felt kindred with these special jungle rocks. Kauai would be just like Oahu, only quieter. How hard could it be?

Plumes of midday heat rose from the sidewalk as I lugged my bags from the carousel. The terminal was small and unfamiliar with none of the fanfare of my family trip to Oahu a few years prior, where pretty Polynesian ladies wrapped fluffy flower petals around my neck and musclemen in grass skirts stroked ukuleles.

I rolled my mom's extra-large red leather suitcase to the curb to wait for Rosa and her husband to pick me up, as Randy had promised. "They'll be driving a silver four-door sedan."

Five minutes. Ten minutes. Fifteen minutes. Nothing.

Thirty minutes. I watched every last person on my flight depart with family or friends in pickups and old cars. I began to pace.

Forty minutes. Fifty minutes. An hour. More.

It was now one o'clock. The ladies who sat in flowered dresses behind the kiosk had long since locked the windows. No one was there but me.

The blood drained from my face like soap bubbles sucked down a drain. Prior to that moment, everything had lined up. As though things like that should happen every day. Cinderella and her fairy godfather Randy lending his multimillion-dollar vacation home complete with servants to pick me up and chaperone me around the island, plus an endless buffet of exotic tropical fruits to gorge on while overlooking the most spectacular of sunsets. How had it not occurred to me that this was all a sham?

Swollen with fear and embarrassment, I tied my sweater around my waist and rolled the eighty-pound suitcase off the curb and into the hot tropical sun. It glared at me mockingly, chucking solar flares on my prairie-girl skin, roasting in the searing heat.

The airport road wasn't even a road. It was a potholed single lane of red dirt and pebbles in the middle of nowhere, with a lone palm swaying in the distance and ocean just beyond. That damn ocean, spitting spindrift, wasn't even blue. It was gray and choppy and snarled with each gust. Kauai was a parched, tropical ghost town.

My stomach twisted. There wasn't a taxi or shuttle bus in sight. Didn't matter, I'd no clue where to go anyway. All I knew was that Rosa was to pick me up and Randy had arranged it.

Dirt flung up around me, and the tiny rocks made it impossible to roll my suitcase through the crud. I'd packed enough clothing for two months and was so over myself I wanted to light it all on fire. Sweat poured from my brow and blisters forged painful balloons on my toes. I saw a police car make a U-turn in the distance and grumbled in shame.

"Miss, are you okay?" the officer asked as he unrolled his window.

"Not really." I couldn't look him in the eye.

"Where are you headed?"

"To a friend's, um—the north shore."

"Do you have a phone number or address, anyone to pick you up?"

For a moment, I got excited, like maybe the officer knew Randy. It was all a mistake and they were the ones picking me up, and Rosa was here yesterday, or coming tomorrow, all a big mix-up. The police would drive me to his house, or Rosa would pull up in a limo, or an extra-large pumpkin with an overgrown mouse as coachman.

"Miss? Hello?"

"Um, I think they got the wrong itinerary or something."

"Who's they? Do you have an address?"

I hung my head low, like it might snap off my neck. "No."

"Really?" His eyes said it all. "Get in. We'll look him up at the station."

The policewoman at the counter clicked and clacked at her giant computer, trying to locate a home on the north shore owned by an alleged Randy Delgard. She tried the north shore, then the south, the west shore, and the east. Nowhere was Randy registered as an owner of anything, not even a studio apartment in Lihue.

"Sorry, this man does not exist in our records. He's not on Kauai."

"For real? You sure?"

"Unless it's under someone else's name," she said, holding back the sympathy that ordinarily came so naturally to the Hawaiian aunties. Probably thinking this blonde-haired, blue-eyed mainlander, who was clearly no longer a child, had no business showing up on her island with no place to go and no one to guide her.

"You sure you don't have a phone number?"

"I can't find it," I lied.

"You flew all the way here with no number or address? Do you even know this person?"

I closed my eyes and held my breath, as though that might make her go away.

"Honey, I've been doing this for thirty years," she said. "I hate to break it to you—"

Tears trickled down my cheeks the way rain slips off a leaf. In no time, I was trembling; I moved my hands to my forehead to cover my eyes.

"Let's call your mother."

"No, it's okay."

Her eyes darkened. "Miss, have you run away from home?"

"Of course not." My temples began to throb as I realized how serious this was. "I love my mom. She knows I'm here. I just—"

"Then I insist," she said, turning the phone toward me, her Hawaiian accent warming. "Dial nine, then one."

I proceeded to punch the numbers, swiping tears from my cheeks, trying not to make eye contact with the three policemen sitting behind her, watching me from behind their desks. They'd laugh about me later.

I cradled the handset to my face and felt the ring ricochet through my ear canal to the walls of my brain as though my entire skull was empty, not a synapse or neuron to be found, just an echo chamber of a very dumb woman-child.

"No answer?" The lady looked at me with concern.

I shook my head. "She's probably working."

Unlike most mothers of young almost-women, my mother would not be sitting at home waiting by the phone to see if I'd arrived safely to the middle of the ocean. She would not have Randy's phone number as an extra precaution, written on her telephone pad or the back of her hand. Hell, I didn't even have his phone number. My mother would not be overly worried or in fear of my fate. She would quite likely not even be home.

It wasn't that my mom didn't care. She was always telling me how much she loved me and trusted me to make good decisions. She was just incredibly, incorrigibly, over-the-top *busy.*

"Shannon, I tell you, I was driving a car by the time I was ten." Mom had told this story a hundred times. "Grandpa said that I should go practice in the field, by myself! I could barely reach the pedals and clutches were impossible back then. By age thirteen, I was playing for most the town's dances and receptions. By age twenty-one, I was married with my first baby, teaching school, teaching piano, I had my own band . . . As for your great-grandma, well, she left Hungary at age eighteen, just she and her sister and a suitcase on a steamship to Canada. Didn't know a soul, didn't speak a lick of English, never saw her parents again. Ever. Can you imagine?"

They were woman, hear them roar! I would be no less capable. No less fantastic. Except, maybe, on this day.

"Where's your dad?" the policewoman asked.

"He's dead," I said, intentionally flat, knowing this always shut them up.

It was the way I'd said it for a while. As though to remind myself of the finality of it: his death, the car crash, the chocolate-brown coffin, the grated skin and dent on his forehead that all the pancake makeup in the world couldn't hide, and worst of all, the large purple bruise that formed even though they said the impact killed him instantly. *Were they sure? Had he felt any pain? Had he known he'd die?* The smell of formaldehyde, the eerily sad organ music, the black clothing, the too many flowers, the tears, his crumpled van, my crumpled world . . . it all flashed before me, the shittiness of growing up with one parent gone and the other living a life so full there seemed little room left for me.

Each day since the age of ten, since that fateful summer, I had wondered: *What would my life be like if HE was still here?*

One thing for sure, I would not be standing in the Lihue Police Station underage and alone, hoping on a thread of a thread for a ride to some Hollywood con artist's tropical estate.

"My dear, Officer Fukuhara can take you to a hotel," the police lady said in her best sweet voice.

"Thank you." I attempted a smile. "But I think I'll go home."

When we returned to the airport, the only counter open was Hawaiian Airlines. In my wallet was three hundred dollars, my driver's license, and a Visa card with a two-thousand-dollar limit. So, I purchased a one-way flight to Waikiki for forty bucks. The lady handed me my ticket and smiled the way people smile at the last puppy at the pet shop that no one wants to buy.

It was then and there it hit me: I would not fail at finding myself. I would likely not succeed either. But this would not go down in the annals of my ancestors—the great women, the great mothers and grandmothers, the great aunts, and all the great, greater, greatest who'd survived God only knew what fresh horrors—as a failure.

Hello, Waikiki! Let's play.

Good riddance, Garden Isle!

I never wanted to see her again.

CHAPTER 4

How do you best exterminate the vile creatures of the world—small, large, visible, invisible, real, illusory—from your sacred space?

a) Call an exterminator. Don't look too closely. Bugs are gross.
b) *Raid!* Be sure to wear a gas mask—that shit kills everything.
c) Pull up your slouch socks, get on your hands and knees, and do a catch and release with an old yogurt container. Choke the gag reflex down. They're just bugs.
d) You don't. This is the tropics. It's called a biome, *people.* Bugs, mold, and parasites are here to eat the decaying bits for you. *You're welcome!*

CHAPTER 4.1

Ayahuasca Journey
September 2021

The Shipibo tribe members believe that one's state of health, both physical and psychological, is dependent on the balanced union between mind, body, spirit. . . . They have another word for ayahuasca, oni, which means wisdom because they see this plant as a great teacher.[4]

Loops. A loop is like a circle. People like circles. Circles represent totality and completeness, and most profoundly, creative energy, like the egg or womb where life originates. Circles are at the infinite nature of our existence.

I always liked circles. But not tonight. Because the dark side of a circle is a loop. An endless loop. And I was in one.

There's no getting out of a loop. My mind had started racing, first a problem, then an answer, then problem, then answer, problem, answer . . . Each time the answer took me right back to the problem at a speed so vicious I could hardly hang on. Then the answer turned out to be no answer at all, rather another passage to trouble.

---

[4] *Grandmother Ayahuasca* by Christian Funder © 2021. Reprinted by permission of Inner Traditions International and Bear & Company. www.Innertraditions.com

The problems of the world came so big, so loud, so gruesome, spinning, spinning, spinning in my mind in a loop of madness. Which took me to a memory of my dad, not a complete memory, just a flash of one, a sliver, a shard.

When my dad died, in an effort to comfort me, my grandmother told me I would see my dad in Heaven. It wasn't a maybe, it was *for sure*. I made her promise me that it was true.

"Swear on the Bible, Grandma. Swear that Dad will be waiting for me in Heaven."

It would be the only thing that got me through his tragic death.

"He'll be there, promise." And she'd hug me, and I'd see that my grandma had turned patience into some sort of high art. This didn't stop the questions.

"How old will I be?" I'd ask her.

"You'll be ten," Grandma said.

"How old will Dad be?"

"He'll be the age he died, thirty-nine."

"But what if I die at ninety, won't I be ninety years old in Heaven?"

It was this particular thought that made me sick with confusion. The idea of living forever in Heaven stuck at a certain age. What child wants to be a child forever? What old person wants to be old forever? And what's the alternative, a heaven full of thirty-year-olds? It made no sense. Eventually, we'd want to grow up or grow old or get young or get out of Forever Land and out of that damn infinite loop.

Conflictingly, I wanted to believe my grandma so badly. I had to. It was all I had, my only hope of ever seeing my dad again.

"Then you'll be whatever your favorite age is," Grandma would say.

Okay, now you're just making shit up. "But if thirty-nine is Dad's best age, and thirty-nine is my best age, then we'll be the same age and he won't be my dad at all! And I need him to be my dad. I need my dad!"

And I'd cry so completely that I felt my heart shrivel into my spine. Maybe that's when my backaches began. Maybe that's why my back broke in that very spot behind my heart when I was eighteen.

In 1979, most families didn't hire therapists. Heck, we barely went to the doctor unless it was an emergency. As I recall, my family never even visited Dad's gravesite but for the time his parents came to visit before we moved away. And when the anniversary of his accident rolled around, we all stayed silent. How very British of us. Though we weren't even a little bit British, except by way of being part of the commonwealth. My blood roots were Eastern European and Nordic, and Canadian, of course. *Oh well—stiff upper lip, keep calm and all that.*

Poor Grandma was my therapist and so much more, and she was running out of answers.

"Shanni, we're not meant to know exactly how Heaven works. God is beyond our understanding. Have faith that Heaven is waiting for you, your father will be there, and it will be glorious."

Forty years later, I sat glued to the ground, lost in a realm where Heaven seemed an impossibility and the answers looped right back to the problem. Over and over, I watched the cycle of life play out on the screen of my mind at a staggering pace.

Birth. Life. Death. Birth. Life. Death. Too many thoughts. All the thoughts.

What's it all for? When your destination is a grave, what's the point? Why get better? Why get worse? Why even be at all? And where is God?

Nothing. Nada. Just a meaningless loop.

Like my mind, my body too was stuck in a loop. I couldn't get enough air. I could barely breathe.

I felt myself spinning off a track, a disc hurtling through space, squirming then wanting to barf. Then the vine would move through my stomach and intestines, and my lungs would expand mightily, like balloons attached to a helium tank, then I'd exhale loudly, as though I'd sprinted up a mountain, then another yawn so big my mouth felt wide as the sky.

So many people who drank the tea got their guts cleansed—puking or diarrhea. It was practically a rite of passage. Not me. How come?

Wait a minute—all this yawning, is the vine clearing out my lungs?

Yes. That was it! She was forcing air in and out, in and out. It began with yawning, then sighing, then yawning and sighing at the same time, and over and over again.

"The lungs are the organ of grief," a teacher had said in nutrition school. "They receive and let go, over and over, keeping the connection to the outer world in balance. If grief goes unchecked, the lungs become blocked and damage occurs."

When I was ten, no one ever asked me, "Are you okay?" Not then, not ever. My family just got on with it, as though losing a father occurred every day. Sure, people die in car accidents on the daily. Which made it impossible for my ten-year-old brain to compute, *Then why am I the only kid I know without a dad?*

Ever since then, my sadness, my anger, my betrayals, and my fears hid in the bleakest caverns of my lungs, never entering the light, blocking that invisible force that animates and gives us life, my breath. Without it we're dead.

I yawned then sighed again. Taking small comfort that maybe Abuela Ayahuasca knew what she was doing, helping me to heal . . . And maybe my grandma did too.

CHAPTER 4.2

Bugger

October 2017

Strange. The grain of rice on the counter appeared to move.

It had been ninety degrees every day for weeks, raining buckets through the night. The humidity was unworldly, how I imagined life would be in the heart of the Amazon, or Pandora, the earth-moon where the Avatarians lived in their bizarre jungle trees.

Everything was moist, the cushions on the couch, envelopes in the mail, chips in the bag, underneath my breasts, all of it.

I swore it moved again.

My feet were killing me. Sore from walking barefoot on the hard tile of our new home and the fact that nobody wore shoes here, just flip-flops, *thongs*, as we called them growing up. "Slippas," as I had better call them now, if I were to ever blend in.

Remove ya slippas at the door. And don't take mo better ones when you go.

I stood beside the sink in as little clothing as I could get away with, a sports-bra top and cutoffs, whipping up a King Kong–sized batch of guacamole as I had almost every day since we arrived. I could have cared less about the bulge of fat that hovered over my shorts, or if I looked cute or slim or even remotely passable, or that I should have been losing weight but was gaining on practically a fruit-only diet. Who does that?

Friends back home were cozying up in cashmere sweaters, boyfriend jeans, and cute boots, having lavish dinner parties in houses decorated for fall. The maple trees would be shedding their red and yellow leaves and the air would smell of cedar and compost. Meanwhile, I was sweating heaps, a faint bouquet of musk around me, nearly naked, feeling pudgy, obsessing over specks of rice on the counter like a lunatic.

"Josh, did you have rice for lunch?" I called out.

"Rice? No. Granola," Josh responded from the bedroom where he was readying for a surf session at Rock Quarry with Tyde and his new school chum JoJo.

"Have I made rice lately?" I couldn't remember.

"Don't think so!"

"What about the taco you ate last night from Paco's?" I directed my voice toward the bedroom; the yelling thing was getting old.

"Nope."

"Wait, there's rice on the floor too?" I walked toward the sliding door, eyes fixed on the tile. "Oh—my—God!"

Hundreds of tiny grains of rice were wiggling toward the light like a school of fish, only it was dry ground, my kitchen floor! There was also rice on the rug, under the chair, around the piano, everywhere.

"Josh!"

"What?" He came careening from the bedroom in a panic, his board shorts halfway up his hips. "What's wrong?"

"Maggots!"

"Huh?"

"You're standing on them!"

Josh jumped from foot to foot like he was doing a Scottish jig.

"You look ridiculous!" I laughed.

"You're the one screaming," he snorted.

"Because—" I swallowed to keep from spontaneously retching. "Now we need to find the corpse!"

Josh gave me his *you're a nutjob* glance. "Hon, they probably hatched from the garbage."

I shivered in dread.

"I'll get the vacuum." He tiptoed to the closet as though walking on hot coals.

"That won't work. How about a wet paper towel?"

"There's too many."

"Gross! You're cleaning the vacuum then."

I carefully got on my knees with paper towel in hand and began squishing the tiny buggers between my fingers. Each time their little bodies popped I got a shiver. It was so gross, hundreds of them, some even hanging, dripping from the counter where the compost sat with two-day-old rotting fruit peels. I'd never seen anything like it. I needed Josh as protector on this one. This had to be his win. My husband, Joshua the Maggot Slayer.

Three days earlier, a giant cockroach blew out of my air-conditioning vent and onto my lap while I was driving to Costco in my shitty new/old car that I bought off a neighbor. The week before that, I found a cockroach gnawing on my toothbrush in the bathroom drawer. Maybe he was just crawling past, but I wasn't about to give him the benefit of the doubt. The only possible food in that drawer was between the bristles of my toothbrush, so yeah, I'd have bet big bucks he was nibbling and pooping on my hygiene tools. I asked Josh to do something about it, but he was too slow. By the time he got three squares of toilet paper folded neatly into his fingers, that roach had slipped into a crack to poop and feast another day.

"Hello!" I heard someone sing-song from the other side of the window screen.

I turned to see a very pretty woman, also in jean shorts, but wearing a top, a designer T-shirt with holes spotting the neckline that made her look chic and broke at the same time.

"You must be Kylie, JoJo's mom." I tried not to reek of desperation.

It had been a month and I had yet to make a single mom friend. Not a one. Not even a hello bumping carts at the supermarket. Now would have been my chance, but I was too busy popping maggots.

"I'll be right there."

I whipped my head around to Josh with a grim face that—if he could only read my mind—said loud and clear: *Under no circumstances do we ask her in.*

Josh looked at me curiously, the way my dog used to look at me when I told her I didn't have time for a walk or couldn't share my ice cream. "What?" he whispered.

"She cannot know we have maggots." I hated it when he couldn't read my code face. "Do you copy?"

"Of course."

I got up to get the door.

"Oh, sexy," Kylie joked, eyeballing my skimpy getup, as I closed the front door behind me, paper towel in hand.

"Ha, I'm not used to this weather yet. It's so hot." I smiled the way moms smile at each other when they first meet. The smile that says, *I've got this all under control and I'm super fun, I never yell at my kids or my husband, we have a fabulous sex life, and so many friends, and my farts smell like roses and I'm really cool, I swear . . .*

"Tyde," I called toward the side of the house, "JoJo and his mom are here."

Tyde came around the corner with the big foam Costco board on his head wearing surf trunks and no shoes. He'd already completely forgotten that once upon a time, in a faraway place called Canada, we wore shoes with laces, and shirts and jackets too. On this one Kauai custom, we'd all adapted rather quickly.

JoJo helped Tyde place the board in the back of Kylie's truck, then piled in the front seat, the two of them laughing about something as JoJo cranked the *Moana* soundtrack. They already seemed close.

"Is your husband coming?" Kylie asked, as that had been the plan.

"Hon—you going surfing?"

Josh stepped out the front door with his hand out to shake Kylie's. "I'm Josh."

"I'm Kylie." She spread her arms wide and embraced him. "We hug here."

"I'll take it!" he said a little too enthusiastically.

My eye twitched. I might have shot a stink eye, but they were both staring and smiling at me as I folded and refolded the maggot towel between my fingers. And anyway, she wasn't like that. I could just tell.

"You need a proper hug too." She leaned in to wrap her arms around me with a big smile. God, she was pretty and with that Australian accent, so posh.

"Oh, okay," I said, sucking my elbows to my ribs in fear of sharing armpit sweat, giving the limpest hug ever.

"The island of aloha," she said warmly, then tucked her hands in her pockets. "So, how are you faring here? It's weird at first, isn't it?"

This was the moment that all new friendships teetered on—the *do I be honest or do I white-lie* moment. The *what kind of friends will we be* moment. Casual pretendship, where we fake pretty little lives, practice phony smiles, and secretly compete? Or, the real deal, lay it all out, ride or die—laugh, cry, doesn't matter because you're my sister so let's prick our pinkies and make a blood bond. All this to be decided in a moment, a glance, a head tilt, a twitch of the nose, the muddy art of reading body language and subtext, energy and auras, the things we women do so well.

She looked, waiting.

Well, answer her, Bozo!

Josh nodded. Both bubbling in anticipation.

Best not disappoint.

"This place is bizarre." The words spilled out in a jumble. "As we speak, maggots are forming a coup d'état in my kitchen—"

It was happening. I was going for it. There would be no stopping me now.

"I'm sweating balls. We don't know anyone. We live in the country. I'm a *farm* wife! There's no kids for miles. I have zero friends. I left a bustling city of three million and I—I—I feel like I'm mildly schizophrenic or taking crazy pills. Do Hawaiians hate white people here? Do white people hate white people here? Do the tourists ever leave? What's up with the traffic? And will the fricking roosters just shut the hell up? I need a chicken trap, no, a BB gun! And storage, I need storage. Where do I buy a shelf unit? Our stuff arrives in a week! A whole forty-foot container of gak! Are there furniture stores?

Or just surf shops, food trucks, and Toyota dealers? This was supposed to be a six-month sabbatical. Really, we never meant to move. Where does a girl get a fresh-baked barbeque chicken around here? Safeway? Man, I miss those. And maple-bacon donuts, do they have those? Only once in a blue moon, but, I mean, yum—"

Kylie started laughing. "Oh my God." Her perfect teeth gleaming, but not in a *you're so pathetic* kind of way, rather an *I'm on your side* way. "I know how you feel." She reached her hand to my arm to squeeze it. "Believe it or not, it'll come together. Give it time."

Josh gave me that *nutjob* look again.

Part of me wanted to crawl under a rock, or nab a cigarette. It was quite satisfying, really, to spill my guts to someone who might actually care. To think that the incredible flurry of activity of the past two months, actually the past seven months—leading right back to January 22 when we put an offer down on this house and turned my temporary wish of a six-month sabbatical into a permanent move—might have been a huge mistake. Possibly the hugest! An enigma wrapped in wishful thinking drenched in adrenaline, with a pinch of reality to hold it together. That poor pinch had a lot on its plate.

"See you guys again soon." Kylie rolled away with the kids in the truck, still giggling from our exchange.

"Bye." I waved again, the feeling of satisfaction quickly slipping into what could only be regret.

Josh had promised to make his way to meet them in the next hour. Coral Quarry was a convenient five-minute drive from our house and well on its way to becoming our favorite local beach. Convenience wasn't something we mainlanders were willing to part with.

"Why'd you say that?" Josh gave me that look again.

He made sure Kylie's truck was well gone before he posed the question. I figured it was coming. I figured I was in trouble.

Not the kind of trouble where you get a good scolding, say you're sorry, and that's the end of it. No, this was more fundamental, like parasites in the bloodstream or rat nests in the walls.

"I don't know." We reentered our maggot-infested kitchen to get back to the job, now checking corners and under carpets for the assholes that got lost. We could not have those things hatching—good God, the swarm of nasty flies that would follow. "It just came out."

"Did you mean it?"

"I barely remember what I said."

Josh pulled out the vacuum and got to it. The sound of the vacuum saving me from any real explanation. I wasn't ready to talk about it. The sabbatical I never got. The six months of nothing but a beach, surf, mangoes, a pile of good books, just us and the kids and nothing else, no business, no family drama, no cancer. He promised. We would leave for Costa Rica or Mexico within the year that his mom died. That would be our reward for all our hard work, not just with his family, but in our lives and the serious labor of six-day workweeks, twelve-hour set days, never knowing if we were coming or going in a crazy business with young kids, a giant mortgage, all of that.

Anyway, it was too late. The deed was done. Fini! *Forty-foot container filled with all our stuff and arriving in a week* done. The moment it arrived, it was official—we've moved. We've left Canada. Gone. Starting over in a new country, packing up everything we owned, all that mattered, selling cars and leaving family—the opposite of a sabbatical. A sabbatical was a rest, not a departure, a reprieve, a time to reflect and be silent and work on ourselves from the inside out. A sabbatical was easy.

"Shan, we still own the house." Josh stepped on the vacuum to shut off the motor. "The renters have a two-year lease. If things don't pan out, we can always go back."

"Of course," I said with none of the fervor that I had delivered in my earlier soliloquy.

"Though, after all the work to get here, I can't imagine going back, but . . ." He trailed off without finishing his sentence.

I nodded again and did my best to look at him with a soft face, instead of the accidental (but I really couldn't help it) bitch face that often adorned me.

It wasn't me, really; I wasn't a bitch. At least, I didn't want to be. I just wanted everyone happy, that was all. And I wasn't sure Kauai could do that. I was bipolar on Kauai. At once it was both weird and awesome, paradise, drop-dead gorgeous and all that, also totally backward and unconventional and there were just so many bugs! I already knew that I would have none of my conveniences, whether it was Whole Foods, my raw milk supply, my car mechanic, or my brother nearby. Kauai was work, major work; we were starting over. Everything from schools and medical, to jobs and finding new friends, not just for me but for everyone in the family. Especially Canyen, who'd been whining since we'd arrived about how much he missed his pals.

The day before we left our village, I caught him at the corner store sitting at a table with his two besties eating Fudgsicles and chitchatting like little old men playing cards. It pained me because I knew I had taken that away from him. We moved to a farm road and I'd no clue if there were boys on this road to play with, and the only corner store was ten miles away. Actually, we were miles away from everything. And yes, we'd wanted that. Privacy. But not at the expense of my kids having friends. We were starting over, and starting over was a bitch, especially when life had gotten mostly pretty darn good back where we had left.

"Why *did* we move, Josh?"

"What?"

"I just . . ." I hunched my back over like a sad clown staring at his big blue plastic shoes. "I just don't know if *we* belong here."

"To escape the damn rat race." I could see the blood rising up his neck, flooding his capillaries, turning him a shade of pink. Josh always started out nice, but if I pushed too much or too hard, a different side of him stood at the ready. "To get out of the grind."

"But don't you think the grind was grinding down for us, getting better?"

How I thought we could have this conversation and still hang on to the levity of our day was naive. We had both been in good spirits, even with a legion of worms crawling across our sparkling home. Tyde with a surf buddy, plus Kylie's visit and the promise of a new friend, added a shiny layer of sweet and hopeful to this strange new world of ours, and now I was wrecking it.

"We wanted this, Shan—a simpler life."

I should stop now. I don't need to say everything on my mind.

"But with your parents gone, it was bound to get easier for us right where we were."

"Yes, but you always say, 'Regret the things you do, not the things you don't do,'" he huffed, exhausted. "When you saw the fruit orchard online, the pineapples, the flowers, this house, you said, 'Let's do it.' Remember?"

"Yes, I guess. I mean, I sort of hemmed and hawed. But it's true, I'm all for an adventure." I paused to catch my breath, my lungs tightening. "But don't you think we needed a rest and not a move? You switched directions on me. One minute we were searching for a place to rent so we could sabbatical, then suddenly we're looking at real estate."

"We agreed it would be easier to sabbatical in the US than a foreign country. Hawaii is both! Remember the hell we went through trying to exchange money in Costa Rica? That was just a two-week vacation. Shan, our finances are ridiculously complicated. Years of tax returns in two countries—seven a year! Who can keep that up?"

I nodded.

"We wanted land. Our own land. It's cheaper here. We saw opportunity and we jumped! Who the hell wouldn't want to live here? The fucking land of surf and honey."

Surf and honey? Aha! That's when I saw it, when I realized what had happened.

Josh, the California boy—the intrepid surfer who never got to do his sport, not since his early thirties, who needed to play hard and be in the ocean—had been planning this his whole life. Hawaii had always been the goal.

And me, prairie girl from a small city near the Montana border, who wanted my life to be an adventure like the women I grew up watching on TV, nothing but big dreams of seeing the whole wide world—

I never felt so alive as when I lived in Los Angeles, waking up in my dilapidated, but achingly cool, bohemian beachside rental in Santa Monica, flitting off to Gold's Gym for a prework workout where on any given day, I might have seen Ray Liotta or Ted Danson. Hitting CBTL at nine for a steaming vanilla latte, off to direct a TV crew in a restaurant on La Cienega or a boutique in Beverly Hills, surrounded by people brimming with that Hollywood *je ne sais quoi*. The weekend would roll around and I'd take off to Mammoth with my ski buddy—a Hollywood agent to has-beens who kept their careers alive by selling home goods and cheap lingerie, making a fortune. We'd sleep at Motel 6 and get our mountain/nature/snow fix, then return Sunday night to do it all over again. It was grand. I was in the center of the entertainment universe, my very own slice of glamour-pie.

And Josh. He grew up there. He didn't care. He only wanted Hawaii. Simplicity. Calm.

Me? I wanted it all.

"I don't know if we thought it through," I said quietly, not wanting to start something.

"We didn't. We felt it. Which is better. Organic. The way you like it." Josh looked at me earnestly. "It's the dream, Shan! People bust ass their whole lives for this."

Nearly on cue, we both took a gusty breath that said, *Let it go.*

"I guess I'm still shaken from the move, getting here."

"Me too." He wiped his hair from his eyes, his wavy mop ever in need of a trim.

This made him vulnerable. I always cut his hair and he was only ever grateful for my snip jobs, good or bad, even the bowl cuts.

"Remember, Shan, moving is a top-three stressor—death, divorce, and this."

"You're right." I giggled, an attempt to elevate the mood. "Well, these maggots aren't going to pop themselves."

Josh smiled his handsome smile. "It's going to be great, hon. Don't overthink it."

I put the Kleenex box down to walk to him for a hug. But it was too late. He'd already flicked the vacuum back on.

CHAPTER 4.3

Spring 2016

This always happened. Gluten-free lasagna noodles, the bane of my existence. You had to drop them just so into the boiling water, then stir quickly, but not too fast or they'd break, then pull the pot from the heat just in time but not too soon, then drain them oh-so-carefully and rinse with cold water but not too hard with the nozzle, and don't burn yourself for goodness' sake.

Anyway, none of that mattered because half the noodles had already split or shredded, and the other half stuck together in a gelatinous clump—despite there not being a sticky gluten protein in sight for at least a few city blocks.

"Who opened that window," Josh's mom said with bony hands firmly on hips, standing at the edge of her kitchen in a puffy blue robe.

Oxygen tubes sat on the space between her nose and lip, like she'd been wearing those tubes her whole life, like the stage 4 cancer was the least of her worries and the real problem was whether the shades were drawn or someone mucked with the thermostat or—God forbid—opened a window.

"Me?" I hesitated, plucking noodles from the strainer, melting my thumbs in the process, cursing the fact that I'd married a celiac. "But, Robin—"

"You know the AC is on. I'm trying to keep it cool in here."

"Cool? The AC doesn't even work," I said, as nicely as I could muster.

I'd been cooking for two hours: chopping onions, frying, seasoning the ground beef on a hot-ass, open-flame stove, shredding the cheese, assembling the spinach and ricotta layer and tomato sauce from scratch. My task was two extra-large gluten-free lasagnas for a party Josh's mom was throwing that night. The other two non-gluten-free lasagnas would be picked up from the pizza place, a quick drive down the canyon, two blocks from the Glendale Target.

We were in Los Angeles. Our third trip that year to see Josh's mom, Robin, who shared the same name as my sister. The temperature outside was 102 degrees. Inside? Death Valley.

"It does work, but you guys keep opening the doors and windows."

"Because we need air. I'm sweating bullets," I said, laying out the broken noodles side by side to see what could be salvaged. "Please, I'm so hot."

"I know my house." She scurried past me, as though she might climb on the sink to close the windows herself, her silver hair standing upright from too many hours in bed.

Poor thing, on round three of an experimental drug. Only this time, it wasn't working. The doctor had warned that eventually this would happen. Lung cancer does that. It tends to win.

She hadn't deserved it. No one does. Robin never even smoked, which was a myth anyway. Loads of nonsmokers get lung cancer, especially women.

Through my studies, I knew that the lungs represented grief. It seemed to me that Robin was dying of sadness from a difficult marriage. Josh said she often didn't feel heard or understood. Which was weird because she conversed well and had strong opinions, right down to delivering to me, days after marrying her son, a pamphlet on how hard it was to get pregnant after age thirty-five. Like, statistically speaking, impossible. I was thirty-four. *Lube up, young lady—time to give me grandchildren.*

The funny thing was, I rarely saw her sad. I never even saw her cry, not about her cancer or anything. But I saw her frustrated, a lot. I saw her boss people around. I saw her angry. And we all know, Anger is Sad's bodyguard, and Anger is damn good at its job. On this, I could relate.

"Robin, seriously, what are you doing?" I was now scooping hamburger meat into casserole dishes, simply wanting to finish. I was so close to my escape from that sweltering kitchen.

"Mom! Seriously?" Josh entered from the garage where he was working on decluttering, sneakily loading Robin's cardboard box collection into the recycling and tossing freezer-burnt food from her forty-year-old Whirlpool upright freezer. That thing was like an Egyptian tomb. Still, nobody wanted Marie Callender pie from 1998.

"The windows need to be shut!" she insisted. "Do you know what electricity costs in California?"

The sun beat across my chest like a spotlight, scorching me with its most dangerous of rays, the ones that made it through the glass, the ones that brought no beneficial vitamin D, just a bright red burn, a mild torching, a precancerous glow. Meanwhile, beads of sweat rounded my cheek onto my jaw and were performing a quick sauté toward my chin.

It had been days of taking orders from her—in honesty, it felt like years. Every vacation Josh and I had was now spent in LA. We'd book Mexico only to cancel it for a last-minute TV show or an urgent trip to California. Eight years of cancer had run through that house. First Josh's dad's lymphoma. Then his too early passing. Now Robin, or Dammy, as the grandkids called her.

"I'm not doing this," I announced.

"Just close it!"

"No!"

And then I did something I never do: I walked off the job. Tossed my apron to the floor and stomped right past her, staging my own mini temper tantrum. Josh followed in solidarity.

"Come back!" she yelled.

"No!" I yelled back.

By the time Josh and I had dashed to the bedroom like a couple of teenagers in trouble, she was calling through the intercom, two flights of stairs away.

"Come back, you two!"

Silence. Then footsteps. Clattering. Good God, she was nimble. She was scurrying down the green shag-carpeted stairs, past the huge plate-glass windows and the giant macramé plant holder with the philodendron dangling to the floor.

I loved that house. All seventies Neutra architecture built into the canyon like a wooden waterfall, plants hanging in thick braided rope, sleek Danish post-modern furniture and artwork worth thousands from their one-time art gallery. All of this was her design, her taste, her stuff, her legacy, her job—that and planning trips, dinners, vacations, talking to friends, delegating, with a phone permanently melded to her ear.

"We've got to get out of here," I whispered to Josh.

Part of me knew Robin couldn't help herself—control was her last form of safety. Yet I wasn't about to give her the satisfaction of an apology or even the chance to talk at me.

That sounds cold. Cancer is brutal. And I was deeply sympathetic. She'd nursed her husband through years of treatments and transfusions, while Tom's body shrunk and his brain slackened and he transitioned from the material to the ethereal. I watched the cycles of vitriol the two once shared melt away as a warm rain thaws ice. I saw their couple-hood redeemed as he came to regularly thank her for sticking by his side with a loving arm around her shoulder and a soft kiss on the cheek. Oh, how she needed that. And I saw her take small pleasure in the idea that one day, once her husband passed, she would hatch a life of travel, fun, and friends with no one or thing to stop her. Peace would be hers and deservedly so. And I saw her robbed of that when she got her cancer diagnosis exactly one month before her husband died. And I wondered about providence and justice and the cold hard realities of life.

"Let's go." Josh slid open the side door of the guest room. "She's coming."

"Shit." I snagged my shorts on the balcony that we were now hopping over in a bizarre game of *escape my husband's mother.*

Josh and I slid down the railing, onto the back deck, around the hot tub, up the opposite side of the house and toward the garbage cans, huffing and puffing from the sprint. We split out the gate and onto the road in front of the house then stopped dead in our tracks, staring at each other with crazy eyes.

"This is insane." I choked up a laugh while attempting to catch my breath.

"So insane." Josh grabbed his belly, also hiccupping laughter. "Let's walk."

We grabbed hands and began a quick stride up and away from Josh's childhood home. Forty-five years old and running from Mommy. I had to stop to contain the giggles, tears now streaming from my eyes. It was all too much.

"Oh God, look!" Josh gulped.

I turned. "No."

Robin stood in the middle of the street in her robe, looking both fierce and harmless at the end of her oxygen tether. Where on earth she had found tubes that long was a feat that only she could have managed. How many packs of premium crush-resistant oxygen tubes had it required for her to make it half a block from her tank? How many customer service agents had to hear her explain the necessity of a tether that would take her to the far reaches of the universe so she could publicly scold her middle-aged son and his wife?

The reality TV producer in me knew I had a gem here, passing up the show of a lifetime: *Dammy and Her Damn Cancer*. Something like that. Robin was made for reality TV and I would know. For the bulk of my career, I'd pitched TV shows as a side hustle. An impossible business, but that never stopped me. I loved the process: the germination of concept, the casting, shooting the reel, my kick-ass partner—I'd no doubt we'd eventually launch a winner. But casting family was a no-go, destined to destroy any chance of peaceful relations, including family dinners, holidays, and more. As it was, most of the time, it wasn't funny.

Josh would come home from work in Vancouver with eighteen missed calls on his phone. He'd show me in defeat. "She's calling to see if we're coming for Christmas. It's September."

I always knew when Josh was on the phone with his mom because he'd be arguing, despite their being thousands of miles apart. Then I'd hum the long-distance TV ad from childhood, "Reach out, reach out and touch someone," and picture the kid on the couch with the broken leg, yucking it up with grandma—only Josh was often pacing, swearing at the walls, and kicking things.

Typically, after calling Josh ad nauseam, Robin would give up and call me. I'd have to explain that I had no clue what we'd be doing on December 14 or March 28 or August 5 because we were TV contractors and jobs could come days before and Josh could be off on a plane to Pennsylvania or South Dakota or France! By this time, my TV career was far less exotic. I might have found myself in a van slogging to Surrey to direct a *Love It or List It* episode, or at a downtown bistro filming rich housewives behaving badly.

"Come inside," she called to us from the street, the curve in her spine looking particularly distorted in the harsh noon sun. "I'm sorry."

"Okay," I said, feeling childish, and walked over to give her a hug. "I'm sorry too."

I was terrible at holding a grudge. Anyway, it was no longer funny and I was no longer mad. And that lasagna was not about to cook itself.

Robin passed away four months later. She had done everything in her power to make a clean break, estate in order and all. It was a fine legacy. She did an admirable job.

Strangely though, Josh never got the closure he needed from either parent. Not an *I'm sorry* from his dad for the rage that erupted when he fought with his wife, or a *forgive me* for being placed in the middle of their battles, or a *thank you* for Josh's effort as protector to his mom when Josh just needed to be a kid.

With two parents dead from cancer in short order, plus two kids morphing and needing all things under the sun on the daily, Josh and I had a front row seat to the Sandwich Generation Roller Coaster. *Buckle up!* Each day brought new challenges that we often didn't feel equipped to handle. Losing parents when you still need them was a quagmire beyond our busy little brains. Which made me wonder if there was ever a time that we didn't need mom or dad. A hundred years old on my deathbed, *I sure wish my mom was here to hold my hand.*

One thing was clear, we had no choice. Life would just keep tossing boulders and Josh and I would keep jumping, or swerving, or shooting Uzis, blowing obstacles from our path. And you know what? Our parents did that; they armed us for life's challenges the best they could. No matter what their temperament—Robin, Tom, Marguerite, Jim—each did the best with what they were given.

Yet there was a sliver of shame I carried. Why hadn't I tried better to channel Jesus or Mother Mary or Buddha, someone, during the tough times with my mother-in-law? Was it so hard to be my best self? The woman was dying for Chrissake!

In her home, I was always a good helper: party prepping, hosting, cooking, cleaning, clearing clutter, getting Robin's extremely belated Christmas cards out just in time for Easter . . . But that was superficial. Anyone could have done that. It was not enough.

Until one day, Josh said to me, "Remember that Christmas when we all drove to Palm Springs, two cars full, and the only adult my mom would drive with was you? We were too triggered, too inside it. She was impossible. But you, Shannon? You were able to step out of the bull shit and just *be* for her. You listened. . .when no one else could."

Hmm. Maybe there was a little channeling going on after all.

CHAPTER 5

If you suddenly had to escape a blazing house fire and could retrieve only one thing, what would it be?

a) The family's heirloom jewelry collection.
b) Computers and such.
c) Your *Wizard of Oz* figurine collection.
d) As long as the kids are safe, wild horses couldn't drag you back in.
e) Your things define you. Run back into that godforsaken house with a giant Santa sack and grab as much sh** as you can get your mitts on.

CHAPTER 5.1

Ayahuasca Journey
September 2021

The ayahuasca, in combination with the healing songs of the Shaman, is said to be profoundly restorative. Before healing begins, energy bodies often appear to be covered with chaotic patterns that reflect the spiritual imbalance of the person.[5]

"Tell the vine to slow down if you need to," Steven's wife, Sarah, had told me earlier, "she'll listen. You decide the speed."

Sarah lied. Or I was too weak. Or doing it wrong. Something. There was no reasoning with Grandmother Aya. No way to slow her down. No downshift. No anti-venom. Quite simply, there was no getting off this ride.

Am I stuck here forever?

That's the thing about being forced into the now of everything. Even in the mundane every day, when things go bad, it feels like forever, but you know it will eventually end. Imagine that on a psychedelic.

---

[5] *Grandmother Ayahuasca* by Christian Funder © 2021. Reprinted by permission of Inner Traditions International and Bear & Company. www.Innertraditions.com

Earlier, while I waited for the Aya to take effect, I had honed my intention. I asked to be shown *how to be* and *how best to serve.* I thought that was a big enough question that it would give me direction in every area of my life: kids, husband, career, community. I thought it wise, generous, humble, *how gracious of me—*

Ha! She was laughing at me. What a joke to think I could control this, her, or that my intention was somehow noble. Abuela had other plans.

I'd become her firsthand witness on the scene of the myriad crimes against humanity and crimes against Earth. Witness to the most heinous acts humans were capable of: gruesome murders, gas chambers, electric chairs, lobotomies, rape, molestation (*oh God, the children)*, vivisection (*the animals*), such gore, devils in dark suits with mangled faces who'd warp into evil puppeteers, strings on fingers attached to an endless parade of workers in gray garb and soldiers doomed to war. Then she showed me robot-like men with Kevlar vests and knee pads, guns drawn, menacing, doing the bidding of a malevolent force bigger than all of us, bigger than her.

Then she took me to lakes turned to poison pits with factories oozing noxious refuse, fish belly-up, whales tangled in drag nets, turtles choked in plastic, earth movers destroying swath after swath of rainforest, old growth downed in a vicious swipe of a gargantuan machine with grisly eyeballs and a steely grin.

Then us, the consumer, our complicity, our apathy, our vanity, our superficiality.

Then she got personal. I saw the brutality of a friend's husband who'd hung himself—the money, the lies, the abuse, the hookers, the private jets, the hunting the mightiest of bucks, the secret clubs, the too good for all of us, and, finally, him swinging from a noose.

Then I saw the man near me raped as a child, and the guy across from him beaten, and him beating his kids, and it went around and around like this again.

I moaned and moaned a death cry. A deep bellow from the center of the earth. Pain. Suffering. Anguish. I felt it in my every pore. Sorrow rushed over me like lava, melting my tissues to liquid while dread sat in my chest like a lead bomb. Heaviness glued me to my mat. I couldn't move; I only moaned in futility. I wanted to puke so badly. Yawning was not enough.

Please rid me of this evil. Let it out. Let it out! Put me out of my misery, please.

All around me retching and I could only moan, wrapping my head in my scarf in hopes that the relentless horror show would pass, burrowing deep into my mat and the grass beneath me like a centipede squirming to escape the light.

No. Not fair. Not a centipede. A centipede is useful, a helper; like a spider, they eat the bugs that bug us. No. I was an ascaris, a parasite, lowest of the low, infecting human bodies, infecting the skin of Mother Earth, taking, taking, taking.

CHAPTER 5.2

Stuff

November 2017

"What's happening?" I woke up, startled, wind sweeping wildly through the room and no clue where I was again. *Dorothy? Is this Oz? Will a tornado take my home? Toto? Josh?*

Each night my dreams took me far away. Mostly strange places that had no zip code. But occasionally, Canada, familiarity, my past.

Strange to think of Canada as my past. I missed the land and my community, but mostly, I missed my friends. With me no longer in the neighborhood, friends dropping by were no longer, with the exception of Kylie dropping off JoJo to see Tyde now and then, and those visits were far too brief.

Four, five, six weeks without a naughty text, a gut-busting laugh, a gossip or colluding of any sort. It was a friendship celibacy I didn't ask for and didn't want. The worst part was that I was alone in this undertaking. None of my friends had left their everything. Normal people didn't walk away from a full life for a mirage of perfection, even if that mirage was paradise. My few close girlfriends from home may have felt the occasional pang of, *Where's Shannon? Oh yeah, she's gone.* But it couldn't have been anything like the dry ache that sat stiff in the middle of my chest, welded to my every breath.

Another gust sailed through, as though the wind was trying to push leaves, twigs, bugs, and birds through the tiny holes in the screens. Kauai had her moods, and wow would they swing. Sun, rain, wind, sun, rain, wind. Scorching. Pelting. Blowing.

You could count on her unpredictability. After a huge gust, she'd send rain. Buckets pouring from the corners of our roof. Then silence. Then a sunbeam. Then a gust. Then a downpour. Over and over again, like a menopausal woman in the throes of great change.

I'd no clue of the time; judging by the light, maybe seven o'clock. I heard Mama K beat the lanai outside our sliding door with pellets of rain, then looked to my right for Josh beside me. "Josh? Where are you?"

Damn, he's gone again. It scared me when he wasn't there when I woke up.

"Your tea, madam?" And just like that, he appeared, pushing open the door with an elbow, wearing the all-too-common Kauai uniform: surf shorts, T-shirt, slippers at the front door.

"Thanks, hon." I pressed myself to sitting, feeling relieved. "What time is it?"

"Time to get up, sleepyhead." He stroked my head.

I reached for the hot mug.

"Guess what?" He didn't wait for me to respond. "I've applied for my real estate license," he said, beaming, already heading for the door, zingy and ripe for busyness. "There's coffee for Her Highness when she's ready."

"Wait, what? Did you say real estate license?" Josh was already back in the kitchen.

I placed the cup carefully on the night table beside the bronze lamp shaped like a palm tree, then swung my legs off the bed to get up, the way old ladies do. There was a full eight inches between my feet and the carpet. I'm tall, five foot eight or nine depending on the day, so it was weird stretching down for the ground to get up. We had a true plantation poster bed with a mattress so elevated I felt like I was in "The Princess and the Pea." Only there was no pea—maybe an ant or a cockroach, but no pea. I wouldn't have felt it anyway. The bed was too soft, like a marshmallow. It sucked me in and wouldn't let me go. Some days I'd oblige, telling myself I needed the rest, deserved it. But really, I was stalling. Now that we lived in Kauai motivating to get out of bed was the hardest thing I did all day. Finding important and meaningful things to do was a close second.

In the kitchen, Josh smiled at me bursting with good news.

"I've decided to sell time-shares." He took a slug of his coffee and set it down like he was banging a gavel.

Ah, I see someone has found their important and meaningful thing to do, I thought but did not say. No wonder he was so happy.

"Seriously?" I sat cupping my tea, slouching across from him at the table, still waking up. "Wait, so you want to go from reality TV cameraman, and all the insanity of that, to high-strung sales? Don't we hate time-shares?"

"Maybe. Sort of," he said from his side of the table. The sun splashed blindingly onto the glass while bright red ginger flowers waved from the window like cheerleaders applauding his decision from the stands. "You know how I love real estate. Secretly, I've always wanted to get my license, and time-shares are easy. It's a part-time job compared to my old schedule. I'll get to meet people, connect with locals, and learn how the market works here."

If I hadn't known better, I'd think that while I lay sleeping, my husband had been beamed aboard a spaceship of reptilian overlords—the only service-to-self aliens that embraced the nastiest bits of corporate-controlled capitalism and rampant greed. The rest of the galactic had figured out that allowing power-grubbing oligarchs carte blanche on the planet was a quick slide to annihilation.

"How hard can it be?" Josh's normally handsome brows arched up into his hairline like Howdy Doody.

Who is this man in my kitchen? And why couldn't the Pleiadians, those wise specters of light, have beamed him up? Instead—*Yes, yes, Kang, feed these stupid humans piña coladas to sell a share of time in a box with a signature on a piece of paper. Brilliant! Next, we destroy Earth! Oh, wait, humans are already doing that. Shall we steal the sun?*

"I don't doubt the absence of difficulty for you," I said, poking an itch in my eye from a lone cartoonish blood vessel that flared when I got stressed, this time caused by the marathon of packing and moving. "It's just, well, it's kind of cheesy. Everyone on this island is either doing it or has done it."

"Not everyone," Josh said with too much vigor for a morning chat.

"Well, that's true. This place is brimming with nutritionists too." I groaned. "Yay me, here comes another 'health coach.'" I bent my fingers into air quotes.

When we made the decision to move here, I thought my freshly minted nutrition degree might be a doorway to a serious business. People come here to get healthy and my plan was to help fill that niche. Instead, I discovered my newfound vocation was as common as the cockroach. *Health coach certifications free in every pack of mushroom powder.* Healer types everywhere—naturopaths, Reiki masters, Ayurvedic practitioners, acupuncturists, breathwork gurus, massage therapists—an entire island of health freaks, alongside timeshare folk, holding hands, singing "Kumbaya," and Josh and I were two more bodies to toss in the mix.

"Uh-oh." Josh glanced at his phone for a time check. "Got to go." He pushed his chair out and stood. "How's my hair?"

"It's a bit much today." I laughed and plopped my head into my hands.

"What?" He giggled.

This was our playful.

"The back of your head looks a little *Dumb and Dumber*."

"Like a bowl? That's on you. You were supposed to cut it." He wet his hands at the sink and patted it down.

"I would have—"

"It's fine. Got to go. Headed to the real estate board to sign up for the exam and get my papers. You got the kids?"

I turned toward the bedrooms and cupped my mouth for volume. "Boys! Time to get up, my sweeties!"

"I ammmm!" Tyde screamed from the bathroom, already upset with me.

"What's with him?" I rolled my eyes, noting that this particular phase of modern boyhood—the angry pubescent bear, the too-quick-to-react preteen, the f-bomb-dropping gamer—was not some passing fancy but rather a latent personality trait rearing its head alongside armpit hair and a cracking voice.

Josh shrugged. "He's all yours," he said, then kissed me on the cheek.

"Wait! I'm happy for you." I kissed him back.

"Thanks, hon."

"Don't you want to know what I'm up to?"

"Sure." He was already outside, tilting his head to peer through the window screen like Ned Flanders over the fence to Homer Simpson.

"Well, I've got to call my one client with psoriasis. She's quite sick. Then I'm going to post another health video, maybe on hormones, or maybe on living here, *healthiest place on Earth.*" I swirled my hands like Glinda the Good Witch, then fluffed the cowl that formed nightly at the back of my head. Thanks to my dark roots, it looked like a muddy straw tornado, impossible to flatten or cover without a fresh shampoo every day (not about to happen).

"Great!" Josh said, starting the truck engine. "Good luck!" He slammed the door, reggae cranking from Kauai's number-one hit music station, Kong 93.5, already his favorite.

A feeling of dread shot through my body.

Stupid container is due in three days. Where will I put everything?

I hate reggae music, Josh loves it. It's an impasse!

Why does Tyde yell at me first thing? Is it those first-person shooter games?

What are we to do with all the fruit rotting on the ground?

Do I seriously have to work the farmers markets?

I left an exciting and very real TV career for this?

With those thoughts, and nowhere to place them, I began the daily routine of serving breakfast, making lunches, driving kids to school, cleaning, sweeping the front and back lanais, then staring at my computer screen. Knowing that when I imagined our new life in Kauai, *and all the places I would go*, it looked nothing like me sitting braless in my pj's at the kitchen table.

Container Day arrived like a tornado. It was due at noon, forty by twenty feet of it, stacked to the gills with stuff, no furniture, just stuff. The kids were bouncing off the walls like Ping-Pong balls.

"What time will it get here?" asked Canyen with bulging eyes.

"That means I get my PlayStation! You packed it, right?" pleaded Tyde. "Right?"

"My toys are coming!" Canyen yelped. "I can't wait!"

My head spun like an Astro Wheel: *Why didn't it sink? Can we deny it's ours? Do we run for the hills?*

Surely, Josh was thinking the same thing.

In a few hours, boxes overflowing with toys, books, clothes, linens, pillows, dishes, knickknacks—as well as loose items like kayaks, fishing rods, bikes, baskets, stools, tool kits, skateboards, and so much more—would land on our driveway. Meanwhile, the painters were still milling about the house at island pace and we had yet to dispose of half the stuff left by the previous owners that now cluttered our garage.

What made today even more daunting was the memory of the last time I saw that blasted container, five weeks ago in Lions Bay. It had been a beautiful late September day. Puffs of white scattered in the sky like cotton balls. A chill in the air signaled this side of the earth had begun its tilt away from the giant fireball in the sky, toward winter slumber. The birds had fled to Florida or Guatemala, minus the hummingbirds who knew fresh sugar water in bright red plastic feeders would be filled for winter (thanks to folks like me, obsessed with the cute little buggers).

At exactly five o'clock, a driver would come connect our unfathomably long container to a semi-trailer, then make his way across the Canadian border and into foreign territory (the

USA), to the largest undefended border in the world, then drive to the Port of Seattle where everything that mattered to Josh, Tyde, Canyen, and me would sail 3,000 miles across the wild windy waters of the Pacific to Oahu, where it would port for a few days, maybe a week, then venture a final 150 miles to Kauai's Na'wili'wili Harbor to complete its journey.

It was 11 a.m. and Josh and I were ready. Ready like we'd never been before. Early, in fact, minutes away from sealing and locking the big box for transport, marveling at our fastidiousness, ready to break out the champagne, when two things happened:

First, a call from my sister in a fit. She was buying Josh's truck and had decided that it was a lemon. *Huh, what now?*

This made me regret so much. Namely that she was now caregiver to my fifteen-year-old dog, Patty, who would've never survived the Hawaii animal quarantine because she was too old and arthritic. Patty loved my sister. So, when Robin offered to keep my sweet dog at her lake house for her final days on the planet, I knew it was the kindest, most generous thing that anyone had done. Bless her big heart.

The day Patty left, we loaded up my sister's car with boxes full of the best of my kids' toys and books (that they were still growing out of, but I had to cull something). I imagined my sister's grandkids enjoying these things as my boys had. Patty jumped onto the passenger seat of Robin's car, thinking herself smart—she would not be left behind.

No, dear sweet Patty, you won't be left behind, at least not by Auntie Robin. But you will be left behind by me, and your beloved family of four.

When my sister pulled away that day, not one week before our departure to Hawaii, I felt I'd played an awful trick on my dog. I cried so hard. It was the most heartbreaking thing I'd ever done.

I hadn't known it would feel like someone ripped my heart in half. I hadn't known that pragmatism loses in a war with the heart. I hadn't known Patty would live another nine months. It was all so damn hard. The good news? Robin loved my dog dearly, and Patty loved her back.

Beloved pets. Crazy humans. *Up. Down. Arrived.*

Second, I called US Customs to double-check all was in order for the border, when the officer asked, "Did you label every box with all of its contents? If you miss one detail, we could turn the truck around or impound it. Also, no wine collections or liquor cabinets, CBP allows one bottle and a case of beer, same for visitors."

Huh, what now?

Suddenly, each box and each item required a number that would match a list. A list that we hadn't known about or made. We'd barely labeled the boxes. Now the driver couldn't enter the US without it. Not to mention our twenty bottles of wine, vodka, whatever from our liquor cabinet that had to be found somewhere in the back of the very full, very carefully safety-strapped container.

Josh watched my face fall then bolted down the ramp toward me, phone in hand, jaw on asphalt in the middle of the street. We'd summited Everest only to find Denali on the other side.

The next eight hours were spent pulling the container apart, opening boxes, labeling everything, with Josh's back breaking and me scribbling madly, Sharpie ink on my fingers and face, calling friends to see who wanted free booze.

My hope was that today on Kauai would be different. New place. Fresh start. Warm salt air. We would be organized, maybe even jolly. And we'd be grateful that every item would find a home in our new home.

"Stop—stop!" I heard Josh yell in his salty stress voice from outside.

I ran to find the semi-trailer cranked in a V attempting to make the corner of our driveway, the edge of the metal container scraping the tall trees like a sharp blade. I couldn't watch.

Tyde and Canyen stood in delight, oblivious. To them, it was Christmas.

"Back up!" Josh yelled. "Okay, now forward. Whoa—whoa!" He wiped the sweat from his brow. "Okay, bring it back again, real slow . . ."

After twenty minutes of tires spinning out and skinny tree trunks getting unwittingly sawed by the top edge of the container, the driver lined it up parallel to our house. Josh signed the papers, snipped the lock, and set up a ramp. Four strange men, plus Josh, swiftly began unloading boxes.

"Kitchen, please," I said, attempting to direct and read the boxes as movers flew by at a breakneck pace. "That's for Canyen's room, over there—"

I'd never seen such a flurry.

"Oh, please, not in the loft, that goes over—wait, that one goes—hang on—oh, okay, no more room in the kitchen, I can't get to the fridge—oh, nope, not there, that goes in the garage—wait, stop, I just need—oh, don't break it, that one's fragile—"

Devastatingly fast.

"Okay, ma'am, sign here," the oldest of the gang said, handing us yet another form and blissfully apathetic to the fact that I could no longer walk through my sweet new home that I'd just cleaned top-to-tail. The same home that, just a few hours ago, had looked so pleasantly uncluttered that I could've lived that way forever.

Now, boxes were piled so high that I couldn't see the stove or open the fridge. I wanted to cry. Actually, I wanted a nervous breakdown but was too pragmatic with my hearty immigrant blood—a German grandpa who narrowly escaped a Siberian labor camp, and a Hungarian grandpa who left communism to arrive to a dust bowl of a prairie with nothing but grit and good instincts. No family. No English. No stuff to bog them down.

"We found it, Mom." Canyen and Tyde whizzed by me with the PlayStation in hand, headed for the TV to connect to their favorite poison. *Maybe we did import drugs.* That online game system should have been illegal.

"I can't believe it. So quickly?" I called out from behind a stack of boxes. "You get thirty minutes each, that's it."

"Okay," they both said, knowing it wouldn't be enforced with this mess.

"Where's Dad?" I asked the boys.

"In the garage putting shelves together," Tyde answered.

It was time to make a choice. Go full catatonic, freeze in a drooling stupor, glued to the green armchair hidden behind the boxes stacked just beyond the kitchen table. Or snap out of it and deal.

After ten minutes of still as a statue, and Josh being the opposite, the mover guy, the good husband, the man of the hour flying by the window like a missile, I got up with box cutter in hand and began. If I didn't like what I saw, I closed the box back up. Before long, every box taunted me:

I'm an oversized gravy bowl shaped like a rooster you got for your wedding—you hated me then, how about now? We're a box of

Christmas gack. You're not going to put Santa Claus or Baby Jesus in a crawl space, are you?

Choices. Questions. Decisions. Hadn't I made a thousand decisions in the past few months? Including one giant life-changing decision?

Stress streamed about the house like a brisk breeze, leaving a wake of boxes, bags, baskets, bikes, and so much stuff. I hadn't noticed, but in the few hours since we'd begun unpacking, a great spirit had quietly slipped through a window and into our home, bringing a shadowy mist with her.

The wind was now gone and the air had turned stagnant. The sun had been vanquished behind cloud cover, which made for a sudden, almost unbearable, heavy heat. It was Madame Pele, Hawaiian goddess of fire, lightning, wind, and volcanoes. Legend says she does this. This creator, destructor, earth-eating spirit had settled into our walls and into our ceilings. Primordial lava slithered into boxes, drawers, and closets. Suddenly, she blew—

"There's too much goddamn stuff!" Josh yelled while juggling a stack of baskets, eyes wide as a frying pan.

"It's not my fault!" I yelled back, yanking the bread-maker from a box.

"We should fucking toss all of this!" Josh yelled again.

"Are you joking?" I said, out of breath.

"My whole life is managing other people's shit!"

"What do you mean? This is our shit. And I bloody-well packed it!"

Josh dropped the baskets to pull his fingers out to count. "I packed my parents' house, me, alone, four thousand square feet in a month, right after they died! Then Lions Bay—the garage, everything outside, the whole container. Then the Hawaii house in August! Before we moved. Remember? I came to check on it? Two truckloads to Goodwill that you never even had to see."

People are ugly when they argue. It's nature's way of scaring off an enemy or predator: scarlet-faced, blood vessels popping from eyeballs, veins and muscles thick with cortisol, fingers twitching, the face hollow and sucked into the skeleton, voice gnarled like a prickly vine. It's all rather detestable.

"I hate it too! Moving here has been nothing but red tape! Exactly what I did not want! I wanted a sabbatical. Remember? Six months in Costa Rica. No strings. No stress!"

"You wanted this too. Remember *that*?"

I no longer had a clue what I remembered or wanted, whether my things, my house, my career, my marriage—it was all a blur.

"Enough!" Josh kicked a basket on the ground, drunk with frustration.

"Stop!" I reached to grab the basket and the towels that spilled out of it. "We're not throwing away good things because your parents were hoarders!"

"You're the hoarder! It's shit we don't need!" Josh's eyeballs shot flames that landed and popped on my face and chest.

"Stop! Just stop!" I flapped my arms at my side. "Why do we have to blow things up all the time? And why is it always my fault?"

"Because you're addicted!"

"Excuse me?" The words bled fire up my throat.

"Shopping! You buy shit we don't need!"

"Look at you! All your tools. Your toys. The kite board, the paddleboard, the prone-thing-*whatchamacallit*," I spat and sputtered.

"Every time you leave the house you come back with bags of shit!"

"Half this shit is yours!" I felt the lie in my teeth; I *was* a bit of a shopper. "Who needs six surfboards?"

"What about your clothes? Sweaters and jeans and fifty pairs of shoes!"

"I *get* to like clothes!"

"I *get* to be a minimalist—"

"This is insanity!"

"I just wanted a shack on the beach!"

I began to tremble. "Stop it! We're exhausted. You're the one who said moving is a top-three stressor—divorce, death, and moving."

"Great, soon we'll be three for three!"

"How dare you!"

The yelling ripped through the house like lightning thrashing a meadow. What began as venting—and how this move was supposed to be about clarity, simplicity, freedom, ease—exploded in a pyroclastic blast. Sixteen years of heartbreak buried in the bilge of our marriage, had just spilled onto the floor. *Surprise!*

We fought like demons. Angry that our life had become about bureaucracy, managing possessions, and fighting for every penny. Angry with a complex world that made us feel alone and unworthy. But especially, angry with each other.

Whose fault is this? It's always someone's fault.

Why does it have to be so damned hard! It's always so damned hard.

Josh left in a fury. Peeled away in his truck, spitting gravel. Possessed by angry gods that didn't want our shit cluttering up their island. Possessed by possessions.

Why don't people just plant a garden and listen? Lie under a tree with legs and arms spread like a starfish to receive all the everything of this land?

Every pore in my body was steeped in anger. Without a place to go, it swirled inside me like a hot soup. The only thing left to do was stomp around in an agony unique to modern humans—the agony of too much. In the past, only royalty could afford so many things from so many places. Now, thanks to malls, Walmart, Costco, and the rest, so many can afford to cram their homes like dirty pack rats.

Josh had a legitimate argument for becoming a minimalist. But his timing was bad—the day our container arrived! Which did nothing to solve the dilemma before us. More important than finding a place for all our things was finding a place for us, the Moodys, on a rock in a jungle, the most prolific land on earth.

A jungle is a perfect ecosystem that supplies everything you need to survive on a silver platter: nonstop summer with a permanent supply of food. You could quite literally land here with nothing and thrive. Our job? To not screw it up with a tornado of meaningless stuff and emotions—baggage and demons from the material world that told us to keep buying, keep numbing, keep distracting, keep fighting, keep on the surface and away from the path of truth.

After ten minutes of circling the house, I sat in a corner to cry, wishing I could have been the one to peel out of there in a dust storm. Nothing came. No tears. No salt from the highest order to leak in puddles of holy water from the corners of my eyes. No angels to comfort me. No mother to hold me or friend to call. Just a drought, along with an endless pile of things—so—many—things—all around me.

CHAPTER 5.3

Spring 2013

Mom kept repeating, "Trip of a lifetime—Shan and Mom to the Motherland!"

Everywhere we went, each new city block, European café, or boutique, and especially the first-class airport lounges, she was blown away. Like she'd never set foot outside the Shire. Though she had many times. Mom was a world-class pianist after all.

Her talent took her almost everywhere Princess Cruise Lines went: Africa, Indonesia, all over Europe. Since the age of twelve, she had performed at countless banquet halls and snazzy hotels including the Ritz-Carlton in Osaka, Chateau Lake Louise, Banff Springs—she'd even toured the UK with a band/singing troupe she'd formed in the seventies. Yet, even with these world-class adventures, each new place we visited together she held with the curiosity of a child, as though it was a freshly unearthed treasure.

It helped that she was accompanied by the youngest of her four, me, her *angel*, she used to say with a laugh, also my middle name, Celeste. There wasn't a person on earth who loved their mother more than Little Shanni. I clung to her every move, exit, and return. Yanking at Grandma's sleeve: *When will she be home? Can I run to her yet?* Waiting for what seemed like hours on the concrete steps of our carport for her to return home from teaching school each day.

Watching her primp for a gig was like being in the presence of a movie star. Quietly commanding, so pretty with turquoise eyes and a broad, beautiful smile that lit up the room. Her dexterous fingers flitted across the piano keys like a butterfly swooping flower to flower. And she was smart to boot, got her doctorate in music education when she was fifty just because.

Forty-three years I'd waited for our first big trip together. It amused me to see my mom so present in the novelty of it. As though she knew at a visceral level that it could never be repeated. Maybe that's what wisdom is: recognizing the frailty of the now, how quickly it becomes the past, and having the peace of mind to lap it up with awe.

I loved this and I needed something to love. Anything. Because our trip of a lifetime had turned harrowing.

"I just wish you could forget about him for a day," Mom said. "He really is upsetting you. I mean physically, Shannon, your poor body."

"I know," I whimpered, blowing into my fiftieth tissue that morning.

My nose had become a faucet. The liquid cascading from my nostrils was not even snot. My body had no time to add the salts and proteins to make it proper mucus. Instead, I dripped water, then I'd sneeze a bunch, then my nose would tickle terribly and drip some more.

"He won't leave you, sweetie. He just won't." Mom sat up on the bed in her nightie with her ponytail hanging loose off the side of her head, the way it always did when she woke up.

The curtains behind her hinted at a blazing ball of sunshine rising on the other side of the window, lighting up the fresh-from-slumber streets of Budapest.

"How do you know?"

"He needs you," Mom said, shooting me a look of *don't argue*, "more than you need him."

This from a woman with a perfect track record of reasonability. When she gave the *I mean it* look, I took heed. Mom always kept her cool, never meddled, and her big goal for us kids was that we blossomed into responsible, kindhearted, successful adults, able to stand on our own two feet, no other human required.

Maybe that's what being widowed at age thirty-nine with four kids does—make it through that shitstorm and you can handle anything. It sounds bad, but when my dad died, Mom had been set free, never to marry again. It was impossible and liberating at the same time.

But not for me. To never have a dad again—there was nothing liberating about that. Though many would have argued it made me resilient, tough, the woman I was today. Only not on this day. This day, I was a snot-bubbling mess.

"He's finally home from his two-month-long shoot, and I'm away. And our pretty little French au pair is there willing to do whatever he asks." Tears streamed down my cheeks as I imagined what this trip could have been if my husband wasn't threatening to leave me. "What if he's packing up the kids right now?" The whole scene felt out-of-body. Me crumpled in a ball, looking tragic on the floor of some quaint hotel in a corner of Europe. And the other part of me, a bird, a hawk, surveying the scene.

There she sits, cornered like a rat, three stories up, a block from the Danube. In the land of her people, her ancestors who'd been conquered so many times by so many armies—Vikings, Huns, Romans, Germans, Turks—that she should have been used to the hardship. Resilience runs thick through her veins, generations of war and conflict and hardship. You can do it! Get up, Princess!

"I can't believe he said I'm a bad mother!" I pulled a row of squares from the toilet paper roll clutched inside my fist, a wool blanket skirting my armpits. I'd slept a paltry three hours and was starting to shiver.

Our trip was a year in the making. First-class all the way, thanks to air miles from all the shows I'd worked on: first Vancouver to Paris, then Paris to Budapest, then Budapest to Vienna, then home. In Paris, we'd go to Moulin Rouge, stroll the Champs-Élysées, spend a day getting lost in the Louvre, drink espresso and break bread. In Budapest, we'd bathe in thermal springs underneath hidden churches, visit Grandpa's family farm with long-lost cousins, eat goulash, explore Buda then Pest, as the city's gargoyles watch from above. In Vienna, we'd see *The Marriage of Figaro* at the opera house and drink champagne because we earned it and had never done anything like it and likely never would again. Josh knew this. Josh knew the stakes were high.

"That's not true in the least. Did he actually say that?" Mom asked.

"Maybe. Not exactly. But he said I should have married an investment banker, a Fortune 500 CEO. 'Just what you always wanted'—that's what he said. What the hell? If I wanted to marry a millionaire, I could have. Remember Peter?" I didn't wait for an answer. "He's worth an easy fifty million now. He would have married me in a heartbeat. Remember?"

Again, I didn't wait.

"So, yeah, *not my MO, Josh! Not that shallow!*" My voice rang singsong like a bratty teenager or an eighties Valley girl. "Then he said I was unemotional. Can you believe it? Too hard, too ambitious, like my career is all that matters. Bullshit!" I blew into the scratchy fibrous tissue.

"Does he have any clue what I've given up? I could be running a production company by now! EP on the *Dr. Phil*

Show, if I suddenly decided I didn't give a shit about humans anymore. But no, I've turned down every promotion for my family. I work half-time so I can *be with my kids*, raise them myself versus some nanny from halfway around the world! It's true, this last year has been more busy than usual, but—"

"I know. I know you," my mom said softly. "You're a wonderful mother. Remember before you met Josh? You said you weren't sure if you wanted kids?"

"Yeah, sorta." I swiped my nose of the watery film coating my nostrils.

"I told you that you have to. It's exactly women like you who should be championing this next generation, making sure they're good critical thinkers, soulful, successful, all of it . . ."

I half listened, deep in my rant, saying all the things Josh needed to hear. "I do it all! I cook every dinner, lunch, breakfast. Every weekend I ferry the kids around: soccer, skiing, hiking, biking. I don't even go to yoga, I *teach* it. It's a frickin' side hustle, extra money for the pot. I barely go out for myself. Unlike so many of my friends whose husbands are home weekends.

"Get this, his mom said I shouldn't work at all. Can you believe it? I should be full-time at home. *Fucking nuts. That's nuts!* Barefoot baking cookies, sexy in the bedroom, helicoptering around the kids like a Stepford wife. Jesus. Go back to the fifties already!"

Mom sat confounded, shaking her head. This was news to her. She didn't know how bad it had gotten. How could she have? Constantly on a ship, totally unreachable by phone, spotty email, busy playing for passengers, touring every port, having the time of her life . . . Who could blame her? Me, I guess.

Often, I felt grandmothering wasn't her thing. She was nothing like my friends' parents who seemed to live for their kids and their kids' kids. Thanks to my three older siblings, my mom had been grandma'd six times over by the time Tyde and Canyen had come along.

But that wasn't fair. How quickly I forgot that unlike most grandmas, my mom had to make a living, into old age. There was no combined income, no retirement, no husband to help her through the golden years, not even any life insurance from way back when the accident happened. She had a boyfriend, nice guy, lots of fun, but he had no money.

"You know, your dad didn't want me to work either." She pulled the scrunchie from the side of her head and began fingering the tangles out of her hair. "But I needed to play or I'd go crazy. I told him, 'Join me, join my band, because I'm not quitting my music.' As you know, he became our drummer. I would've preferred someone more qualified, but—"

"But?" I said, too fast, too sharp. I hated it when Mom referred to my dad as though he had let her down, like he wasn't good enough. Each gig they played, Dad moved her heavy equipment and set it all up, did the sound testing and fixing. He worshipped her and would have done anything for her.

"Nothing. It saved our marriage." Her eyes became glassy. "Those were hard times."

"It's all hard times, and he was a good dad *for Pete's sake.*" An expression my dad had often used, it shot off my lips like a cannonball aimed square at my mom. "He sure loved you. He would have never left you for wanting a career."

I huffed then stood up and felt my pajama bottoms slip down my hips. I'd dropped an easy five pounds.

I should have seen this coming. Marriage is impossible. Now mine was in the dumpster. Weird. Because casing out drama was literally what I did for a living—finding holes, searching for conflict, unearthing breaking points in people and relationships—that's reality TV.

Two months earlier, Josh and I had done something we'd never done before. Both of us took big shows that would have us out of town and away from the kids at the exact same time. We grappled with the decision. In the end, I told him, "We can do this. I'll hire an au pair and pay her extra. I'll get friends to help. Don't worry, I've got it handled. Promise!"

The show I'd been offered was a game changer. Finally, I'd ascend the ladder from director to co-executive producer. In a parallel universe, I'd already have been running things, like my LA cohorts. Even my former assistant had become an executive producer for Bravo, tripling my weekly draw. I told myself it was okay that I hadn't *made it* yet, that having babies stalled me, that I chose to be home half-time, more than half-time (except this last year), that this time was precious and I'd never get it back. Anyway, I'd take building Legos with my boys over schmoozing network execs any day.

And things were shifting. My kids were seven and five, now full-time in school. My star was on the rise, and I was guiltily enjoying it. People were calling me to speak at film festivals and on TV panels. CBC National had me defend *Here Comes Honey Boo Boo* to the *Boston Globe* TV critic who claimed society's gluttonous appetite for reality TV would be the end of this great country, akin to the fall of Rome. He was right, but I defended my industry admirably anyway.

What were the odds it would come crashing down at this moment, on a floor on the Buda side of Budapest, blocks from the Chain Bridge and the funicular and so many war memorials? Everything I'd worked for—the calls, the accolades, the unexpected second blooming of my career and my ability to juggle it all—crumbling like Budapest's legendary ruin bars.

It reminded me of the eighties Enjoli ad emblazoned in my memory. The blonde vixen in her pencil skirt *bringing home the bacon and frying it up in a pan,* making it look easy and loving every minute of it. Only in my version, Husband was in a chokehold with a silk tie his mummy bought him, their hot steaming turd of a marriage shooting flames from the oven. *You lied, Enjoli! "Have it all," my ass!*

Little had I known that seemingly innocent perfume commercial was not for my mother, or any of the busy working mothers of the seventies. No, that ad was for me and all the other little girls who thought, *Yes, please! I want to have it all. Girls can do anything boys can do and better!* I even bought the T-shirt!

In the end, I limped away from my game-changing show a week early because I needed to get home to stop my marriage from burning to the ground. Only to depart from my husband and kids eight days later for this trip, with dinners in the freezer and playdates arranged, while my marriage sat stuffed in a drain pipe like a festering hair ball.

Fate wasn't going to let me have it all like some stupid commercial. Instead, I charred my wings on the sun and cried my face off. Then I did what I never did: I quit.

Upon my return from Europe, I was supposed to supervise the edit. I quit.

Then the next show that I had taken for the summer, another biggie. I quit that too!

I quit it all, then said to Josh, "Okay. I'll stay home. For us, for our marriage, for you, for the kids. If that's what our family needs, I'll do it. It's all about us now."

And instead of receiving me with arms wide and loving, he said, "We'll see."

That was at the airport before my departure flight for what was to be, and should have been, my most fabulous trip with my mother. *Fu—!*

Josh had used the D-word only one week prior. He meant business. It was in the middle of my biggest shoot with the whole cast and crew, and I cried and nearly barfed while my friend rubbed my back and fed me rubbish like, "It'll work out," and "He won't leave you." I'd never been so scared in my life, except the day my dad died. I quit something on that day too.

"Shannon, listen to me. He's wrong!" my mom said in her stern voice. "You're a great mom. You left your career in LA to live in Lions Bay to raise your kids in the best place you could find." She then straightened her nightie and began rifling through her suitcase for a bra. "What's he thinking? I taught full-time and played every weekend. I was always working. I had to."

"Yeah, you were never home," I said with too much fervor.

"I was home."

"Well?" I said, puckering my lips and squinting, knowing this was not the time, but also, if there ever was a time for truth, it was now, with my life served up hot and sticky on a wet paper plate. Which had me wondering if it wasn't precisely that truth of being left to fend for myself that created the tough (dare I say *hardened*) woman standing there today. "I felt pretty alone in my teens, Mom. I felt alone a lot. You weren't there."

"That's not true. I was there."

Pretty much true, I didn't say out loud. The hurt needed somewhere to go. Who better than my mother? *Why am I being such an asshole?*

Mom dropped her head and pretended to look for something in her suitcase. Her best defense had always been no defense. Retreat. Turn away. Don't engage.

"When we moved to Calgary, it was just you, me, and Troy," I said, flinging my favorite blouse into a corner, my face flushing with heat. "You *chose* to play every night instead of teaching school during the day. I'd get home from school as quick as I could just to see you. I'd watch you put your makeup on. I got twenty minutes of you, then poof—you were gone to work for the night."

"I was making a living!" my mom spat with rare anger. "If I had been a cook or a maid, you would've felt sorry for me. I'd be a hero! But because I was playing, you kids thought it wasn't real work. For God's sake, Shannon, I was raising four kids alone, paying bills, doing what I was called to do! Never did I bring men home or party or drink. I was careful. Making good money. Affording you and your siblings a beautiful home and more. I was doing my bloody best!"

My childhood flashed before me as I pieced together who I'd become and why I'd become her. So many of the hurts of yesteryear: my dad killed in an instant, my widowed mom working nonstop, my siblings gone rogue, my chubby puberty, the catty whispers of so-called friends, my bestie asking for a fight after school at the bike racks (*bike racks!*), the near-constant flush of insecurity, the parties my brother Troy and I threw and the drunken nights of forgetting, the morning I woke up in horror to puke on my pillow, underwear on the floor and blood on my sheets, my mom away and unaware. It was a tomb of abandonment flooding into the present like a bursting damn.

You're an ice queen. You don't even like to be touched, echoed in my head in a loop. Josh's tone had been so cruel. It sliced right to that little girl who only ever wanted to hold her mother's hand. *It's their fault! Mom. Dad. Both of them. But he's dead, so it's on her.*

"Love is a verb, Mom, an action," I spat back. "Not a thing we say to make people feel better. It's a feeling we create in others by *being there*. Time spent. Hugs and touch. Real love is when we hug so hard, we squeeze the sad right out of our kids. Moms are built for it. And if it wasn't for my lack thereof, I wouldn't be destined for divorce. I'd be a better wife, a softer, more easygoing woman who prefers intimacy with her husband to the rush of directing a room full of people. Maybe if I was hugged more, I could've loved him more and *that's* the problem!"

Mom swiped a tear from her eye as she dug through her overflowing fuchsia suitcase. The one we barely fit on the Paris subway that I had to pay a homeless person five euros to carry up the steep stairs, from the underground to street level, while Mom waited up top to be sure no one snatched the rest of our bags. The one I dragged up and down five flights of ruby-red shag carpet at our Parisian flat in the Saint-Germain-des-Prés district. The same one I got her for Christmas as part of a designer set because I knew she loved pink, and I only ever wanted to make her happy.

"I'm sorry, Mom." My voice was cracking, tears flooding my eyes. "It's not your fault."

"No, I'm sorry. I'm sorry I hurt you when you were young." She walked toward me for a hug. I stiffened. It was true. I wasn't used to hugging. Josh was right.

"I did my best," Mom continued. "Four kids. Raising you all on my own after your dad died. I loved you so much, but yes, I was busy with so much responsibility. I did the best I could. It's all I can say. Except that I couldn't have loved you more." She squeezed me again.

"You've never said that, Mom, the part about not being around." My head pounded hard, like someone had taken a vacuum to my brain. "Thank you."

"Let's try to have a good day, okay?" Mom said, doing what she did so well, finding passage through the muck, pretending I hadn't just been a total jerk.

I stood up to brush my teeth in our tiny bathroom and felt my stomach grumbling. It had shrunk to a peanut. I wanted to reach for my mom and hug her again, to hold her heart and let her hold mine. I wanted to get past words, past history, and past bullshit. I simply wanted to be loved and I wanted my mom to understand: *How can I be loving to Josh when I'm so incredibly unloving to me?*

None of that came out as I was already taking my frustration out on my teeth, pressing into the gums and between the cracks as though that would clean up all the misunderstandings and half-truths and claiming of ground and boundary breaking between two people. This wasn't Josh's fault or mine or my mother's or my father's. This was marriage, the most complex relationship two people could have.

"The cousins are meeting us at the *palacsinta* shop in ten minutes," Mom said, looking smart in skinny jeans and a flouncy blouse. "It's a long walk."

"Okay," I said. "Almost ready, but I don't think I can eat." My stomach rumbled on cue.

"Stop it. Palacsinta is your favorite!"

Mom looked pretty even when she was mad. It crossed my mind that I might look like that at her age. Genetics—only she was prettier. Then I thought how lucky Josh was because I was going to age well. Then I got mad, because despite my shortcomings, I knew I was a catch and it wasn't all my fault. *I'm not an ice queen. I'm a good human and a fan-frickin-tastic mom!* And now, that same person who didn't appreciate me was keeping me from enjoying one of my favorite things on the whole planet—crepes, the food of my Hungarian ancestors, my lifeblood.

"Shannon, come on," my mom said, spritzing her blonde strands. "You will eat!"

My grandma had made palacsinta almost every weekend of my childhood—eggs, cream, flour, a stick of butter for the pan. Long, fresh fried rolls stuffed with brown sugar and cinnamon, I'd gobble them up, licking my lips, begging for more. It wasn't about the food; it was about the woman serving it. Grandma. She knew. Food equals communion. It's a display of love, just like touch, just like time spent together, just like my mom working her ass off so her kids could have a good life.

Twelve years Josh and I had been a couple. Twelve years of me in the kitchen baking gluten-free cookies, gluten-free turkey stuffing with gluten-free gravy, finding new ways to make gluten-free squares and desserts of all kinds, for him, my celiac husband, with love. Food was my love language and Josh had gotten heaps of it. Did that not count?

"Actually, Mom, I think I can eat," I said with renewed energy, slipping my feet into my runners and standing a little straighter.

"Fantastic! Let's go get palacsinta." Mom threw her purse over her shoulder and flung open the door.

CHAPTER 6

Emergency Alert. Missile inbound! What do you do when you're told a nuclear bomb is headed for your home?

a) Go underground. Thank God that you "invented" the world's number-one social media app because your apocalypse bunker is the size of a small city and all your billionaire friends will be there.
b) Drop the kids down a manhole, women and children first, because chivalry is not entirely dead. Grab a few cans of soup and some blankets—we're going back to basics.
c) Run naked through the streets screaming, "The end is nigh! Jesus is coming!" For once, you'd be right.
d) Laugh. It's a nuke, for Chrissake! Best go out with a smile.

CHAPTER 6.1

Ayahuasca Journey
September 2021

The Shipibo believe that every physical body is covered by these designs that are invisible to the untrained eye. . . . In ancient times, when heaven was closer to earth, everything was covered in these patterns . . . the trees, the rocks, the flowers, on animals and on humans, and that illness is a disruption of these patterns. . . . The Shaman achieves a second sight and becomes able to see where the energetic disruption of the pattern is located.[6]

Abandoned. That's what this was: humanity alone in the universe. Godless. Friendless. Weak. So weak. Unsupported. Helpless. The incredible trauma of this world. Stuck in a vicious loop. Repeating for eternity.

The patterns were fast and geometric, intricate in neon rainbow shades. Then they'd warp to light speed and turn awful, disfigured, malevolent. I'd open my eyes and hope for the calm coolness of nightfall in our quiet clearing in the jungle.

Please! Some goodness.

---

[6] *Grandmother Ayahuasca* by Christian Funder © 2021. Reprinted by permission of Inner Traditions International and Bear & Company. www.Innertraditions.com

But the patterns would land everywhere, anything that had a heat signature (people), and anything white or with a hint of light (the tent). I'd squint and squirm and pray for it to stop. Eyes closed. Eyes open. It didn't matter. The patterns were all over, haunting me.

Steven and his team milled through the tent, checking on us. But they too had turned menacing with dizzying zigzag patterns all over their bodies and red devil eyes.

My body prickled as though being stabbed with hot pokers and I began to shiver. My body was freezing. But only pieces of it. Then I stopped shivering and felt the incredible prickly heat again. Then cold again. Hot, then cold, then hot. And in specific places: my right shoulder, the tops of my legs, my ribs. It happened so fast I didn't have time to think.

No thinking. Only feeling. And pain. Not the physical pain of childbirth, the ripping apart of bones and flesh, rather an emotional tearing, frightening cosmic fractures that I didn't understand. Whatever was happening was beyond my body/mind comprehension. This made it worse. All I could do was take it. Go through it. All the hurt my cells ever carried flooded through me in prickles and tingles, and patterns, patterns, everywhere.

I moaned and sighed and yawned, stuck to my mat, and prayed to the heavens, to God to protect me: "This is the house of the Lord. I command all darkness leave. I am light. I am goodness. No evil shall enter this vessel for I am the house of the Lord."

I didn't know what else to say. I knew I needed to learn to pray better. But it was all I had in my prayer lexicon.

Please—I need contact, light, someone to touch me. Please, bring me a person. Show me! I need another innocent being to ground me and prove that God is with me. A good human or an animal. Any animal. I'll even take a bug. A cricket.

Reality was out of my reach. I saw the theater of planet Earth. The games. The lies. Hidden truths all around. *We can't trust our senses!* There was no other plane of existence. Nowhere to go. Just this moment, the horrible ugly now. I hated it and felt this deep in all the places. Every cell in my body was experiencing it within me, feeding back the pain of the world. Each fractured part of me shattered in time. It was all inside me. It was me. Only me. Inescapably, hopelessly, me.

CHAPTER 6.2

Comets

January 2018

Ten-year-old Canyen frowned as he climbed into the car at the turn-about in front of the school. I'd been stuck behind a long line of trucks and SUVs waiting for him, so I assumed his mood was because I was late, per usual. Or perhaps it was the gray cloud that had hovered over the island since October, sulking and draining and rarely budging, keeping us soggy and leaden.

"Maikai can't come over today," Canyen said gloomily.

"Why not?" I perked up my voice, as though that might help.

"He said he had soccer."

"What about tomorrow?" I asked, the perk dampening.

"He said he didn't know."

It was at this point I wanted to jump out of the car and yell to anyone in earshot, "Who wants to play with my kid? Come on, I need a warm body! And by the way, he's awesome! He skates, makes his own gumball machines out of Legos, is hilarious and can repair his own RC car. Come on now—any takers?!"

It was January and Canyen had made a handful of sort-of friends at school. Most were unavailable for playdates given they lived in Kilauea and we lived on a farm road a five-minute car ride out of town. After school, the K-Town Boys, as they were called, cruised the hood on skateboards or bikes with whomever was around. Due to geographical constraints, so they said, Canyen was seldom invited.

Kilauea parents were like seventies parents—they popped out latchkey kids, street-smart, with an edge. Kids walked home from school, grabbed a PowerBar and a banana, then cruised the hood looking for bros to build a skateboard ramp or hit the Menehune Mart to mooch Slurpees. I actually liked that, except when it came to my son not being included.

It broke my heart every time. Canyen would load into my car after school and I'd go through the standard list of Kauai things to do: "Want to hit the beach? Want to grab Dad and surf? We could hike or go for a bike ride . . ."

Half the time it was raining, which meant trekking trails were drenched and slipperier than an oil slick. Add to that record-breaking humidity and it was hard to imagine spending time outside at all. Not so smart of us to ship our bikes and all our hiking paraphernalia from the mainland. It all sat molding and rusting in our garage along with so many other things inappropriate for life in a jungle.

For the first time ever, I wondered if my go-for-it/try-anything-once attitude was my worst quality versus my best. *I know, let's move to Hawaii, that'll fix everything!* Sitting in the rubble was my youngest son.

Nighttime, I'd tuck Canyen in, read a story, and he'd ask, "Why did we move here?"

Stumped, I'd think for a moment, then call Josh.

Josh would enter the room and try to cheer us up with his thumb and pinkie extended and middle fingers tucked. "We're here for the simple life, kids." *Shaka!*

Secretly, I'd roll my eyes. That damn simple life was going to run the show now no matter how hard I fought it. *What's so damn great about simplicity anyway? I like my layers, my complexities, they make me interesting*, then I wondered if I was Kung-Fu-gripped to my past.

Josh would tell the boys the story of Hamana Kalili, the sugarcane worker who lost his middle three fingers in the mill. Unable to perform his job, he was moved to guard the sugar train. In order to give the all clear for passing trains, he'd wave his mangled hand, thumb and pinkie swaying in the breeze. Thinking this hilarious, local kids imitated him, and because Hamana was a nice guy, it stuck. A hundred or so years later, here we were, still doing it.

My goal was to find a way to convince Canyen and Tyde (and, more critically, me) that slow and simple was better than what society had conditioned us to—success at breakneck speed. Still, I couldn't shake the thought that living in Kauai was like dating a supermodel: pretty on the outside, gorgeous actually, but a few crayons short of a full box. So much of what I took for granted on the mainland did not exist here.

First, a proper mall. There was not even a bookstore. Shopping was limited to Costco, Safeway, surf shops, and boutiques. To be fair, the boutiques were cool, loaded with island-themed tchotchkes, locally made jewelry with Tahitian pearls and tempered gold, an array of beach cover-ups and colorful dresses, and bikinis with micro bottoms to fit the tightest of rumps. Buying a bathing suit in Kauai was perilous. Even with their deceptively flattering skinny mirrors, stepping into a changing room was like shoving your self-esteem in a wood chipper.

Second, aside from Costco and Walmart, there were no chain stores. Arguably, a good thing. But it also meant many things required shipping, and many things could not be shipped: computers, lithium batteries and anything that used them, aerosol cans, including my favorite dry shampoo. It would all have to be lugged in a suitcase the next time we flew from the mainland.

Third, there was no downtown, or skyscrapers or buildings taller than a coco palm, which, according to Kauai municipal building code, *no building shall be*. Again, maybe a good thing. But it also meant gatherings took place at the beach, the beach park, a backyard, a front yard, or a park near a beach. There was little culture to be had, and almost no reason to own nice shoes. Which, considering the nonstop fighting over what to do with the ramshackle Coco Palms property, begged the question, "Why not turn that into a cultural center?" Surely all could agree that promoting Hawaiian culture and gatherings would be the best use of sacred land.

Fourth, there was no real newspaper (I know, but I am a Gen Xer and I do like a good broadsheet once in a while). They had the *Garden Island*, but it's no bastion of journalism and I'd no clue where to find it—a gas station? Who goes inside gas stations anymore? Unless on a road trip. And I missed those too.

The longest road trip here was a two-hour drive along the Kuhio Highway to the other side of the island, at which point you hit a dead end because *that's it!* One highway, one road, single lane, around the entire island that didn't quite make it around the island because of the towering, indomitable, and utterly stunning mountains that ran the Napali coastline. This on an island that (including tourists) housed a hundred thousand people at any given time, and as many cars.

There were hardly any sidewalks. There was no indoor entertainment for the kids when it rained, like a trampoline park or a climbing gym or a proper theater with reclining seats.

Most outfits catered to tourists, especially the hotels with their luxury vacation pricing on everything from coffees to zip lines to the spa. And I realized that just saying so made me an entitled asshole, begging another question, "Why the F move here in the first place, ha'ole?"

To which I would have said, "I don't F-ing know!"

There was so much I missed about my old home that some days I wanted to cry. But I couldn't. Tears wouldn't come because I didn't actually feel sorry for myself. Instead, I felt like an old sea hag, dried up and soggy all at once. And who even cared but me?

Ha'oles were a pest here. That's what they called us. Not to our faces, not usually, and maybe not everyone. But you could feel it like a bad stench, the dog that just rolled in dead pig. Tourists? *Aloha!* New residents? *Go home!*

I told the boys, "The goal is to blend in. Don't look so fresh off the boat. If anyone asks, we've lived here for years."

Tyde would say, "Not doing that, Mom. Everyone in my class is from the mainland. Half the class is new."

No wonder they hate us.

My actual response: "Well, always be respectful. Address adults as auntie and uncle. That's what the local kids do out of respect. They look after their own here. It's the village."

Then Canyen would ask, "How come we don't call people auntie and uncle back home?"

Because people back home forgot how to belong and how sad is that?

My actual response: "Here locals treat their neighbors like family. This is how it should be. We come with aloha or we get off the rock."

In Hawaiian, *ha* means "breath," *ole* means "without." Ha'ole means "without breath," not truly alive, soulless, a ghost.

Stating the obvious, it's an insult. Strangely, however, it was the white people who I'd heard use that term the most, some being mean, and some self-deprecatingly, calling themselves ha'oles, insult and sarcasm rolled into one.

Maybe Kauai wasn't so *supermodel* dull. What did I know? Except that when Canyen hinted that he wanted to move back to Canada, I understood.

His reasons? Playing in the woods, five-cent gummies at the store, hot chocolate after soccer games, sleepovers, every day a fun activity, new shoes at the mall . . . innocence. All I wanted for him was a version of that too. Instead, on a sleepy Saturday morning in January, we got my phone squealing loudly like a siren—

BALLISTIC MISSILE THREAT
INBOUND TO HAWAII. SEEK IMMEDIATE
SHELTER. THIS IS NOT A DRILL!

"What? Is this a joke?" I stared stupidly at the face of my phone, the kids already in the midst of a balls-out Nerf war.

Plain as day, all caps, a text from the Kauai Emergency Management Agency:

BALLISTIC MISSILE INBOUND!

A fucking nuke! Headed for the island? Jesus, are we going to die? Where's Josh?

My head pounded as I mouthed the words *shit-fuck* over and over again.

At 8:07 a.m., every person in possession of a cell phone, staying or living in the state of Hawaii, received that emergency alert.

Wake up, Hawaii—your lives are over!

I stood at my kitchen sink, dumbfounded with bedhead, still in pj's that my sister gave me—a Mickey Mouse tank top with a red breast pocket that said, "Hey Mickey!" Thinking, *Am I gonna die in this getup? What does one wear to Farmageddon?*

Before I could process, my phone chirped with texts:

"WTF?" from a Silicon Valley mom I had met at a meeting for Tyde's school fundraiser. "Did you get that crazy warning? Missile inbound!"

Though I barely knew her, she and I had commiserated about how surreal it was to pack up our lives for Kauai—arriving within a month of each other. I thought we might be friends, but she'd canceled three coffee dates in a row only minutes prior to our meeting. "Sorry, I'm sick," or "My kid's sick," or "My dog's sick," with an epically long text to explain.

"Are you panicking? Do you have a bunker? I've got Clif Bars and energy drinks. I expect this in LA or New York, megalomaniac central, but here? If I were a terrorist, I would not hit Kauai. Maybe Vegas. Has Kim Jong Un lost his mind? F-ing North Korea. Like, seriously!"

I closed my phone and gulped a vomitous gulp.

Is this how it ends? We move thousands of miles only to be fried by a potbellied fascist? We'll be smoldering clumps of ash in minutes.

It had been four months since we'd packed up our lives and left safe, mostly neutral Canada—for this! War-mongering U-S-A and what I'd just learned (as in just this minute) was the most militarized group of islands in the world. The Pacific Missile Range Facility (PMRF) was ninety minutes from my front door! The world's largest instrumented, multi-environmental range that included 42,000 square miles of *controlled* airspace.

Kauai was not so innocent and definitely not so simple.

My heart leapt into my throat like a giant toad. *I better call my mom, say goodbye.*

My reflex was to suck in a huge gasp of air, chug-a-lug. I'd been instructing yoginis in my twice-a-week Lions Bay yoga class to do so for over ten years. *Inhale deeply, fill the lungs, open the mouth, exhale and sigh, come on, ladies, release it, let me hear you roar!* Oh, to twist back time to when my biggest concern was who to beg to pick up my kids because my shoot day had gone two hours into overtime. The problems of my past so trivial now.

I looked and listened and made quick note: no sirens, no screeching cars, no horns, no sign of panicked neighbors, no yelling, no helicopters, no planes breaking the sound barrier, no Josh.

Josh?! I imagined him weeding the pineapples. *Well played, Josh, well played.*

Slivers of hope ran through my mind: *Maybe it's not real. Military mistakes happen all the time. Cuban Missile Crisis anyone? Besides, it'll never make it. Anti-ballistic aircraft will blow it clear into space. We have the PMRF for God's sake! This is the US of A! World's largest military. Come on, Trump. Get it right. Now's your chance!*

Meanwhile, a hundred miles south on Oahu, panicked parents were stuffing their kids down storm drains. Tourists, ordinarily bent on piña coladas and beach buffets, were pushing and shoving their way through thick cement stairwells into hotel basements, hunkering down for a nuclear holocaust, screaming and wailing and making final calls to loved ones.

Keeping my horror from the kids, I googled what to do. I had no clue. Note: *Internet is working. Good sign.* Second note: *Not on the news. Another good sign.*

Meanwhile, Tyde and Canyen played "Hostage" with a medium-sized teddy bear in the center of the room, carefully guarded by Canyen with his prepubescent skinny boy arms draped around a plastic orange, white, and blue semi-automatic Nerf rifle, as stray foam bullets whizzed by my head. The irony was not lost on me.

"I got you! I got you!" Tyde yelled.

"You missed! You missed!" Canyen yelled back.

From one website: "Seek immediate shelter indoors. Do not drive anywhere. Do not run. Move away from windows. Get underground. The goal is to put as many walls and as much concrete between you and the radioactive material that will soon be outside."

Third note: *No basement. No bunker.*

From another site: "You're toast. Forget about escape unless you have a government-built, military-grade bomb shelter designed for presidents, heads of state, the elite .01 percent. Step outside, open your arms wide to the sky, and be prepared for the ultimate suntan. It'll be the last one you ever get."

Eureka! *Zuckerberg has built a Vatican-sized bunker? Maybe he'll let us in!*

Then—*Fat chance, plebs. Time to get good with God. We're about to be one with the sun.*

Indeed, if a nuclear bomb hit, we were goners. No one would survive. I'd seen pictures from the fifties of kids huddled under desks during military air-raid test strikes and found it laughable. Radiation and unfathomable heat would blast from the detonation site for hundreds of miles. Pure horror. The image of Hiroshima post-nuke was etched into the minds of every literate human on the planet.

It scared the hell out of me. A nuclear blast creates a fireball a mile in diameter, as hot as the surface of the sun. Radioactive fallout would be carried for miles by jet stream and surface winds. It would be a shitstorm of epic proportions, like swimming in molten lava. *Toast*, indeed.

I called for Josh outside and quickly evaluated the scene. The walls of our new home were almost entirely made of windows, with a wide-open floor plan—the main reason we chose it. Our garage had mostly solid walls of wood, gypsum, fluffy insulation, and a few windows, no concrete, nothing bunkerish on our property at all!

Do we drive the truck into the garage and huddle inside its shell? Exactly how long do we huddle? Three months? Who gets the deadly task of dumping the poop pail and grabbing snacks, which line the shelves of our garage precisely for moments like this? It'd be like eating uranium.

Suddenly, I had a vision of holding my boys as their bodies melted from the inside out from radiation sores, rocking back and forth in the truck, hugging them, stroking their silky hair, crying, wishing us all dead. It occurred to me that mothers in various parts of the world were forced to do this every day—Syria, Rwanda, Pakistan. Dreadful stuff. I recognized this feeling, a collective horror, the worst that every human shared.

The kids still deep in their Nerf war, I walked out to our lanai congealed in fear yet strangely open to my fate, which, given our bunkerless open-floor home, was hopeless. I looked to our chunk of beautiful earth: the St. Augustine grass that sloped toward the orchard; the tropical trees that dripped of fruit, the bounty of which I had never experienced as my own; the succulent red flowers of the ginger plant flickering in the breeze; the white hunchbacked egret sitting lazily atop the pomelo tree like a grumpy old man, or was it an angel, I couldn't decide; the floppy-eared goats and their sweet spotted kids bleating in the distance, just past the pineapple grove. It was so bucolic, so peaceful, that past the fear, I could muster only gratitude, unimaginable that the scene inside the truck could be my new reality in minutes.

"Look at this place," I said half out loud. "Mine so briefly."

Josh sprinted toward me from the compost area at the back of our three-acre parcel, panting. "Did you see the text? What in hell!"

I yelled, "Jesus—you're here!"

And just like that, with eyes glued to our ostensibly omniscient, metal-polymer, microwave, satellite-linked device, answers arrived:

> MESSAGES 829-32
> This is the Kauai Emergency Management Agency. There is no active threat and no action is needed at this time. The Hawaii Emergency Management Agency is investigating this false alarm. Repeat. False alarm.

Another giant exhale and all was right in the world. Or was it?

One thing for sure, I was wrong about Kauai. As a first line of defense against America's Pacific Rim enemies, she was anything but dull. She was a formidable shield. Which made her people, by no effort of hers, sitting ducks for some butthole tyrant's war game.

The inbound missile was no false alarm. Something very big was averted and we ordinary folk would never know what or how. And despite Mama Kauai's incredible fecundity and fierce squalls, she could not protect us from the incredible hubris of man. If once she'd decided *who stayed and went* on her mystical isle, she'd lost her edge to the forces of greed and power.

Beyond the annual war games of the US military that sent toxic chemicals and lethal sonar deep into the Hawaiian ocean (beaching her largest, most sensitive creatures), on land there was another pox, a village of meth heads stealing cars, bikes, purses, and private mail. Each looking for a fast buck and a hit, living in tents and pooping on beaches, while who knows how many Hawaiian-blood families lived below the poverty line, no longer able to fish (let alone inhabit) the shores that billionaires like Zuckerberg now called home. Former public beach trails were now armed with surveillance cameras and security guards, right to the edge of Zuck's two-hundred-acre (and growing) plot.

Twenty minutes south of this, the former Coco Palms was a rust pile. Stuck in a three-decade-long stalemate, blighting Kauai's original historic port—a beautiful windswept bay with white coral sand fed by the Wailua River and crystal blue waterfalls from the belly of Mama Kauai herself.

This once pristine island was the poster child for disparity: $20 million beachfront manors equipped with private chefs, maids, and gardeners, contrasted with a service class unable to afford a studio apartment. Josh told me about a saleswoman in the time-share office who lived in her car with her twelve-year-old son. "Just until I catch a break and get my windfall."

Hawaii was loaded with dreamers, idealists, moochers, and vagabonds, content to live in an old car or a van. Many claimed to live off the land (because who needs a house in this climate?), only to leave their dilapidated vehicle on the side of the road, six months later, stuffed with refuse, as they escaped to their next adventure. *Mahalos, Kauai. Sorry about the mess.*

Worst of all, this place never belonged to the US. As a Canadian, I understood this better than most Americans, maybe even my husband. We were the tiny mouse sleeping next to the giant elephant—*Don't piss him off!*

Queen Liliuokalani was overthrown in a coup d'état by the Committee of Safety (always with the *safety*), composed of seven foreigners and six resident ha'oles—white folk the enemy, again. It mattered not that tyranny and injustice knew no color or boundary.

Few knew the extent to which many Europeans were persecuted in their homeland. Fascists and communists killed my great-grandfather and great-uncles and took their land and sovereignty. Those who survived were forced to start all over in a new world, a dust bowl of a Wild West prairie considered uninhabitable by the ruling men who placed them there. And that there was the problem, the corrupted elite, the greedy oligarchy. Not skin color. That's just melanin, an enzyme, some have more, some have less, but we all have it.

Recently, I'd joined a Canoe Club, curious about this ancient sport and tradition. I'd also wanted to meet new friends. I was too embarrassed to tell Josh that at practice, a local girl (and a force in the canoe) hocked a loogie on the ground as she walked by me, barely missing my foot. I was about to compliment her on her paddling strength, but she'd already made a judgment. What did she know of me besides fair hair and a skin color lighter than hers?

This island, this microcosm of our planet, of Gaia herself, teeming with life, vibrating volcanic energy from the center of the earth, was broken. And me, a prairie girl from the most arid regions of Canada, born in a bitter winter during howling dry winds, was weirdly now a part of her, feeling broken just as she, trying to make a home, yet belonging nowhere.

That evening, while I tucked Canyen into bed, he looked at me with sad eyes.

"Mommy, I miss my friends so much." A tear rolled down his cheek. "Do you think we'll ever move back?"

"Well," I said, my breath shallow and nervous, like I was about to step off a cliff, "Dad says we give it two good years." I kissed his forehead. "But—"

"But?" Canyen pressed. "Mommy, but what?"

They say, in a family, the mother is the barometer of the household. She sets the temperature of the room. If it's a warm, sunny 70 degrees, it's because of her. If it's a broiling 113, that too is because of her.

Alarm bells rang in my head: *Don't say it, don't put it out there, not yet, too soon . . .*

But patience was never my strong suit. "Well, sweetie, if things don't get better . . ." I hesitated. "We might, w-we might just go home."

CHAPTER 6.3

1970s and '80s

Grandma always told me to pray. According to her, it was the best thing I could do when scared or sad or just uncertain. For me that seemed to be often, at least the scaredy bit. Me and my insecurities were like too many peas exploding from a pod.

"God is always listening," Grandma would say. "He's waiting to hear from you."

"All those prayers." I'd swipe my forehead. "He must be so busy."

Then I'd kneel down beside my bed, clap my hands together tight, and recite the Lord's prayer. Messing up the "forgive us our trespasses" bit because what even was that? Then stumbling over the "in Jesus's name we pray" finale because I thought I should just pray straight to God, straight to the top, the chief, the big kahuna.

Grandma would gently correct me and tuck my straggly blonde hair behind my ear like I was Shirley Temple on the Good Ship Lollipop. Only I was long and stupidly tall for my age; where my friends were stretching out of their baby fat, mine was sticking in all the wrong places, rendering my belly button a sad little slit.

But with Grandma, I always felt special, even cute. She was either teaching me, loving me, or feeding me, and every once in a while, shooing me onto her front steps with a long stick of freshly snipped rhubarb and a bowl of sugar.

Her favorite topic was the Bible. For Grandma, just as God was 24/7 on speed dial in our prayers, so was the Devil.

"You need only ask and evil spirits will enter your life just as easily. People do that, they summon the Devil, the fallen one, then regret it."

Cue every last hair of every last follicle on my taut young epidermis standing on end.

Grandma would explain that Lucifer was once a very beautiful and powerful angel. One day, while strumming his harp and singing a most melodious tune, he challenged God's authority. He wanted to be God's equal, the COO of heaven. God said *Homey don't play that* and cast him down where Lucifer ended up lording over Earth. Not a bad gig, but being an ambitious type, Lucie used the opportunity to collect as many souls as possible for Hell and is still working on it, tempting the sheeple into depravity with shiny things like fancy corporate jobs, private jets, and hookers, something like that.

"Wait, if he's here and God's up there, wouldn't that make Earth Hell?" I asked, wondering if old Beelzebub was hiding in Grandma's closet, waiting to add me to his club of demons because I stole my sister's newspaper money to buy a Snickers and ten Mojos last Saturday.

"Gosh, no," Grandma would laugh.

"What about the starving children in Africa?" I'd ask. "That sure looks like fresh hell. Those big bellies gotta hurt so bad, fat and skinny all at once. It makes me so bloody sad!"

"Shanni, you shouldn't say *bloody* or *fresh hell*."

"Dad says it." I shrugged, picturing the Biafran kids on the TV set Saturday mornings after cartoons, and poor Sally Struthers (who must've gotten fired from *M.A.S.H.*) begging people for money. I'd have given her every last penny in my piggy bank if I'd had any. "Why can't we give them our food, Grandma? We have so much."

I never understood those big stomachs. Clearly they weren't getting dinner at home then a second one at Grandma's like I was. I bet those kids swore all the time. *Damn stupid world. Damn stupid government. So bloody unfair.*

"Listen Shanni, Hell is eternal damnation, where people go when they die if they choose evil, if they choose Satan over God. We're not supposed to love our things more than we love God. It keeps us from what matters like family, love, and kindness."

My eyes grew wide as Frisbees as I swore up and down that I would never choose the Devil. Even if he offered me a lifetime supply of fresh-baked chocolate chip cookies, the Barbie Dream Home *and* Camper, and my very own kitten farm. *Team Jesus all the way!*

"Also, don't ever play with a Ouija board," Grandma would scold. "That's a direct line to the fallen angels."

And she'd say all this as though sharing her Hungarian goulash recipe. Like I wasn't about to rip open the Yellow Pages and sign up for a nunnery, or a self-defense class, or hire a personal security team, like President Jimmy Carter on the six o'clock news.

Grandma would then tell her favorite story of the two Indian girls who lived with her when I was in grade 3. On a lark, they spent a night at the cemetery with a couple guys and a Ouija board. One of the boys, Johnny, had a broken leg in a cast. They thought it a good idea to ask Mr. Ouija if ghosts were real. Adding to their query, "Prove it."

Four sets of hands hovered over the toggle of the mystery board with eyes shut and intention set, anticipating something grand. In moments, a cloud-white vapor began to rise from the grave plots. The teenagers wondered if they were seeing things. *Perhaps it's just a mist.* Then came the moaning. Quietly at first, then a cacophony of horrors as the vapor took shape and ghosts rose from the gravestones.

"*Aaaaaaah!*" they screamed and fled for the car, frightened out of their wits, squealing tires and ripping away as fast as they could. Only they'd forgotten something: Johnny. The poor guy was hobbling behind on his broken leg, crutches feathering the ground for flight, scrambling up the chain-link fence like his pants were on fire.

Tears of laughter streamed from Grandma's face each time she told the story. I, however, sat frozen, promising myself to never step foot in a cemetery, let alone touch a Ouija board.

No wonder I slept with a light on. In summer, if I got to bed before the sun set, which was 10:30 p.m. in Southern Alberta, I could sometimes fall asleep without imagining a cluster of demons under my mattress. Most times, I slept with the lamp on and my Siamese cat Tip-Dip lodged in a headlock so he couldn't take off. God forbid the Devil messed with him. With a running start, Tip-Dip could climb clear to the top of our backyard telephone pole, and that was after Mom had him declawed for wrecking the furniture.

Scary stories aside, Grandma was my beacon, my cook, my doctor, and a soft place to land.

One summer day, while playing hide-and-seek, I hid under a cement staircase. When I got up to run home, I hit my noggin so hard my head cracked open and blood rained down my face, just like in the movie *Carrie*. It coursed from my eyebrows and chin, ruining my favorite white halter top with the macramé strawberries on the pockets. I'd sliced it so good I couldn't even feel it for five minutes. It was confusing, all that blood and no pain. Geographically, the incident happened exactly between my house and Grandma's. To whom did I run? Grandma.

When we moved away from my grandparents to Calgary, I was twelve years old, two years after my dad died. Mom, my brother Troy, and I were off to the big city to live in the house my parents had bought just one month before Dad's accident. It was being built when he died and had now sat empty nearly two years. All I could think was, *If only this house had been built sooner.*

Back in Medicine Hat, my sister had gotten pregnant and moved north to have the baby quietly in the middle of nowhere. The plan was to give him up for adoption, which she did not do, and who could blame her? My nephew was perfect, with tender blue eyes and a big round head like a cabbage. My brother Marc stayed behind to live with my grandparents and take courses at the college. So, it was just me, Troy, and Mom moving to Calgary and not at all how things were intended to be.

It was one of the hardest things I'd ever do, to leave my grandparents. But I had to go. I had to get away from stupid Medicine Hat.

Tracy, my best friend in the world, had dumped me for a dumpling named Colleen, who only wore violet, the same color as her eyes and the splotches of her pale blue skin. Worse than the fact that I'd been dumped, Tracy had become quite cruel toward me. Being twelve, I saw no way out. How would I survive another year of knives hurled at my back? Also being twelve, I figured Grandma would be around forever, waiting for me open-armed whenever needed. And if she ever were to die, I'd turn her into a robot because they would have the technology by then, and it would be cool, not creepy like it sounded.

Seven years later, I had become a young woman, fit and eager. No longer an outcast. No longer chubby and insecure. No longer scrounging for friendships and dreaming about boys I could never get. No longer needing Grandma to bake me cookies or pour iodine on my wounds.

It was summer. Being Canadian, that meant sunshine and long-awaited heat. The dog days were to be embraced with zeal. Get out of the house, strip off your layers, run through sprinklers, break into pools, tube down lazy rivers with six-packs of beer trailing on a rope, wear bikinis with too much padding in the bra, beaches, bonfires, sunbaked cheeks and shoulders. . .

I was nineteen years old and in the throngs of my best summer yet. He was tall, muscular, more of a Jean-Claude Van Damme versus an Arnie, with cocoa-brown hair cut Caesar style (as was the look), smart as a whip and hot as the summer blacktop. His name was Greg.

I'd never ever, like *ever*, felt so lucky. How had I landed this guy? Even my mom's boyfriend would marvel at Greg's good looks and bright white smile.

"That boy sure is an Adonis," he would say.

"Well, that girl is no chopped liver," Mom would add.

But Mom's boyfriend was right; next to the grade-A tenderloin, I was a T-bone.

One month into our relationship, I'd never been so happy, or so madly in love. This, I disguised, because those are the lessons of the pubescent outcast: *Play it cool.* Junior high taught me that.

Three years as the not quite nerd but definitely not cool kid; the chubby but not enormous girl (because people weren't in those days); the new girl with a widowed, too-busy working mom and no friends (because moving means leaving who you love and that's a whole thing). It didn't help that my mom permed my hair once a year to give it *volume* (like I cared about volume). The actual effect being that I looked like a chubby poodle who overcompensated with thick black eyeliner and too-snug jeans.

Thank God I discovered the *20 Minute Workout.* Between bouncing around my living room to T&A shots of hot chicks doing aerobics and not having Grandma nearby to feed me second dinner and brownies on the daily, by high school I had slimmed down to a real size 6 and was starting to actually look like my mother's daughter.

Greg and I had just spent a week at his cabin alone exploring each other in ways that only curious young lovers could. It was in this blissfully sweet state that we got the call from my sister that Grandma had collapsed and was being medevaced to Calgary—

She might not make it through the night!

"What?" I scream-cried, horrified. This was far worse than any devil under my bed.

Mom, Troy, and I raced to the hospital in shock. Just two weeks earlier, I'd visited Grandma and she was as she'd always been: in her garden, cooking, teaching, loving. I couldn't believe my eyes. Tubes up her nose, connected to a mask covering her mouth, connected to more tubes pumping oxygen. Long needles in both arms connected to a different set of tubes filled with electrolytes dripping from silicon sacks on tall metal hangers. Wider tubes poking out the sides of her rib cage, connected to her lungs, pumping yellow fluid into bigger tubes, and her face sunken and gray.

And yet—she smiled. Her face lit up when she saw us, as though nothing of this earth could stop her spirit from shining through.

"Oh, Grandma," I said, swiping tears and placing my hand carefully on hers, "I love you so much."

She nodded, unable to speak, and motioned to write. Quickly, Mom pulled paper and pen from her purse and handed it to Grandma as we all held our breath . . .

Knowing Grandma's depths, I fully expected the wisdom of the ages to pour forth on that page. All the questions I'd ever asked—*Why are we here? Who is God? What happens when we die? How did they build those dang pyramids?* Because all along I suspected life wasn't actually about owning the nicest house, or the most expensive car, or having fancy friends, or chasing fame—no matter what the TV tried to tell me.

Instead, Grandma wrote furiously an addendum to her will, updating it to include the latest of events, like transferring my car back to me for a dollar. *Sign here!* A year earlier she'd put my car in her name so I could afford insurance (no thanks to an accident and too many speeding tickets) and ended up saving me $2,000. Then she scribbled something about my nephew, six years old, and how we all needed to pray that my sister would find a husband and father for that sweet boy. She wrote and wrote until her fingers cramped and our eyes grew soggy in grief.

There was no poor me, no swearing at God, no huddling under the covers, just a readiness to accept, come what may. As the rest of us stood there, confused and small, appearing solid, acting solid, but liquified, actually vapor, tears melting our skin like acid. It hadn't been ten years since Dad. Meanwhile,

Grandma had more light streaming from a single eyeball than the bunch of us had in our collective bodies.

That night, Mom and I prayed for hours. My uncle, Mom's brother, even prayed and he was an atheist. "A man of science," he always said. I told Greg to pray too. But I suspect he was also an atheist, which, before this day, hadn't mattered much. Now it did. Death without God would be unspeakably bitter.

As was her way, Grandma defied the doctors, specialists, and their prognoses. Those in the various labs who saw her chart could not believe she'd lived past three days. The cancer so ubiquitous they couldn't identify the organ of origin. Foiling them all, she lived three more years, at home, in her house, where Grandpa had been waiting when she was airlifted.

When I visited, Grandma and I would talk for hours and I would massage her arm, swollen with edema. She'd thank me profusely, as though she was a burden. My heart would swell like her arm, overflowing with tenderness for her, and hurt and fury at God.

"Grandma, if God is good, why does He allow this?" I'd ask.

"This isn't his fault. We have free will. We get to choose how we live."

"There's nothing free will about you getting cancer. It makes no sense!"

"It's near my time. Everything for a reason."

"You're too young. You never smoked or drank. You're so kind. First Dad, now you?"

"I'll see your dad in Heaven," she'd sigh. "I loved Jimmy like my own son. It will be beautiful beyond our imaginings. Someday, we'll all be together again."

"How do you know there's a Heaven? How do you know it's beautiful? How can you still believe after all we've been through? Your land stolen by the government, all that money gone, the troubles with your business, Grandpa suddenly dying in a car accident while you're sick with cancer—Life is rotten. And God allows it."

"It's also sweet. God allows that too," Grandma said, untying her hair with her good hand from the knot at the nape of her neck. Her bun unwinding from its black-silver swirl that resembled the starry spin of the Milky Way, worn the same way every day since I could remember, her once hearty body thin and curved next to my straight lines and lean muscles.

Can't I just give her my vitality, the fire that burns the heat of a million tiny suns inside every one of my cells? It's yours, Grandma, take it!

"Life is meant to be bittersweet, and that's why there's the promise of Heaven," Grandma said. "Earth is a training ground. We can't know joy without suffering. We grow or we shrink. For those with faith, there is the ultimate reward." She hesitated. "And, if I'm wrong, well, no harm done." She shrugged as her eyes smiled.

"So, you're not sure?" I asked, pondering and disappointed at once. This was not the answer I'd expected from the wisest woman I'd ever known.

Grandma tilted her face to the yellow light at the center of the ceiling, held in a pearly glass dish with its dust and tiny black flies lying listless on the edges, then smiled at me with that most gentle of smiles. "I'm hedging my bets on God."

CHAPTER 7

Whose advice would you trust most to get you out of a life-or-death bind?

a) A priest or pastor
b) A psychic
c) A quantum physicist
d) Your doctor
e) A child
f) Grandma
g) Other

CHAPTER 7.1

Ayahuasca Journey
September 2021

We have forgotten what religion is. It comes from the desire of the human heart to connect with something much greater than itself. . . . It's about experience and transformation that dyes the soul beautiful colors, which are then reflected upon the world. We have severed our shamanic umbilical cord that connects us with the divine. . . . True insight comes from within . . . and this is where plant hallucinogens enter the picture. They don't tell you, they show you.[7]

The room was silent. With that continued all manner of inner atrocities, in waves, like a flood tide, filling me with fresh horror each time.

I began to sob. All I could do was curl up and release the salty liquid that leaked from my eye sockets to seemingly no end. Turning me into my own river. Each cell a tide pool, drenched in the sorrow and suffering of this planet. And, worst of the worst, none of it, not one bit of it, made sense.

---

[7] *Grandmother Ayahuasca* by Christian Funder © 2021. Reprinted by permission of Inner Traditions International and Bear & Company. www.Innertraditions.com

Why do humans live in a state of war? Why do we kill? Why do we hate? How can we be from God, from pure love, ultimate source, when we're so cruel?

Me, a card-carrying member of this dumpster fire of a society. Our potential, our greatness, our light-being soul-fire diminished to a spark, a speck of a spark. Like robots programmed to repeat the lies of government-sanctioned spin doctors. Hollow mantras to satisfy our every lust. People everywhere fixated on desires that reached no higher than money, power and fame. . . While they watch, amused by us, all-powerful in their thrones.

We think we're free, but we're not. We think we're fortunate, born into normal-ish (whatever that is) first-world homes, yet asleep to the truth of the atrocities around us, just beyond our borders, just past our zip code—*No please, don't tell me, I don't want to know. My life is too good. Your misery will only bring me down!*

Because why? How? What could I ever do to stop it?

Such a nobody. That's what I felt. Useless. A grub. A milk-fed maggot with no excuse.

Why hadn't I touched my family more? Loved them more? Why had I held back the one most important thing we all had smack in the center of our being, in the base of our heart in an unlimited supply if we'd only just look? The one damn thing that makes us human—love!

Visions came of me as a young girl, sitting on the grass in front of my singing teacher's home after my lesson. All the girls in my class had been picked up but me. An hour later, the next group of girls all picked up but me. I prayed not to cry as the weight of young eyeballs burned holes in my back, my gaze glued to the ground. Then it was dinnertime, no more lessons, no more girls or happy parents picking up happy children. The sun was setting. My face held stiff against a wobbling chin and glassy eyes, while the corners of my mouth turned to the cement, yanked and pulled by a force beyond gravity.

That day I changed. I became someone else. Innocence evaporated as I walked the train tracks home, up high on the hill alone. No one to witness but the gopher scrambling for his hole. Crying. Swearing. Repeating words I'd promised never to say: "Shit. Fuck. Piss. Damn. Hell. Shit. Fuck. Piss. Damn. Hell." Fearing eternal damnation—

Worth it. It felt so good to let it out. To release the anger that I'd bottled inside. Anger I hadn't realized I held, so raw and ragged and hot. Had I sealed my fate? One year later, my dad died. Innocence gone and sadness turned to anger turned to glue. *Fuck!* My new mantra. Another mantra for the low-vibe nothings.

That word seemed so powerful then, powerful and horrible, a *bad* word. It carried too much of the ugliness of the planet. *Never take the Lord's name in vain. No profanity. It's all a test. You pass—Heaven. You fail—Hell.* Programmed into us, pounded into us—the threat of Hell—critical to our dissolution of self. That's where fear takes us.

A true child of God has no need for profanity and no need for fear. Hell is the opposite of Heaven and love is the opposite of fuck.

In a deluge of angry psychedelic visions, I saw that every time I had ever said that word, I invited the lonely, the sad, the mad, the desperate, which created a mask emblazoned on my face like a tattoo, the mask of a bulldog who's broken inside, splintered into a thousand pieces.

I saw me as a child running home from school by myself, speeding on my bike from the swimming pool along the streets of Riverside, hair tangled and wet, rain smashing the pavement in front of me. That was the night I was struck by lightning—I was right there again, reliving it as an innocent, totally inside of it, inside of her, Nature.

The bolt bounced off the pavement in front of my tire, zipped up through my hands and chest, along my neck and to the crown of my head. I was mildly electrocuted and saved by my bike, by big fat rubber tires. Now, I felt it all again. My legs spinning faster and faster, riding as fast as I could, dripping from the deluge, speeding home to tell my story. Maybe now I could finally be Supergirl, someone special with special powers granted from God himself, the light in the sky.

But I was the youngest of four. Nothing important to say. I would spend the next forty years trying to prove the opposite, working it from the outside out. Because inside work wasn't something my generation did, at least not the latchkey kids.

I wept for her, yearning to go back in time to hug her and never let her go. Sobbing until my head felt drained of moisture, every cell squeezed dry, my body curled tight into a ball like a baby duck burrowing under its mother.

Only there were no feathers, no down, and no one to hold me, just the inexplicable loneliness of the eternal now. A forever mirror, bouncing light back and forth and over and under, all within me—I was the hologram. I was the projection. It was me. Within me. Only me. And the only way out was to die.

I surrendered to the vine. "Do as you please."

CHAPTER 7.2

Mighty Swell

March 2018

The rain kept coming and the brown water never washed away. It made for a creamy beige froth on the waves that left a fizzy yellow scum line on the shore. At this rate, I'd never learn to surf. We couldn't even dip our toes in the water for the bacterial count, let alone body board or rope swing. Which meant there wasn't much to do besides watch movies and hunker down. Hard because, to us, island life was all about the water. It was the reason we'd moved.

The trails, too, had become mudslides. A short jaunt uphill was taking your life into your hands on the "Hawaiian Ice." The roads were slosh puddles. There were barely any sidewalks to begin with, so a neighborhood stroll was out. Seemed all the people on the entire island had disappeared into their homes to wait out the seemingly endless barrage of weather.

I wondered why we had automatic sprinklers when there was absolutely no need. It was unfathomable to me that the incredible rain that had begun mid-October had barely let up six months later. Countless times I checked the weather in Vancouver: sun, partial sun, occasional rain, and sun. *Sun! What the heck? Vancouver's never sunny in spring.*

Meanwhile, in paradise, downpour after downpour. Kauai was the queen of flash floods. She had monsoons.

Back home, higher elevations would at least get snow out of the deal. The kids would lose their minds, throw on ski pants and a jacket, run up the road and toboggan our neighbor's nerve-racking driveway covered in fluffy white flakes. Mild temperatures meant the steep sled track would quickly ice off into a luge, while the kids whipped into snowbanks with grins so wide they looked like Halloween pumpkins. But here, in Kauai, it was wet, just wet, and muddy, uncomfortably so.

Canyen took it the hardest. I would pick him up from school and the grass field (that he wasn't allowed to play on anyway, because *them's the rules*) was a mud pit. That mud was dragged onto sidewalks, classrooms, and all over legs and clothes. I couldn't wear nice shoes. I couldn't even wear nice flip-flops. They'd get destroyed by the muck that was everywhere, toes caked with red dirt under toenails and in knuckle grooves.

In Lions Bay, I'd become used to complaining about the rain. With its perpetually dark skies and debilitating short winter days, it wasn't uncommon to go weeks without a sliver of sunshine, not a beam. By February, friends would drift into weather depression, their skin an off-putting shade of gray, dragging their bloated bodies out of bed. For what? More rain. This was the last thing I'd expected in the rainbow state. It would've been just my luck to be the one person to move from Vancouver to Hawaii to get Seasonal Affective Disorder.

SAD, indeed. Meanwhile, little Canyen got himself a blistering case of staph.

It began with a rare cloudless day on the Wailua River with Canyen's new friend Keanu. *New friend, hurrah!* The two were an instant hit. *Huck Finn meet Tom Sawyer. Tweedle Dee meet*

Tweedle Dum. A better match could not have been dreamed up by Mark Twain himself.

In a few short months, the two enjoyed wet days fishing for bass in grassy reservoirs, tarp surfing on skateboards on the front carport, chasing RC cars in the mud, boxes and boxes of organic Fudgsicles and bunny pasta, and too many sleepovers to count. Keanu was one grade younger than Canyen and as fun and funny as the day was long.

Lisa, his mom, was equally captivating. We became fast friends, roasting in our beach chairs, drinking kombucha with a splash of gin, soaking up the exuberance of our boys amidst the jaw-droppingly pretty Wailua River as it wound down from the middle of the island and Makaleha's emerald peak.

Once revered as a ritual site for Kauai's ancient inhabitants, the river teemed with jet boats and tourists paddling canoes and stand-up paddleboards for the Fern Grotto or various waterfalls. At her mouth, where river spilled into ocean, sat the Coco Palms, surrounded by chain-link fence and black tarp, a burnt-out shell of its former glory, reminding guests, perhaps mockingly, paradise is not what you think.

Lisa and I would lounge with our backs to the blighted hotel, slipping in and out of the shade from the highway overpass as necessary. Our boys would splash around the river mouth, taking turns on Lisa's husband's homemade foil board, then balancing on bloated tree trunks that lingered on the shoreline with roots jackknifed to the river bottom, forming small dams.

For the first time in ten months, laughing came easy. Lisa enlightened me to the various mom cliques on the island, from territorial ha'oles to the *titas* who wanted nothing to do with them. After twenty years of teaching kindergarten, she seemed to know almost everyone. Meanwhile, I regaled her with stories of working in reality television. Laughing it up, until one afternoon, when she noticed Canyen's chest.

"Have you checked that?" Lisa asked, which surprised me—she wasn't the nervous type.

"I'm just sort of noticing it myself." My heart jumped. The scab was the size of a quarter.

"Has he had it long?"

"I saw him scratching the other day. But he's always scratching. He's a picker." I laughed the way we'd come to laugh, like screwballs, Lucy and Harriet.

"Get some Hibiclens on that." She became serious. "Especially after swimming in this slew."

Sure enough, a few steps off the shoreline, you couldn't see your toes through the water. The olive tinge of the river suggested it was awash with microorganisms.

"What's hippie-cleanse?" I laughed.

"You goof," she giggled. "It's antibacterial wash. I use it all the time. They sell it at Longs. Go grab a bottle on your way home."

That night, Canyen soaped his wounds with Hibiclens in the shower. He had so many mosquito bites and cuts and scratches that I could barely keep track. Truth was, we were all a little festery. The heat, the moisture, the bugs, the mold, the fungus, ours was an island teeming with life-forms in every size and dimension, worst of all, the microscopic.

"Time for bed, sweetie. Let me get some tea tree on that," I said, pulling my favorite homemade salve from the drawer and dabbing it onto his chest wound. "Does it hurt?"

"Nope," he said, undeterred.

"How long have you had this, anyway?"

"Not sure. It's itchy."

Once the melaleuca oil soaked in, I sprinkled BFI powder over it, Josh's mom's remedy full of zinc and minerals to help the skin form a scab.

"I love this smell," he said, chin stuck to his chest as he watched his tiny fingers spreading the powder over the sore, innocently trusting all would be well.

"Will he be okay?" Tyde stood behind us, toothbrush hanging from his mouth, readying for bed after being kicked off the game system by his dad.

"Mom?" Canyen looked at me with big eyes.

"Of course, sweetie." I said, hiding my uncertainty.

Canyen was so little; I had a feeling he might never grow up. Unlike Tyde who'd grown a foot since we'd arrived and had developed a snarky teenage tongue. Which made sense, given he turned thirteen in February, officially placing Josh and I into the madness of screenagers.

Tyde was such a loving boy. But I hated the first-person shooter games. They brought out the devil in him, along with a never-before-seen sibling rivalry with his brother. Every time Tyde clicked on the screen, a slew of chemicals raged through his bloodstream, endorphins, cortisol, and testosterone peaking with every hit. Canyen was yet to be drawn with such enthusiasm.

Tyde would tell us that the game system was the only way to connect to friends back home. Mom guilt? Check! So, we let him. Knowing we had pulled our boys from their first friendships, and a village that coddled them, to a bigger village that (with the exception of Lisa and her boys) had yet to embrace us.

Tyde would lock himself in his room and scream profanities at the screen, assuring me it was part of the play. "All the kids do it, Mom!"

Oh, of course honey, then it must be okay!

About once a week, Josh and I threatened to smash the PlayStation or run it over with the truck. It was war: parents vs. children, parents vs. video games, parents vs. the purveyors of violence and smut.

"I'm worried about Tyde," Josh said as we crawled into bed.

"Me too. At least he's not playing *Grand Theft Auto*," I sighed. "I'm so glad we've held off buying an iPhone. Plus, he got that job at the Juice Hale. Maybe he'll be okay."

Josh flicked off his lamp. "I am proud of him. I love that he's husking coconuts and making shaved ice. But seems the second he gets home—video games. We moved to get away from the goddamn game system, and those wet, gray winters."

"Ugh, I don't miss Vancouver winters," I added, twirling my hair into a knot to avoid overnight pillow tangles. "At least here, the sun pokes out between squalls. We get vitamin D."

Indeed, here nature beckoned at every turn. She was unavoidable. You had to love the outdoors or you might as well live in a New York City high-rise. By any standard, the temperature was pleasant, rarely above 88 or below 68. The ground was soft. My kids had discarded shoes. Their feet were now tough as cowhide, connecting them to the charge of the earth every single time they stepped outside. Our windows were almost always open with trade winds blasting through like a sage clearing, ridding the air of unseen toxins.

We were in it whether we liked it or not, and our physical and mental health could only benefit. I prayed that somehow this countered the toxic trance of electronic games.

"Speaking of," Josh said, "what about Canyen's sores?"

"He'll be fine," I said, flicking off the lamp.

"I've seen people lose body parts surfing river mouths." Josh flipped to his stomach, bunching the pillow between his arms and already tangling the sheets so they favored his side. "It's dangerous."

"I'll keep my eye on it," I said, yanking the sheets back my way.

"I heard a story at work." Josh lifted his head to whisper. "I don't want Canyen to hear."

Josh proceeded to tell the story of a coworker from the time-share office whose friend's wife got staph from the water. Being young and new to the island, she didn't think much of it and left it unchecked. A month or so ago, her leg turned septic, then so did the other. Eventually, both legs had to be removed from the knee down. She's now in a wheelchair: two kids and a fresh move to the island to start a new life. The price? Her legs.

"Maybe tomorrow take him to the doctor, Shan."

"Okay," I said, turning on my side, now doubting the natural approach that had come to define me and my manner of managing my kids.

The next day, I brought out the big guns, my hundred-dollar-a-bottle ozonated garlic and oregano oil. It stung like a bitch, reeked to high heaven, and killed any microbe it came into contact with, according to countless studies. At first, Canyen's wound was shrinking, then it seemed to expand, like both were happening at the same time, undulating in slow motion like *The Blob*. But, in three short days, the wound scabbed dry. I'd won and Canyen smelled like a tub of garlic hummus.

Until, two days later, Canyen began scratching his legs like crazy. Small red sores were cropping up everywhere. How had I not noticed?

"This definitely looks like staph," the doctor said with a worried look. Canyen had seven or so fresh wounds on his legs, all from over-scratching and picking mosquito bites. Each of them red and angry and growing. "I can swab it if you like."

"Yes, please."

I shuddered to think my free-range parenting had gotten the best of me—

What if he loses a leg? If only he had antibiotics from the get-go. Stupid me. Stupid mother. Worst parent ever. My heart crumpled into my chest with worry. *I did this. It's my fault.* Not just my natural topicals and healing tinctures, trying to play medicine woman, too proud and all that, but suggesting to Canyen that we might move back to Canada the night of the bomb scare. *Am I nuts? How careless of me!*

Words are too powerful to toss about so sloppily, a mere step away from manifestation. First thought, then word, then action. Shazam! Thoughts become reality!

Canyen's staph infection was the universe conspiring to get us back to Canada, answering my call. A sensible place where health care is free and gnarly pathogens don't take the legs of healthy young mothers or children, where festering heat and bugs and rotting cesspools aren't even a little bit of a thing. The guilt was overwhelming.

That night, Canyen drank his pink antibiotic drink that would flatten his gut biome and do all manner of damage, but at least it would kill the staph.

While I smothered his wounds with antibacterial cream, I prayed for the proliferation of sores to reverse, that the malicious bacteria would lose hold of my sweet, sweet boy. We had a clean vessel on our side, a vigorous young temple. Canyen was just ten years old and programmed to grow and heal above all else.

The fan rumbled above Canyen's bed, creating a soft, steady breeze that lightened the load of the clammy air. Perspiration stuck to my skin in tiny beadlets between my breast and armpits. I wondered how long it would take to acclimatize to Kauai. Possibly never.

"Mom, can you tell me a *good* story tonight?" Canyen asked while snuggling under the covers, his hair damp from the shower, wearing shorts and nothing else.

"What's wrong with *Wildwood*, sweetie?" I kneeled at the side of his bed to keep cool. "We've been halfway for months. Let's finish."

Canyen pleaded, "I want you to make up a story like you used to. That's my favorite."

The ceiling fan shot stray hairs onto my face so they stuck to my lashes and lips. "Okay," I said, fluffing his hair and smiling. "Here goes . . .

"Once upon a time, there were two boys who lived in the forest up a steep mountain trail, enclosed with tall cedars, giant firs and hemlocks, luscious ferns and primitive mosses with spooky names like Witch's Hair, Wolf Lichen, and Liverwort."

"Mom, this sounds like *Wildwood*," Canyen said, annoyed.

"Give me a minute," I laughed. "Each day, these strange plants would pump an unusual gas into the air that swirled into a dark purple smoke that, if you dared to follow the trail, would lead you to the enchanted part of the forest where magic happened, where dwarves roamed and children could talk to trees and fly and hold their breath underwater for hours."

Tyde entered the room and curled up beside me like a kitten. I knew to take a moment to digest the preciousness of the scene. Times such as these would be more and more rare. Plus, it was the only instance I could count on both boys to be quiet and pensive.

"Keep going, Mom," Tyde said. "I love this story."

"Okay." I shifted to get comfortable, one hand on Canyen, the other around Tyde. "One day, two boys named Tillbert and Canahuck stumbled upon a giant moss-covered rock."

"Mooooom." Tyde elbowed me playfully. Canyen giggled.

"The rock was the size of a van. It shimmered a wondrous shade of chartreuse and looked like a giant's throne, glistening in the dappled golden light of the forest, as though nature had conjured its very own royal emerald living room with a green shag carpet, soft and squishy and begging to be nuzzled. Only underneath the throne's mossy facade were large jagged rocks that shot up like spears. If the boys weren't careful, they could get spired. Suddenly, they noticed a large toadstool with a bright orange frog on top. He ribbited, as frogs do, then said, 'Open it.'

"Under the giant mushroom was a lever for a secret door that led to a passageway that burrowed deep into the mountain. Guarding it was Mr. Dwarf, with his stubby round nose, a long red beard, and a pointed hat that folded beneath his chin. He told the boys if they could guess the password they could enter the magic tunnel—"

"What would they find?" Canyen asked, wide-eyed.

"Well, they'd find rainbow taffy slides, marshmallow trampolines, and the granting of one wish by the great spirit of the forest. But first, they needed the password."

The boys looked at each other in wonder.

"Tutti Frutti!" Canyen exclaimed.

"No, silly—open sesame pickles," Tyde said with assurance.

"You're both right!"

"Mom, this story is always about me and Canyen. And I know exactly the rock you're talking about in Lions Bay. It's at the top of Trudi's Trail."

"You got me," I said, tickling them both, seeing that Tyde—though tall and growing strong, his voice deepening and bones thickening—still loved my tales too.

"Skip to it then—what's your wish, boys? What do you ask of the jungle?"

"I just want Canyen better." Tyde hugged his brother, cozying up to him with a sweetness I'd not seen between the two in a while.

The next morning . . . nothing.

The day after . . . nothing.

So, the following night, after smothering Canyen with all my concoctions, as well as the pharmacist's concoctions, plus green drinks and yellow drinks and pink drinks and more, I made a deal with God. I prayed harder than I'd ever prayed and made a promise that I planned to keep.

"Dear God, I'm sorry we don't talk regularly. Forgive me. I know that somewhere in the recesses of my brain, I moved here for you. There was no finding you with my fancy life in Vancouver. I was too distracted, too driven, too out of touch. Now I'm here, we're here, my little family. And it's not a retreat or a sabbatical or superficial in any way at all, we moved for a reason! To get in touch with myself, at least try to, my meaning, your meaning, the meaning of it all. Like, who are you? Christian? Hindu? Great Spirit? Does it matter?"

I stopped myself. My mom would be appalled by this prayer.

"I promise, if you heal sweet little Canyen and keep him whole—no festering limbs, no surgical saws—I will devote myself to the quest to know You, to be closer to You. I know this is what it's all about, connection to higher purpose, higher power, the highest! Whether I do it here, or back home, or wherever doesn't matter. I'll take your lead. Please?"

I waited as though to get an answer.

The breeze stiffened. The hair on the back of my neck stood tall as I bowed my head into my hands. "In Jesus's heavenly name I pray," I said, still not understanding why people prayed in His name when already praying to Him, but today it felt somehow more official. "Amen."

The next day, progress.

The day after that, more.

And the day after that too.

Canyen was getting better. And with that, I had struck an accord.

CHAPTER 7.3

2011

"Mommy, Canyen broke my Lego again!" young Tyde cried from the playroom.

Into the kitchen, Canyen came careening around the corner with a chunk of Lego Hobbit Town in his tiny grip, socks slipping on the hardwood, making way for the protection of my legs. I was chopping cucumber for our nightly veggie plate and putting final spicy flourishes on Josh's favorite dish, chili con carne.

"Canyen, no." I placed the knife on the counter and attempted to pry his chubby fingers from what looked like a small brown bridge and a plastic tree squished beside it. "Give me that. You're not to wreck your brother's Lego."

"But it's mine, Mommy. My Lego," Canyen pleaded, four years old.

Yes, it was, but Canyen often asked his big brother to help him build his various sets. And Tyde, with a God-given knack for architecture or engineering or both, just sort of took over. Sometimes it worked out and everyone was happy, but more often than not, it brought out a rivalry that yoked at my gooey mommy core, two feisty wolf cubs in a scrum.

"He always does this!" Tyde sobbed, attempting to grab the pieces from Canyen through my legs, both boys crying and yanking at my jeans. "He always wrecks my stuff."

This was hard. I couldn't stand to see my boys brokenhearted and hurting each other. As though to add to the fuss, rain pounded the roof and gushed from the gutters like miniature waterfalls at every corner of the house, feeling ominous. When really, it was just a typical February night on the West Coast.

The dead of winter in Lions Bay meant the sky was dark by four thirty and outdoor playtime was impossibly rare. This wasn't the Hundred Acre Wood of *Winnie-the-Pooh.* Storms here meant giant cedars could come crashing down and demolish a house—a friend down the street lost her whole top floor. A decade or so ago, one deluge swept five homes that sat snug along a riverbank into the sea, taking its occupants, two young beautiful brothers, never to be found.

I tried not to think of such things. Our home was a good distance from the streams that turned to torrential falls in the winter. Furthermore, we were propped firmly atop a very large granite rock, one-quarter the size of our house. When we bought our Timbertop home, the inspector said, "Not to worry, this house isn't going anywhere. Your neighbor, on the other hand, is slowly slipping down the mountain."

Ordinarily, the nonstop rain would have me depressed out of my wits. Having swapped the near perfect clime of sunny LA—where we lived a quick jog to the gleaming California coastline and its meandering beach walks that spanned Marina Del Ray to Malibu—for a tree house on the side of a mountain and perpetually soggy winters in the Pacific Northwest. But it had been more than five years since we'd moved, and Josh and I had long since affirmed this was a far better place to raise kids than LA. Plus, every mother knew, children light up a life, no matter where or what the gloom.

Josh was freshly home from a long run on a Canadian B-grade version of the *Amazing Race* (he got his reality TV start on the very first season of the US original), exhausted after two and a half weeks of fourteen-hour days with a single day off in the middle. Still, he was in good humor, happy to be home. Also, happy his mom let him off the hook to go to California.

Lately, Josh had been alternating coming home to us with trips to LA to see his parents, his dad wrought with cancer but handling it like a champ. A year ago, Tom had been diagnosed with leukemia. The oncologist said it probably began as melanoma. Tom had just had his third chunk of cancer cut out of his shoulder. The wound was long and deep and added to his many scars that, along with his fuzzy mop, mustache, and beard, made him look like a friendly pirate. In typical Tom fashion, this didn't slow him. He and Robin were prepping a sail to Catalina to catch ahi and drink buckets of red wine with friends at Cherry Cove. I was simply grateful not to have to share my husband.

Josh and I had work to do. It was tax time. The worst.

Though the two of us paid our mortgage and credit card bills each month, we had the habit of not putting aside money for the government. Each year, as April inched closer, we felt the money crunch deep in our bones, wondering where we'd find thousands of dollars to pay both the US and Canadian governments with our seven tax returns.

For me, money stress showed up as lower back spasms, three inches below the spot where I'd broken my spine at age eighteen on a trampoline. For Josh, it appeared as acute neck and shoulder pain, in the same place he held the camera for hours each day at work. To solve this, every spring, our line of credit took a massive hit, as did our nerves, our resilience, and our joy.

The house was quiet now. The rain had slowed and Josh had distracted the boys by drawing funny faces on the scrap paper kept in the corner of our breakfast nook. The kids picked through the veggie tray, dipping in a sauce I'd made with herbs, lemon, yogurt, and avocado oil mayonnaise, while scribbling with crayons and glitter glue. I slipped onto the bench beside them, feeling the sweet simplicity of the moment as a happy flicker in my heart.

"Mommy," Canyen blurted, his eyes serene. "I picked you from the clouds."

"What's that?" I said. "You want to draw clouds?"

"No, I *picked* you from the clouds, Mommy." His eyes grew intense while sandy blond curls framed his perfect chubby chin.

Josh shook his head with a look of *don't ask me* and Tyde barely looked up from his glitter glue masterpiece.

"What do you mean, you *picked* me?" I smiled.

Canyen was a trickster, a contrarian; I wondered what he was up to.

"Before I was in your tummy, I saw you from the clouds and I picked you. I chose you, Mommy."

My face went flat. *He's remembering. Oh my God!*

This was a conversation I'd dreamed of having with my children, insight into the crossing in and out of this world, the material plane vs. the ethereal. *Where do we go when we die? Where do we come from before we're born? Tell me about traveling through the birth canal? And what the heck is déjà vu?*

"Why me?" I said carefully, my fingers trembling, speaking tenderly, not wanting to snap the delicate thread of this conversation. "You could see me?"

"Yes, Mommy, I watched you from up there."

"Up where?"

"The clouds."

"Heaven?"

"Clouds, Mommy, the sky."

"And you picked me?"

"Yes, you needed me." He smiled, no clue he'd just broken some physical law of the universe for a glimpse into Heaven. "I watched you." He hesitated.

I couldn't interrupt. This had to come from him, untainted and pure.

"I wanted to help you, Mommy, to be with you. I picked you."

Blood filled my face as my heart pumped wildly. I wanted more, more description, more details. His words were simple, unabashed, flawless, the best he could deliver for four years on the planet.

Josh, unable to resist—who could blame him—asked, "What about Dad? Did you see me too?"

Canyen looked to Josh with warm hazel eyes. Six-year-old Tyde now listening intently, gripping the table and giggling. "You're funny, Canyen."

"Yes, Dad, you too," Canyen said, eyes fixed, cheeks rosy red.

Josh nodded with satisfaction, then looked down to his food.

"Tell us what it was like in the clouds," I said. "What did you do there?"

"I watched." Canyen picked up his fork. I could feel the moment slipping as he pushed sweet potatoes around his plate. "I waited."

No, no, no, no, let's stay here forever, more of this, more of heaven—I wondered if I should grab a camera to record him—*No, too late! Maybe we can relive it. I'll ask him to say it all again. I'll ask more questions. Oh my God, oh my God, oh my God!*

It was too precious, too rare, and I'd no choice but to sit there and hope to memorize every breath of it.

"I waited for you to be ready, Mommy." He looked up, thinking. "Then God put me in your tummy."

My face softened like butter in a pan, and I felt this unbreakable connection to the three precious beings before me. Lucky me. Who was this mystery child, acrobat contortionist, warrior rebel, contrarian boy of mine? Had we flown magic carpets together in ancient Arabia or sailed the ocean in Viking ships? Was he swept from the heavens from the future or the past? Had he lived 12 lives or 202? So many questions. But I didn't want to speak, only to listen.

"You weren't ready the first time."

I looked to Josh and whispered under my breath, "The first time?" I racked my brain, attempting to decode what that could have meant.

Josh gave me another bewildered look.

I covered my mouth and leaned into Josh's ear. "Oh my God, the baby in between."

The month before I became pregnant with Canyen, I miscarried. Nearly three months along with zero red flags. The timing would be perfect, a June baby. Until one night, lying in bed, I keeled over while my insides twisted like an old telephone cord. I ran to the bathroom and out it splashed into the toilet without a fight, just *splat*. Three in the morning and it felt like something had sucked out my insides.

The air was still and eerie, the house silent. Josh was dead asleep. I couldn't wake him. I was too frozen in fear. Lifeblood dripped heavily from between my legs as I stared into the white bowl. Alongside the crimson mass I thought I saw a tiny pink blob that I'd carried and grown for ten weeks, a still aquatic human nearly the size of a Polly Pocket doll.

And what did I do? Flushed her! Because, what else? My body had rejected her, or she rejected my body, or planet Earth, or something.

She. Because she was a girl. I felt it in my heart. The girl I cried for when I discovered I was having another boy (Canyen) four months down the road. An excruciating cry, I wailed so loud and long, like it was the last chance I'd ever have to bring through my daughter, my best friend, my soulmate, because it was. At thirty-eight years old, I would not try again. We would have two children and that was that. Two boys would have to do. And we would be okay, because that's what we were given and Grandma always said, *God gives us what we need, not necessarily what we want.* And I would accept this with a modicum of grace.

Despite my longing, after Canyen was born, I felt at peace. The miscarriage and Canyen's subsequent entrance was meant to be, divine timing, in that order and just like that. His little being was not some random roll of the dice; I was never meant to have *her* at all, for reasons I had yet to discover.

"Mommy?" Canyen peered at me from behind those sweet round balls in the center of his head, waiting for a response.

As though my thoughts weren't swirling madly enough, I was struck again with another remembrance. There wasn't just a *first time*, as Canyen so casually mentioned. There was another, so many years ago that I'd nearly forgot or purposely buried, when I was twenty-two and my first love, and subsequent on-and-off boyfriend of three years, got me pregnant. I never told anyone. Just him. Barely adults and the two of us to be parents . . .

Nature did not have her way. I was interning at a TV station in Denver, and he at an IT firm in Calgary, and this made for a difficult summer and a terrible delay and too many feelings to feel. As soon as I could, I drove seventeen hours home to Calgary, wrought with morning sickness, to land in a clinic on a Friday morning, alone and wanting it over—with not enough love and not enough remorse for such a bitter end—and aborted as soon as I could.

The next day my oldest brother got married. I stood as a bridesmaid, sipping champagne with my boyfriend, as though nothing even remotely momentous had happened to us the day before. Was that her too, picking me from a cloud? Was it Canyen?

Oh my.

Just when I thought I'd sorted it all out with God, I was hit with the mind-boggling mess of it all. This side, that side, souls from Heaven, souls on Earth, spirit, body, flesh, and blood. Had Canyen watched me race to the clinic? Had either of my boys, in their journey from Heaven to here, witnessed me make my too many mistakes, my young and foolish, aloof and ambitious, shirking the rules of creation? *Oh, the mysteries to one day be known.*

What about that part of me that watched over me and witnessed my trials and tribulations? Does she wonder why I'm not kinder and wiser, softer and sweeter, less judgy, less harsh? And why do answers to our deepest questions only beget more?

"You just weren't," Canyen said with his little boy lisp.

"What?"

"Ready." His voice was babyish yet ripe with wisdom. "Then I found you again, Mommy."

"Found?"

"I chose you and I waited for you." His smile pressed his cheeks into dumplings as little teeth poked out from behind his lips. "It was you that I wanted."

"Wow," I said lovingly. "I'm honored."

"Then I got inside your tummy . . . *boom, boom, boom.*" He rolled his hands over each other. "And that's how I got here."

"*Boom, boom, boing.*" Tyde bounced his shoulder off Canyen's. "*Boom, boom, boing.*" He did it again, swaying playfully, having had enough of this strange conversation.

"That's beautiful, Canyen." I gazed softly at my boys, no longer hungry, wanting to linger in that mystery space where secrets live and love is born over and over again.

Canyen shifted as though pulled from a distant dream back to the world. "*Boing-a-boing-a-boo-ba.*" Canyen wiggled then poked Tyde with his carrot.

Tyde held up a celery stick in Canyen's face. "On guard, mister!"

And the two began a veggie-stick swordfight, laughing and forgetting and remembering and melding into that sweet spot of innocence. If only we could have stayed there forever. If only.

CHAPTER 8

What do you do when the rain keeps raining and the storms keep storming and you feel like you just might drown?

a) Build an ark. Invite a male/female pair of every species, collect a handful of good humans (if you can find them), and off you go to new lands.
b) Seek higher ground (like really high), and buy four stand-up paddleboards from Costco just in case. Cross your fingers the nonstop storms eventually pass. *I mean, it has to, right?*
c) Dive into a bucket of cheese fries, or a bag of weed, or whatever your pleasure. Numb the pain. Nothing else matters anymore.
d) Book four one-way tickets to Canada. Leave now. This is a sign from God—you're not meant to be here.

CHAPTER 8.1

Ayahuasca Journey
September 2021

The person is thrown into the depths of consciousness that previously had been blocked by the disciplined mind, and if the ego resists, it can feel like drowning. Forgotten memories and repressed trauma from which the ego sought to protect the individual might be revealed and relived, and there is nowhere to run.[8]

"Shannon, are you okay?" Sarah appeared like an apparition vaporizing in the mist. I could barely open my eyes.

Is she floating? Is she good or bad because that's all there is? It's all black-and-white, kindness and evil, and zigzag confusion.

"Are you real?" I managed to say, my words slow and sloppy, glued to my tongue.

The harder I looked, I saw she could be Mary, mother of Jesus.

Is it really her? Either way, thank God she wears white—that way I know she's good. Wait! What if it's a trick? Oh please, no! The Devil in disguise come to finish the job . . .

---

[8] *Grandmother Ayahuasca* by Christian Funder © 2021. Reprinted by permission of Inner Traditions International and Bear & Company. www.Innertraditions.com

"Yes, I'm real," she smiled.

Draped in a white gown to her feet, a scarf wrapped around her head and long dark hair cascading past her chest, Sarah certainly did not look evil, at least not like the men in the tent. She looked like a saint, beautiful and pure.

"I can't move," I said, barely audible, my mustard sheet tangled about my legs and my hair strewn across my face like straw. "I feel sick."

"Here, puke then." She handed me my bucket while I leaned in to spill my body over it.

"I can't," I said pathetically. "What's wrong with me? The demons won't leave. I'm stuck. I'm stuck here!"

"You've got to puke. It's the only way out of the loop."

"I can't." Tears had crusted onto my eyelashes, and I could hardly see. "Just can't!"

"Let's take you to Maestro," she said, perhaps exasperated, I couldn't tell.

"I can't get up." I'd never been so weak, tears drizzling down my cheeks. "I can't move."

"You must." She placed an arm under my back to pull me forward into a seated position.

Abuela makes it such that you can't move. People would probably do stupid things if they had proper use of their arms and legs. Like those TV ads from the eighties of kids on acid, teetering on the edge of a building, speaking gibberish, arms wide, thinking they could fly.

Ayahuasca wasn't like that. Maybe acid wasn't either, and they lied. Either way, I had no inclination to be physical or test my strength or flying ability. I only wanted to lie there and hide under the sheets, away from this planet of horror.

"Come on now, it's your time." Sarah tucked her scarf to one side to pull me to standing. I felt a tinge of gratitude. She was the first and only thing that grounded me in the slightest. She was clear and forthright and knew what she was doing and maybe even cared.

"Okay," I groaned, and for a moment, I was able to stop the tears and focus on my legs.

They felt like noodles dangling from my torso. I could barely stand, let alone walk. I felt a hundred years old, like a cripple, and she was my nurse, guiding me down a tunnel of darkness to God only knew where.

Sure enough, it was the center line of the tent, on the grass and between bodies. It was still planet Earth. I hobbled along, tripping on blankets and puke buckets.

Sarah held tight and somehow got me to Maestro where I dropped to my knees on his mat then slumped over to hide my head, that big round thing at the top of my body that housed all my stories. I tried to hide like a child under a blanket, as far away from Maestro as I could be while still on his mat—embarrassed. Unworthy. Wanting it to end.

Sarah rubbed my back and began to sing, which made me cry again, releasing and sobbing, rocking back and forth. So much trauma, draining, draining. Every few moments I'd lift my head, but it was dark and all I could see were shapes and colors, Sarah in white and Maestro a great brown blob in the center.

CHAPTER 8.2

Into the Heart . . .
April 2018

Everything I needed to know about Daniella sat overflowing in the back seat of her car: a warm crockpot with a fresh-baked barbeque chicken, a tiger-print bra, flip-flops, crayons, her daughter's coloring books, a pair of pumps, a single neon striped running shoe, clothing that hadn't yet made it into a bag, a bag, blankets, a pillow, books of various sorts, a hairbrush tangled with her long black hair, empty containers, and a clipboard. It was like staring into her brain, all scattered and interesting.

"So sorry, my love. My car's usually much cleaner," she said, rolling her *r*'s, making room for my canvas duffel and sleeping bag. "This is going to be so great."

"Weren't we supposed to be there by now?" I asked nervously.

"Yes, darling." She slurred like she was painting the air with her velvet voice and thick Peruvian accent. "It's fine, though. I've worked with Aguirre for years."

"Bye, Tyde! Bye, Canyen!" I waved from the passenger window. "Be good for Dad."

"Bye, Mom," the boys yelled, freshly home from school and busy perfecting kickflips on their skateboards.

I attempted to settle into Daniella's Subaru wagon as she backed down my driveway, narrowly missing our volcanic rock fireplace of the porte cochere before scraping the hearty areca palms that bordered the neighbor. Already, I wished that I had driven. But I needed this, to let go of the reins, for someone else to guide me through whatever it was I'd gotten myself into.

Daniella and I had met a month earlier at a conference for an MLM superfood line that I had considered repping—anything to get out of the house and meet people, even the dreaded multi-level marketing. Watching *Real Housewives of New York* wasn't going to cut it anymore. How I'd mistaken that for a social life was depressing. I justified it by having directed a season in Vancouver. Scarily, I'd grown so tired of fish-lipped prima donnas battling for alpha status that I was considering a pyramid scheme. *Oye.*

I was instantly taken by Daniella. Tall, statuesque, warm almond eyes, dark lashes, no makeup, self-assured, and with that, a rebellious activist heart, as though to armor her allure with a sharp edge.

"I hate Monsanto!" she said. "You know they practically own the entire west side. That's where they do their testing. Heaps and heaps of glyphosate poured onto the land."

"Really? Here?" I replied. "I had no idea." I then proceeded to tell her about the time the kids and I marched in a Vancouver rally, Tyde and Canyen holding signs taller than they with pictures of cancerous rats with gruesome tumors.

With that, our friendship was sealed. I'd never met anyone like her. The two of us had coffee dates, juice dates, practiced yoga together in the tree house that Josh and I built on the back of the property (with a plan for me to teach one day), and even attended an anti-Monsanto rally on Rice Street in Lihue with thirty other people, older hippie types and a few moms.

"Is there yoga there?" I asked, fastening my seat belt, already hot, always hot, tights and bra top snug against my body like a weighted blanket, hoping for comfort in the areas I thought I knew so well. "Maybe raw food or green juices? I could really use a cleanse."

Jesus, I may well be the only person I know who'd commit to a two-day retreat without a clue what it entailed.

"Yes, honey, but most important, the plant medicine." She pursed her lips into a smile and raised her eyebrows, her former beauty queen features as lovely and exotic as her voice. "It's powerful."

"You mean the jungle plant from the Amazon?" My heart rate jumped. "The one that makes you puke? Do I have to do it?" *And what will Josh think?*

I told Josh it was a yoga retreat. A white lie. I was sort of famous for my white lies. I got it from my mom, the master. *For the good of all! Sparing feelings and all that jazz.* Baloney. My white lies so often crept up to bite me in the ass.

"No, you don't have to." Daniella patted my knee like I was a child, despite us being the same age, forty-nine years and no longer counting. "Aguirre is brilliant."

We rolled along the single-lane Kuhio Highway, the only highway on the entire island, toward the sunset, the end of the earth, to Ha'ena, the hip happening North Shore where world-class surfers and movie stars like Pierce Brosnan and Ben Stiller had beach mansions. The clouds hung low as though threatening to pour, as it had for weeks—actually months—while the sun poked sharp white rays through the cracks between. Oddly drab for paradise.

"Daniella." I looked to this woman I barely knew, who I suddenly realized I had entrusted with my psyche. "I'm sort of . . . I'm a little scared."

"Don't worry." She became serious. "Mother Ayahuasca will take care of you . . ."

Daniella! Where are you? What the holy hell am I doing? Shit! I'm at an ayahuasca retreat! Is this legal? Are the cops coming? Wait—Aguirre, which voice? There are too many voices. Oh my God, help!

It was seven o'clock and already dark out. I was bundled in a stack of Mexican blankets alone on a mat on the floor of a back bedroom in a $10 million beach house, as far as one could travel by car northwest on this sweet Pacific isle. I had taken a small capsule, a mild herb, then went outside and took a puff of a joint. A joint! Something I never did. But the guys offering it were so mellow and cool that I suppose I thought it was part of the experience.

I could hear Aguirre, our guide, repeating, "Clothe the voices. Clothe the voices. Give them a name. They are not who you are." But my mind was racing.

Little had I known, weed was not allowed. Rightly so, it had me steeped in paranoia, the conversation in my head so enormous and loud. And I was scared yet cozy, weirdly cozy. And it was dark, very dark, but for a lone Jesus candle flickering in the wind from I didn't know where, because the windows were shut and so were the doors. Yet the house was so airy and open.

I tried to focus and silently prayed that the bald, smart, chubby dude from the communal area didn't come back to check on me. I was vulnerable in my current state and needed to be alone. Earlier, he had grabbed my hand and peered into my eyes in a way that mildly creeped me out, then asked if it was okay. To which I replied, "I can handle you." Which was my super mixed message way of saying, "Please let go."

He didn't. But at that point, I had already lost my words. A nice woman from LA said this was normal. I was starting to *feel* into my heart and out of my head. *People think too much and talk too much, but never feel enough.* The goal of the evening—the goal of the *kanna*, the small herbal pill I'd taken a few hours earlier—was to birth out of monkey mind into heart brain where words mattered less.

Only I couldn't. I was at the circus, and my brain was on a Tilt-a-Whirl with two clowns, a contortionist, and Dumbo.

In all my life, all I'd ever *taken* was alcohol. No coke, barely any pot, no acid, just booze. And, for the most part, I enjoyed it: the lightness of being, the laughs, the can-do anything spirit of it. Only, for the last decade or so, the price for such a night had become too high: headache, fatigue, the effects of self-inflicted poisoning.

Kanna, on the other hand, is a very gentle, psychoactive, mood-lifting succulent from South Africa loaded with precious CBD. Other than a pretty plant, its role on earth is to relieve us screwy humans from depression. Not the occasional *I'm sad*, but the shoulder-gripping heavy heart that won't go away. *If only I'd stuck with the damn kanna!*

"Are you okay, honey?" Daniella asked when she found me tripping out in the back room, alone with my jabbering, highly critical chorus of inner voices.

"Not so much," I said. "I really am a disaster."

"No, honey. You are not," Daniella said emphatically. "Weed has a shadow side. You shouldn't have smoked it."

"I didn't know," I whimpered, and let her stroke my hair, something I would not normally have done. It felt too condescending or needy or something very not me.

"It's okay. It just doesn't mix with kanna," she said warmly, like she was talking to a child. "Aguirre gives us kanna first, before ayahuasca, because it's a gentle heart opener. Those guys aren't supposed to have pot here. I'll talk to Aguirre."

It was then I realized, Daniella wasn't just some regular retreat goer, she was part of the facilitator crew. Her job was to cook the midnight meal—which explained the chicken in the pot in the back seat of her car—and recruit newcomers such as myself, and comfort us too.

"I don't even like pot," I said, feeling back in high school.

"Don't worry." Daniella leaned in to hug me in her motherly way. "It'll wear off and the kanna will do its thing. You will love it."

"If you say so." I eased into her embrace.

After a few hours, as Daniella promised, the pot wore off, as did the paranoia, and I was able to feel the kanna. Eventually, I'd become clear enough to identify the voices in my head, per the exercise. I gave them names like Bitchy Babe, Scaredy Cat, Funny Girl, Judge Judy, GoGo Chick, and so on. The more I listened, the more I saw the noisy herd for what it was: a script, a program. *Oh my God, I'm a robot, an NPC, just following the programming! WTF?*

During his sermon before we began, Aguirre told us, "The *real* you is innocent, open-minded, nonjudgmental, pure love . . . that's the *real* all of us."

Did I need the kanna to see that?

Probably. Actually, 100 percent. My authentic self was the listener, the observer, that peaceful place of knowing, and I needed to experience that to know it.

By ten o'clock, it had worn off. I told Aguirre I no longer felt a thing. He placed a hand on my heart and the other on my back. "Do you feel this?"

"Yes," I giggled, "I feel your hand."

He laughed. "Tell me this, do you feel lighter, calmer, softer?"

"I think so."

"Do you always feel that way?"

"No."

"Then you feel it," he laughed. "It's subtle. The plant has its own intelligence. It merges with yours to give you what you need. It's all information."

I shrugged my shoulders and smiled. "Okay, Boss."

"Humans and plants have lived in harmony for millennia. Your body also knows what to do, if you let it."

I liked his features, strong and wise, like an owl. His yellow-brown eyes glowed warmly like kerosene lamps, revealing a mischievousness that met with mine.

"You're a good lady." He laughed heartily, then pondered what to do with me.

From the corner of my eye, I spotted the tar-colored ayahuasca brew sitting in a jar by the fireplace and wondered if I should try it, which scared the hell out of me. Most of the other guests had partaken.

Aguirre had said that ayahuasca translated to "vine of the soul," and many called it the Mother Vine. Under its influence, it was possible to reach other dimensions, see beyond the veil, and create a deep spiritual connection to nature, life, and God. After listening to his pre-sacrament lecture, it occurred to me that it might well be time I buried my fear.

What was I missing in my gentile existence of husband, two kids, and a family in suburbia? Are we not placed on the planet to expand and grow? And what of the numbing we humans do each day—shopping, music, screens, TV, alcohol—obsessed with what we eat but rarely thinking twice of what we put in our mind.

Being there, with Aguirre and Daniella, by no accident of chance, it had to be time. I wanted so badly to cure the craters in my heart after forty-nine years of living, the hurt left over from my father being ripped from my existence; the anger buried in the recesses of my gray matter toward my mom for not managing my pain, for working too much with so little time for me. Then my husband, often away, on a plane, people always leaving me, never holding on.

Am I not good enough? Was I never good enough?

Why had I craved success like a bad habit? Not one of my accomplishments ever satisfied me or garnered the attention that I longed for, no matter how big or bold. The disappointment of leaving my career, a profession that defined me, that I worked tirelessly for, then dropped like it was nothing. Like it hadn't required all my smarts and creativity, just *see ya! Goodbye!*

Then my boys and the guilt that I was screwing it all up. The sadistic promise, as foretold by many, "No matter what you do as a mother, one day your kids will be on a therapist's couch complaining about you." And my marriage, which ambled along like a donkey on a dirt trail, swatting flies with its tail, going through the motions but numb to its load, in spite of a transoceanic move to paradise.

Josh and I had run from our life. We'd left abruptly and fixed nothing. We'd bandaged our wounds and never actually healed. Was I ready to face this?

If not now, when?

Aguirre stood in front of me, holding my chin in his hand, squinting at me, peering past my pupils, deep in thought. "Hmm."

My synapses collected together like a choir: *Please, please, please . . .*

"Okay, I have something for you." He reached into his medicine pouch, sitting safely on the counter. "Let's open your heart."

"What?" I said. "But the tea is over there." I pointed to the fireplace in the living room.

"Not today. I have sassafras for you," he said, emphasizing the *sss*, his eyes holding a special glint.

"But—"

"But?"

"*But*," I pleaded. "Ayahuasca? I need to grow. I need to be better—"

"You don't need a bat to the head, Shannon."

"But I do. I need to go deep and fix me."

"Trust me, this is deep." He pressed his hand to my heart.

"Okay," I peeped, still unsure what I'd signed up for, fighting for something I didn't understand.

Aguirre was an early-sixties doctor, guide, and former child prodigy. He left Peru at age eleven and by nineteen had a PhD in psychology. Now he worked full-time with plant medicine, encouraging brave folks to "let the intelligence of the plants guide their experience." Outside of retreats, he and his team of lawyers worked tirelessly to break through the red tape of the FDA, hoping to legalize plants like mushrooms and ayahuasca for medicinal purposes, sacred plant medicines that had been used safely for centuries by Indigenous cultures around the globe. Herbs that healed the body and mind with no noxious side effects when used appropriately. "Contrary to popular Western belief," Aguirre had told us earlier, "ayahuasca is used to *cure* addictions, not create them."

Aguirre handed me a capsule. "Okay, my dear, time to soften."

I placed it on the back of my tongue and took a gulp of water.

He patted me on the back. "I like you, Shannon."

"I like you," I said, again feeling like a child. "And thank you."

Thoughts bubbled up from Thinky-me: *What am I doing? Will this kill me? What would my friends say? My mother? Will I go to Hell? Christ, can I* not *be dramatic for once?*

Given the carelessness with which I had guzzled alcohol in the past, this simple act of ingesting a dehydrated plant in a capsule hardly made me horrible. Every party, every dinner, every get-together, wine was the guest of honor and we'd take her any way she came—white, red, blush, rose, pink, bubbled—with no such thing as too much. Guilt? *Puh-lease.* Thankfully this voice was swiftly shut down, by whatever force I did not know.

A weighty ambience swirled the room, cradling the bodies that draped the couches and mats and thick blankets. Souls bared, hearts held, vulnerable, soft, silent, all was safe. There was no judgment. Nothing shady. There were all types: engineers, entrepreneurs, housewives, a film editor, a masseuse, a guy who looked after a taro patch, and a handsome couple who looked about forty. I realized that we were all here to heal, everyone, not just in this room but in every room, everywhere on the planet, healing.

When would I have this opportunity again, with these people, in this space, intimately cared for? It had taken moving to the outer reaches of a remote Polynesian outpost in the middle of the big blue earth, where kahunas once tossed innocents into volcanoes (was that true?) to satisfy their gods and the lucky lived to pluck fresh fruit, and surf long thick slabs of Koa wood, reveling in manna from the gods, dancing under the silvery light of the moon . . .

While I waited for the medicine to take hold, I drifted into the kitchen where Daniella was preparing fresh baked bread and chicken stew for later in the evening when the effects of the medicine would be worn off.

"What did Aguirre give you?" Daniella asked.

"It's called sassafras." I shrugged. "Apparently, it's empathogenic. I just learned that word. He said it's *heart opening*."

"Ah, it is." She pressed her lips into a smile.

"No ayahuasca for me," I said, smiling back. "Maybe another time."

"Aguirre knows best," Daniella replied. "Ayahuasca is an important sacrament, revered in my country as a cognitive tool, communion with universal mind, the one that connects us all." She said this carefully, speaking like a teacher, which I loved. "You know . . ." Her gaze landed on me, her body sturdy and confident while I leaned into the kitchen island for support. "It can rip consciousness wide open."

"Wow," I responded, feeling inarticulate. I knew so little of this world, not just the plant medicine but my own inner landscape and the cosmos of God. I knew only what I'd been taught by my grandma and the church, and there was so much more. Plus, I felt childish, because I could be so naive. The big career girl starting all over again, not only in my heart but also in life. Kauai was a reboot. Though I didn't know it at the time, my move away from mainland life was my heart inviting me to try something new, something outside the conventional.

"In Peru," Daniella continued, her eyes on me as she stirred her stew, "when kids go through puberty, the tradition is to travel into the jungle for a multigenerational plant medicine ceremony to connect with our families, the earth, and the universe."

"That's so beautiful," I replied, feeling a warmth flush through me. Perhaps the medicine was taking effect.

I thought about my sixteenth birthday, gathered around a bonfire with the party crew from high school. My friend and I chugging tequila from a bottle, chasing it with root beer, thinking ourselves untouchably cool, then staggering home, laughing our asses off. No ritual, no prayers, no chanting *ommm*. Though I did purge that night—potato chips and tequila, no demons.

"We've created a planet of separation, but we are one," Daniella continued. "Plant medicine lets you see this. But ritual is key, set and setting, along with an experienced facilitator like Aguirre." She leaned in toward me. "Are you okay?"

I grabbed my belly. "I feel sick."

"Your eyes are dilated," she said.

"But I didn't drink the tea." I latched onto the kitchen island to keep myself upright. "I thought this was gentle."

"Here," Daniella said, taking my hand, "you should lie down."

Candles flickered along the hallway. We shuffled down the corridor quietly with not even a creak from the floor. I was disoriented. It felt like a scene from the movie *Eyes Wide Shut*, all spooky and nonsensical. A shiver ran up my spine. *Am I playing with dark spirits? Grandma warned me about this. Dammit! Now I'm in it! She'd kill me. What's that stupid movie about anyway? What's their game?*

It hit me then that Josh and I got out of LA just in time, that all my moves had been a progression on a cosmic chessboard to further my soul's journey: Medicine Hat to Calgary, Calgary to New York, New York to Vancouver, Vancouver to LA, LA to Lions Bay, Lions Bay to Kauai. None of it random. All spawning trials and growth.

My stomach lurched and I was hit with a flash of cold. My body began to separate from my mind and feelings. I ached with loneliness. It was in my bones, like I was all there was and I didn't belong to anyone, anywhere, just a creepy hallway with rotten movies and a meaningless career that fizzled into obscurity. A breeze came out of nowhere and swept the room with indifference. Nature didn't care, not one lousy bit, and even that was profound.

"Will I be okay?" I whispered to Daniella, wanting to be held and loved and left alone at the same time.

"You will." Daniella released my hand at the bedroom. "Shall I stay?"

"No, it's okay," I whispered. "Thank you."

A small pull-out couch sat alone in the corner looking boxy and stiff. I propped the pillows to lie down remembering that minutes earlier I'd had a fizzy electrolyte drink. As I flicked the blanket to cover my legs, my stomach released a satisfying burp. The sickness dissipated, which made me feel silly, a baby with a burp, dramatic over a little gas.

Outside the window, my eyes locked on a palm tree backlit by a streetlamp. The orange light was oddly soothing. Except for maybe this street, Kauai had no streetlights that I knew of, so I could've been anywhere—a hotel, my mom's house, my childhood bedroom, another planet.

The silence felt harsh. I needed people. Contrarily, I needed to be alone.

My right hand found its way to my heart and my left to my belly as I fell into the quiet for an hour or two or more. I did not move. I barely breathed. Then slowly it happened: I began to feel alert, luminous. My head-speak, that had been so cacophonous, shrunk to a single loving voice and I was outside myself again, watching, in two places at once, as though everything mattered and nothing mattered at all.

My heart hurts. It's heavy and hot. Is this a heart attack? No, I'm too healthy. What is it? A sharp pain, like a knife. I'm all alone. No one will find me if I die.

I'm scared. My heart feels so hot. Oh God, it's burning! There's a bonfire in my chest. My fingers are on fire. But the rest of me feels good, perfect. So strange.

What time is it? I don't want this to end. My heart is aflame. Will I explode?

Oh God, that's it! My heart is cracking open. Closed for so long, encased in rock. Now it's bursting through, like lava bursting from the cone, black rock crumbling all around it. Amazing!

Can I stay like this forever? Tyde. Canyen. My boys. I love my family so much it hurts. And Josh, dear sweet Josh. I have only love. I'm wide-awake, and it could only happen here, in this way, on this island, Mama Kauai. Wow. You're amazing. Thank you. I love you . . .

Early the next morning, Josh came to collect me. I worried what he might think—his wife off tripping in Ha'ena, while he did the real work of managing the farm and the kids. How quickly self-consciousness returned. I tried not to let it, wanting only love to shine through. I was changed, or so I hoped. I was also a realist and wondered how long it would last.

"So, it was good?" Josh asked.

"Very much so," I said, unsure what else to say. Not ready to speak, still feeling the weight of words as clunky and insufficient.

Josh backed the truck down the cobbled driveway as blobs of rain splattered the windshield, the wipers unable to keep up. "That's quite the house. Was the retreat expensive?"

"Half price for me," I said, wishing we weren't already talking about money, and wishing it wasn't still raining, "thanks to Daniella. I didn't have to pay for a bedroom because I stayed in my sleeping bag on the mats."

"Nice," he said, sizing me up, noting my softness, as though he maybe got what just happened. "I'm glad you went, Shan."

We sat in silence, my mind in an altered state, wistful, hazy. Josh was quiet too. I thought of the three words repeated throughout the retreat: *set and setting*, and *integration*. By leaving early I had missed the integration. I didn't know what that involved, but it felt important.

Our truck rumbled down the highway and over skinny single-lane bridges, while rain poured and thick gray fog filled the dappled spaces of the jungle. It was eerily lovely. A Hawaii few tourists could know, a dark wet paradise, weathered and eroded, drenched in what had to be Mother Nature's tears.

After a while, Josh spoke: first about the work he did on the farm while I was gone for two days, then all that still needed to be done, then our bills and how we should really be on a budget, both of us, but he meant me. It felt like razor blades to my ears. I wanted to tell him he should've come to the retreat and he would have seen that none of it mattered. At least, not in a way that we made it matter, in an exasperating *never enough/us against the world* kind of way.

But I couldn't speak. And he wouldn't have understood. So instead, I listened, hoping he could *feel* who I'd become, as my gaze followed the lines of the trees like it was a dream.

CHAPTER 8.3

. . . Of the Storm

Two days after Daniella's retreat

"Mom, Dad, are we going to die?" Tyde scrambled into our bedroom with his blanket, pillows, and a look of terror. It was two o'clock in the morning.

The sky flashed silver, then white, then black. It was the dead of night, but every second or so we could see the entire landscape like it was the middle of the day.

Kaboom! A blinding flash of bright white, pure earth energy. The clap of thunder rattled our eardrums as though storm clouds had gathered inside our very home. *Snap! Crackle! Rumble!* Then darkness, black all around, and repeat.

It was textbook apocalypse. The stage had been set with Kauai's months of on-and-off rain, flooding here and there, bridges closed for a morning or a night. Nothing too serious. Most of us thinking there was no way this could last. There couldn't possibly have existed any more water to fill any more clouds. The island had had enough, the rain was done, the soil saturated, parking lots and beaches a soggy mess.

But we were wrong.

Upon us was a deluge. The supersonic roar of thunder gods sending shock waves through dirt, tree, rock, home, animal, lighting the whole expansive night sky as though by quasar, a brilliant galactic nucleus. Lightning so grand it flashed in sheets the size of mountains, not bolts. Mother Nature, Pele, Zeus, something or someone clicking the lights on and off for hours in frenetic rhythm, the entire sky, island and maybe ocean, obedient to the wrath of nature. Heinously loud thunder battered our ears like mighty symbols clanging, followed by a conciliatory rumble. The booming voice of a venomous power, roaring and burbling as though heralding, "Get off my planet, parasites!"

"I'm scared, Mom." Tyde shivered. I tugged him close. "Will our house catch fire? What's happening?"

It was days after my retreat, and I felt I'd awoken a Kraken. Somehow, I (*yes, me*) had upset the cosmic order through my teeny glimpse into eternity. Was it something I wasn't meant to see or know? Imagine puny me, impacting the order of things. The timing was uncanny: the eye of the storm directly above us, a wrathful god peering down from the hereafter. *Don't mess with what you don't know, babe.*

"Mom, Dad, get Canyen. He's alone in his room!" Tyde shivered. "We need to get him!"

"Let's let him sleep through it if he can. How is that kid asleep?" I looked at Josh, then thought better of it. "We should wake him."

"Yes, Mom," Tyde stuttered. "Please."

The room lit up—four hundred, eight hundred, twelve hundred watts. Each of our faces frozen in a flash of fear. Then—*kaboom! Crackle, crackle, crackle.*

"Dad, is our house going to start on fire?" Tyde asked again, gripping Josh's arm.

"There's way too much rain for anything to start on fire," Josh said.

I wondered if that was true.

"Mom," Tyde said, his voice shaky, "please, get Canyen."

"Okay, I'll check on him," I said, just as another incredible clamor hit alongside the deafening beat of rain.

"Dad, the house!" Tyde pulled at his blanket in a white-knuckle grip. "Dad? Are we going to float away?"

"Buddy." Josh sat up from his pillow and reached an arm over Tyde to pull him closer. "This house is built for storms. We have a natural moat. The rain drains toward the orchard and forms a river back there, our own stream. You boys boogie-boarded it the other day. Don't worry, we're safe."

"Okay, Dad." Tyde sniffled but didn't cry, already so brave.

I kissed him on the cheek and felt my heart melt for his innocence, already a leader, more worried about his brother than himself, sharp as a tack, protecting Canyen in his older sibling way. Despite the fights and arguments, I always saw Tyde come through for his brother when he needed it most. Why did parents forget that? How could Josh and I not see that our boys never meant to do bad or wrong? Their hearts were pure; at least, they were once upon a time. It was our job not to ruin that. We had a duty to mold and shape our children into the best possible version of themselves, to take the sand in the clamshell and guide it into a brilliant salty pearl. But by God, the stakes were high!

I slipped out of bed. "I'll be right back."

The carpet felt moist on my feet. Everything felt damp for as long as I could recall: clothing, bedding, furniture. I felt around for leaks, hardly able to believe the house was still standing, and made my way toward Canyen's room. I found his little face partially tucked under his pillow with his body curled into a ball, fast asleep.

I couldn't wake him. For what? To be frightened out of his wits? Instead I stood at his window, dumbfounded, watching the rain fall in relentless, almost cruel torrents. Mother Nature had lifted the sea and dropped it onto our island and there would be no relief—at least, not for many hours.

The Ha'ena retreat flashed through my mind. *Imagine if this had happened a few days earlier? Might we have been swept to sea?*

After tonight, I was beginning to understand how quickly the effect of the plant medicine faded in the wake of reality. I didn't have the tools or the know-how to keep it flowing. Like the time my favorite hat blew off while I stood helpless on the cliff's edge of the Kalalau Trail; I'd literally watched it take flight over the ocean like a balloon, getting smaller and smaller until I couldn't see it anymore.

"Surrender," I heard Aguirre say. "It's your journey to experience. We take the medicine into our daily lives."

I closed my eyes and placed my hand on my heart, envisioning my heart cracking open along with the sky cracking open, while Canyen slept silently just a few feet away and Tyde snuggled with his dad on the other side of the wall.

It was beautiful, really, this small family Josh and I had created, afloat in the storm of the century in an ark of our own making. Not a real ark, to be sure. It didn't matter where we called home, or if it was about to break off in the middle of the ocean, sending us adrift on a chunk of lava with no clear view in sight. We had each other. We had answered a call to a foreign land and a whole new life.

"Shan!" I heard Josh call from the bedroom. "Everything okay?"

"Yes." I tiptoed back into bed and placed an arm across Tyde's belly, reaching my fingers to Josh to hold his hand. "Canyen's fine. He's fast asleep." I tucked my head into the pillow. "There's nothing to do now but rest."

As it turned out, other than the island's high ground where our own home was perched, nothing was *fine*. In a period of forty-eight hours, five feet of rain fell on the north shore of Kauai, blowing doors on any previous record. That two-day rainfall was one foot shy of the total annual, one year's worth in a weekend, thirty-six inches overnight! This when the ground was already saturated and couldn't hold another drop.

Nearly every bridge north of Hanalei had been swept to sea that night, guardrails, concrete, rebar and all, landslides the length of football fields. Homes, cars, boats, and belongings all yanked from precious terra firma into the big blue Pacific, never to be recovered.

By some miracle, no one was killed. Not even the guy who lived high on the bank near the end of Hanalei River whose home slipped into the torrent. Bet he thanked his lucky stars that his anxious bladder had him on the outdoor potty during the split second his house collapsed like a box of wet matches.

The next morning, we sat at our kitchen table collecting our jaws off the floor, shocked and hypnotized by the live Instagram videos from residents and shop owners as they wept in fear, documenting the rising sea. Hanalei's Dolphin restaurant had its employees on the roof waiting for rescue as the island became part of the ocean, separate no more. Homes on twelve-foot stilts, protected by their height, had water pouring in through cracks and seams while children cowered in a corner or on a table, helpless and horrified as the grimy brown water rose and rose, seeping through walls and windows, people stuck on their roofs for the night until help could come.

The Instagram reels were devastating. People sharing their homes disintegrating around them, with social media being our only source of news. Maybe this is what they had in mind when they invented Instagram: *Hey people, let's share the real rawness of life!* versus butt and boob selfies and picture-perfect families looking deliriously happy.

Helicopters from Hawaii's National Guard buzzed overhead all day, rescuing stranded families from Ha'ena, Wainiha, Lumahai, Waipa, where cliff met ocean, where the Kuhio Highway once snaked (as in just yesterday) along the mountain ridge, and many an unfortunate home once sat. Because of the complete lack of news coverage, we had no head count on the number displaced. All we knew was that this was a state of emergency, the likes of which we'd never seen before. Kauai was a disaster zone. The army was coming. So was the Red Cross. And countless millions of dollars of damage had befallen people's beloved North Shore.

CHAPTER 8.4

. . . Aftermath of Mud

The days following the flood

"Are they stuck?" Canyen pointed to where mountain met sea and what must've looked like the end of the earth to ancient Hawaiians. "Can the people who live there get out?"

"I don't know." I held my hand over my eyes like a visor, looking to the deep green rim of mountains that separated the north from the west side and the shoreline that disappeared around the corner.

Thin lines of waterfalls cut the emerald cliffs like broken hoses, as we watched people jump from boat to shore with their few belongings, looking forlorn.

"I think only by boat," I said, taking in the flurry of volunteers as they ran to and fro, "but there aren't enough. The Zodiacs can only take a handful of people at a time."

Two days after the great rain, the bridge to Hanalei reopened. It would be the only north shore bridge to open to the public for at least a year. Those of us who'd survived unscathed wanted to help, so I loaded the kids for Costco, packed up the food and Tyde's friend Jowen, and headed to Hanalei, stumbling on a bucket brigade at Pavilions Beach.

"Boys," I called to Tyde and Jowen, "please get the food palate and bring it over." I stood behind a stranger's truck that overflowed with toilet paper, diapers, bottled water, juice, dried goods, and canned food.

"I also brought fresh fruit from the farm," I said to the woman who looked in charge, feeling a tinge of pride. "There's star fruit, avocados, tangelos . . . I heard people are already sick of the Spam and Wonder Bread from the Red Cross. Not exactly healthy."

She wasn't biting. "Thank you, it's all appreciated," she said tightly.

I stepped away to get out of her hair. Who needs some chick acting whole-food heroic after homes had been swept to sea? And not just homes, but cars, washers, dryers, carpets, bicycles, skateboards, kayaks, even buffalo were taken adrift in the monsoon.

"Where will they go?" Canyen asked, slipping his hand into mine.

"I guess some people will stay with their friends elsewhere on the island, maybe some in the community hall in Kilauea," I said quietly. "They've set up beds there."

"My teacher said the mud's full of bacteria," Tyde said as he finished dropping off the food. "A girl from school had to go to the hospital. She needed an IV."

"That's a bad infection if they're getting IV antibiotics," I said.

"I know, Mom," Tyde said, asserting his maturity.

"It kills all the bugs in your gut, good and bad—"

"There's bugs in my gut?" Canyen asked.

I laughed. "Yes. You know that. Like staph, which you had and which is serious, silly." I grabbed the boys' shoulders to guide them up the beach and out of the fray.

"Mom, that girl from my class, she lost her home." Tyde pointed toward the river mouth and Black Pot Beach where *South Pacific* was filmed.

"That's horrible, honey. Which one is hers?"

"It's the big one by the pier."

I gasped. "Those are $10 million homes."

"Her family owns a few," Tyde said.

"Wow. A few?"

"Yah, I think the hospital is named after them."

"The Wilcox?"

"I think so," Tyde said. "My teacher said her family were missionaries."

"Mom, is Kauai going to be okay?" Canyen's eyes blinked from the glare of the sun poking out from behind a cloud.

Tyde and Jowen were now scrambling to get on top of an upside-down SUV, partially floating in the lake that had formed beside the pier. It was hard to imagine a week ago, our truck was parked there loaded with surfboards and towels. I looked out to the pier that stood intact.

The landscape had been completely transformed: Huge divots claimed the beach where water had channeled fiercely to shore, desperate to weave to source. Multimillion-dollar homes had buckled into giant sinkholes alongside chunks of road that disappeared overnight. Exposed pipes and fallen wires draped precariously onto the sand, while masses of asphalt caved into pools of standing water, a danger to anyone in the vicinity, including us. The brick bathroom building that I'd used not one week ago had crumbled to rubble, alongside three vehicles that sat mangled like Godzilla's playthings.

"I think so," I whispered, wondering if it was true.

"Mommy," Canyen continued, "are you and Dad going to be okay?" He looked at me innocently, each pore on his sun-kissed face overflowing with concern.

"Dad? *Your* dad and I?" *Like he had another dad.* "Honey, we're fine," I scoffed. "Why would you ask?"

Were we okay? Or were we slipping and Canyen with his still-so-near-to-God wisdom was the first to know?

"You sure, Mama?" Canyen looked at me again.

Now that I thought about it, Josh and I were often on each other's last nerve. He wasn't the happy-go-lucky salesman/hobby farmer/surfer I'd hoped he'd be. And I wasn't the soft, healing goddess/yoga nutritionist/surfing *wahine* he'd hoped I would be.

Due to the weather, and whatever else, I'd barely begun surfing, despite that being one of my top three reasons to move. I had yet to launch my nutrition business, or yoga in the tree house, and lack of progress made me impossible. When the kids were babies, I couldn't figure out why I often felt cranky home alone with them. It made no sense. I loved them so much. Then I joined a gym. Which helped. But things really improved when I went back to work. Even though it was on-and-off/part-time, it gave me purpose beyond being a mother.

Now, I had no gym, no job, and—compared to before—almost no social life, despite my couple new mom friends. Even Kylie, who I'd had much hope for, couldn't find time to get together with four kids and a husband often away; so we were relegated to quick hellos when picking up or dropping off our boys.

Moms everywhere in a plague of busyness, except, at this point in time, me.

Back in Lions Bay, I'd be busy with my girls, dressing up for a dinner party or a fancy night in the city, maybe a concert, or a comedy club. We'd hike over the root and rock of the mountain that held our homes, or go for a ski at Whistler, or coffees in Squamish to sit in comfy lounge chairs and share secrets. Anytime we needed consoling, a friend was a minute or so away by car, women who knew me. When that wouldn't do, the forest was there to hold us.

But who here had the time to carve out a new friendship? Would I have been worth it given most new arrivals were so quick to leave? Would I too be gone in a few years?

Add to that the super casual, let's-meet-at-the-beach, potluck culture, and invites seemed few and far between. So, I got to watch my social life—once brilliantly fun—die a quiet death. That's what cancer is, isolation. That's what cancer cells do, detach, so as not to infect the others. Worst of all, it felt self-inflicted.

Josh, on the other hand, complained about not enough time on the farm and too much time on his parents' estate, accounting, bills, and selling time-shares. Life in sales seemed to trigger the ball of stress that sat dead center in his chest, winding him up like a tinker toy, reminiscent of our worst days in television. Which made me wonder where he'd placed his brain, because time-share's a racket. We left Canada to be rid of rackets.

Josh had said the guys at the top of the hierarchy, the *gold-chainers*, would vet the guests most likely to buy, making ridiculously large commissions, while the guys at the bottom (Josh and other newbies) twiddled thumbs with the yahoos who came for a free zip-line tour, making zero commission. According to local surf lore, once upon a time the surf lineup went from dudes wearing puka shells to dodgy time-share guys in gold chains calling guys off waves and throwing punches. Around the same time, the island's jungles and fields were being divvied up like pizza pie for greedy developers to build time-share hotels. Legend has it, this brought the wrath of Mama K, such that in 1992, Hurricane Iniki destroyed the place, leveled it. *Because of time-shares!* Whether it was true or not, their energy was distinctively unwholesome.

Strangely, Josh was now part of that legacy. If anything was clear, he was no gold-chainer. He was a puka shell kind of guy and his work was feeling more and more like drudgery.

Further, my car (aka Roach Motel) had broken down, prompting us to buy and ship over a barely used, very cute Mini Countryman from Honolulu sight unseen. As I drove it away from Na'wili'wili Harbor, a gasket blew. I hadn't driven it five minutes. Now that cuteness was in the shop to the tune of $1,200. As consolation, the Mini dealer offered me a rental van that morning, but Josh wouldn't drive me to pick it up, claiming he was *too busy* selling bloody time-shares to give me a ride.

So, I hitchhiked. At my age! People drove by laughing, honking, giving me shakas, or outright ignoring me. But no one picked me up. Maybe I looked homeless, soaked from rain and sweat, sticking my thumb out in rubber boots and a plastic jacket, wrapped up like an Oscar Mayer Wiener with dancing stick legs.

And yes, it was Josh's fault: the car blowing up *and* the hitchhiking *and* the angst from the flood *and* my no social life *and* no career *and* anything that's ever bugged me. Because that's what we do to our loved ones—blame them for everything!

This was all fertile ground for a fight of epic proportions that began at seven o'clock this morning and still sat unresolved. Like most of our arguments, I don't know what started it, or what it was even about, but it had something to do with tallying our utility, how nothing had changed, how we were both stressed as ever, and WhyTF did we buy a farm on Kauai anyway?

So much for my heart-healing retreat.

"Canyen," I said as we worked our way up the Hanalei River to the Canoe Club, his curious trajectory now making sense. "Did you hear Dad and I this morning?"

"Yeah," he said sadly. "I just don't want you or Dad to die."

My heart skipped a beat. "Who said anything about dying?"

"Like your dad. Then you, Grandma, and Uncle Troy moved right after. You were alone with no other family. It must have been so lonely." He blinked earnestly.

"Oh, sweetie, that won't happen. No one's going to die." I kissed him on the cheek.

Dead fish with eyes swollen out of their sockets littered the grass, some still alive and squirming in pothole puddles that ran the dirt road. As we drew closer, I saw the wreckage. Several six-man fiberglass outrigger canoes, once beautifully aerodynamic, lay twisted and lifeless on the rocks and dirt, crushed by the force of the river, torn and shredded into a pile for insurance adjusters to assess. Giant tree trunks, weighing thousands of pounds, had swept beneath the building and through the storage area by the Herculean force of rushing water. I wondered what equivalent force could possibly remove them.

The Canoe Club had been a safe haven for me. Even though I didn't belong, I liked it. Two nights a week for a few hours, it was just me, the river, and the steady tribal beat of women quietly in sync—*stroke, stroke, stroke*—paddling with the water, just as ocean-going Polynesians had done for millennia. A fragile reprieve for a vestige of my former self where I could get away from those who knew me too well and just sink into the scenery, imagining myself part of an ancient warrior clan.

"You want to help?" said a man in overalls caked with dirt.

"Absolutely," I said. "We have four sets of willing hands."

In as few words as possible, he directed us away from the club and toward the little green church in Hanalei to scrub and oil the pews with a few old ladies who were polishing walls. Somehow, this felt fitting.

That night, after one o'clock, Canyen crawled into our bed. Josh was fast asleep, exhausted from his two jobs and the now incredible ominous energy of the island.

"You okay, sweetie?"

"Mommy, I want to go home." Tears rolled from his cheeks.

"But Keanu? Your new best buddy. And school? You seem happy."

"I like Keanu, but I like Lions Bay better," he cried. "I miss it. I miss my friends."

Silence. Sadness. Regret. It moved through my body the way the rain dug ruts in our driveway, big muddy, red river divots. My muscles hardened as I considered my next sentence.

"Okay." I looked at Josh to make sure he was asleep. His mouth was slack and he was breathing heavily, bundled into the pillow like a hamster.

"Okay, what?" Canyen whispered, as I swiped his cheeks and pulled him closer.

"Okay, after two years, let's go home."

My little boy's happiness was on the line. No longer could I envision our staying. *We came. We saw. We tried.* No conquering. Conquering is a relic of imperialism that never served anyone. Certainly not Hawaii. Nope, the Moodys would chalk this up to experience. A grand adventure. The prolonged sabbatical I never got but wanted before we were swept up in a whirlwind of a move.

"Thanks, Mom." Canyen snuggled into my form like a spoon placed neatly in a drawer. "When will you tell Dad?"

"Soon." I looked to Josh face down under his pillow. "Just not yet."

The changes to my heart, and whatever happened to me on that incredible rare night in Ha'ena, were drifting away with the debris from the squall, back to the cosmos, hitching a ride with the sun.

"Why, Mommy?" Canyen traced his fingers on my face the way I used to trace my fingers on his.

"Because Dad is the sun and I'm the moon," I said, not knowing what else to say, when what I felt was:

Because Dad loves it here and I don't. And I have no clue how to cross that divide. And it's going to be so hard—telling him, packing again, moving trucks and oceans and container ships . . . It could kill us, this fragile thing called marriage. And I too can't take the storms, the rain, the mud, the lack of anything even remotely big city, the dearth of friends and family, people who know me and understand me, my kids, and my quirks. I miss a chill in the air, the northern forest and my lone hikes where I figure out life and play with the possibility of who I might still become, walking soft moss trails amongst towering cedars in a trance, as though I have a lifetime ahead of me, longing to feel a part of something familiar. I don't have that here, this feeling of being deeply rooted like a mother tree glued to the earth's capillaries and ancestral life force, to the place I call home. I miss it terribly, and I miss my mom . . .

"It's our little secret, Canyen, for now."

PART 2

CHAPTER 9

If *father* is the divine protector, and *mother* is the divine nurturer, what do you do when the sharks are circling and neither is there to save you?

a) Make peace with your maker. Not even Mike Phelps can outswim a shark.
b) Cross your fingers that you remembered to wear your Sharkbanz*—it mucks with the shark's brain so you don't become lunch. **Won't work on great whites.*
c) Channel everyone's favorite spirit animal, the dolphin. Many a dolphin pod has saved a sorry human from the jaws of a shark.
d) Get angry and punch that damn thing in the chops with everything you've got. Legend has it, this can work!

CHAPTER 9.1

Ayahuasca Journey
September 2021

The urge to transcend the self is a principal appetite of the soul. Carl Jung argued that the sacred element was essential to healing. "The approach to the sacred or numinous is the real therapy, and inasmuch as you attain to the numinous experience you are released from the curse of pathology . . .[9]

As I wept, my body began to sway to Sarah's song. Energy swirled up my spine, tickling my vertebrae like feathers. Perhaps it was kundalini rising, from Sarah's heart to mine, beautiful song energy coaxing divine feminine and divine masculine to wind up, up, up.

Is the medicine activating ancient technologies? Are the Vedic energy centers of lore real? Had to be, I felt my chakras clunking into action after decades of stupor: root, sacral, solar plexus, heart, throat, third eye, crown.

With my body bent over my knees, my head trundled back and forth, forehead to ear, then forehead to other ear, my spine loose and limber like the grasses in the hills of my youth. The

[9] *Grandmother Ayahuasca* by Christian Funder © 2021. Reprinted by permission of Inner Traditions International and Bear & Company. www.Innertraditions.com

energy needed somewhere to go, so I felt my tears beginning to float away like bubbles in the breeze.

Out of nowhere, I released a giggle. A giggle! How strange. But I didn't giggle because it was funny. I giggled because that was the loop. Cry then yawn then cry then yawn then cry then laugh? Was crying my puking? Was yawning, crying, and ill-timed laughter my purging?

"You need to sit up." Sarah tapped me. "Please sit up for Maestro."

"Huh?" I whispered, face smooshed into the sheepskin at the base of Maestro's mat, liking it there, wishing she'd just keep singing.

"Look him in the eye, it's time."

"I can't." My eyes cast blearily at her, my head barely off the ground, afraid I might giggle again, or worse.

"*Om-gom-gudda-budda . . . om-gom-gudda-budda . . .*" Maestro chanted over and over, perfectly still but for the sound driven up through his lungs and windpipe, striking vocal cords, then throat, reverberating off tongue and lips, synching with the heartbeat of nature.

My senses pinged as emotions wiggled through me like voles in a tunnel—each one its own sentient being. Laughter. Sadness. Fear. Disgust. But oddly, not anger. There was no anger. Not all night. Anger was usually so near my surface. Instead, my heart was soaked in sorrow and it was so awful that it was funny instead of maddening.

Did anger need to get out of the way for sadness to burst through? I don't even know if I'm sad anymore. I think I feel only shame, incredible guilt. Anger would be better. Maybe all along, she—my inner bodyguard—was protecting me from this most heavy of emotions, the worst of all of them, shame. I should be grateful, grateful for my anger. And that's why I laugh. Because it's ridiculous. And now laughter is here to save me, just as anger has saved me all this time. Or maybe, I'm just nuts.

Finally, I'd stopped crying. Weird because, moments ago, I felt like I would cry forever and leave this world drowning in tears for all the hurts of man. It had been years since I'd allowed myself to cry. Clearly, I needed to drain, to cleanse my spirit, my soul. It was the least I could do for those poor kids in their hovels, starving, begging in the streets, orphans beat up by adults meant to love them, boys with machine guns groomed to be killers, bloodshed, rape, slaves of every color and generation forced to make trinkets to satisfy first-world thirst for cheap things. Had I really been feeling sorry for myself in this world of horrors?

"Shannon," Sarah whispered again, then nudged me.

"I'm too weak." I hid my face, unwilling to meet the maestro, still too deep in shame.

Facing Guillermo meant composing myself, putting on a mask, the mask of reverence, humility, respect. Because that's what he deserved! But I was too deep in regret. Plus, my mind was playing tricks on me. No—*she* was playing tricks on me.

Abuela! Damn her!

"You must," Sarah said in a stern whisper, like a mother scolding a child.

Suddenly, every fiber of my being wanted to run, to get away from her and Maestro to find my boys and hug them, but first, make sure they were alive. *Yes, alive!* Time was weird on the medicine. The present was all that mattered. And in that present moment, the people I loved the most were far, far, away, maybe in another dimension—

I need to tell them how much I love them. I need to hug them and never ever let them go.

Sarah pulled at my shoulders one last time. "Sit up now or back to your mat."

Enough, you big weak dummy! They want to help you.

Slowly, I pressed to my hands, my back hardly holding me from collapse, then wobbled to my haunches, legs folded beneath the weight of my torso, hair trickling across my face, feeling ever so weak, then attempted to focus my eyes on the man before me:

What am I looking at? A frog? A tree trunk? A thousand-year-old man?

He chanted, powerfully, as though not from this world, a mountain shrunk to Buddha before me, holding the wisdom of the ancients.

If once a regular person, he was no more. Years of strict diets and plant medicine, alone in the Amazon, fighting his own demons and the demons of the world, he had morphed into something else. He'd experienced things most of us could never fathom—astral planes where time was no longer, celestial spheres with inexplicable beings from other realms, dimensions where plants speak and aliens listen and who even knows but he? Through his Shipibo lineage, he'd become shaman, maestro, curandero, traveling the world in ceremony, on the sacred path of Mother Gaia and her medicine.

Meantime, on Earth, he sat before me in the exact position as when we'd met hours earlier: cross-legged, rounded, toad-like, white T-shirt and scarf wrapped around him, glowing in intricate designs from my visions imprinting on his clothes like rainbow worms wriggling under a freshly lifted stone, behind that, his face chocolate brown like the earth.

Are his eyes blue? How am I able to see this?

His eyes were soft and open, glazed like jelly doughnuts a deep shade of aqua, as though he could see right through me, straight to my soul. It was like staring into a lake or a black hole—empty, vast, bottomless. There was a small candle lit beside him and tobacco burning. Smoke swirled around us. None of it felt real. Yet it felt too real, frighteningly so.

Every cell in my body was on high alert, speaking and listening and watching and feeling, all at the same time, trillions of them. They spoke to the grass, every blade, and the grass listened and sat in place meaningfully, a green carpet to soothe us.

Guillermo paused to take a deep breath, then started over again like a machine, "*Om-gom-gudda-budda . . . om-gom-gudda-budda . . .*"

I wondered if it was a dream and I'd wake up with Josh cozy beside me tucked under his pillow, as he liked to do, Canyen snuggled up on the rug. But that wasn't the truth. The truth was I was sitting before someone or thing I didn't understand who might not even be real. Perhaps a wonder of nature—half plant, half man, half spirit from the other side.

But what *side?* Whose side was he on? Because somewhere filed away in the dusty synapses of that infinitely elaborate circuitry of my brain, I heard my grandmother say, "Shanni, what on God's green earth are you doing? *This* is devil's play!"

CHAPTER 9.2

Surf and Turf

July 2018

"Today's the day," I said, whipping off the covers, smothering Josh in our tropical-print duvet that once housed all manner of feathers but was now a thin shell of its former self thanks to a new home in a new climate. "I'm ready to surf The Cove."

"The Cove?" Josh grumbled, literally embedded in a tangle. How he could so thoroughly destroy his side of the bed in less than seven hours of unconsciousness was beyond me. Sheets untucked, pillowcases off, drool on the mattress, while I'd barely carved a dent in my memory foam pillow. "Are you sure?" he continued with a note of distress. "The Cove gets really—"

Er-er-roooooo, a wild rooster crowed as my ears rattled in turn.

"What's that, honey?"

"Are you sure?" Josh said clear and slow, like he was speaking to my mother. Years of music had fizzled the fine hairs of her cochlea such that my spouse, my siblings, plus their spouses, as well as my mom's partner/spouse of twenty years and me, had all become expert enunciators, painstakingly shaping each consonant, vowel, and syllable into our verbiage and speech, then into our delicate marriages. "It was giant—double overhead the other d—"

Er-er-rooooo! Again, the alpha rooster from the lychee tree crowed. But this time louder, as though daring my husband to dust off his BB gun.

They did that, those feral beasts, all day and in the middle of the night, not just the crack of dawn. The wild hens were quiet by comparison, huddling under bushes with their chicks, kicking leaves and dirt with their feet and beaks, looking for bugs, the occasional chirp or peck to a younger hen to keep her in her place. Meanwhile brazen roosters *cock-a-doodle-dooed* nonstop. Quiet for maybe three hours of the day, from 8–11 p.m., the rest of the time, *Er-er-rooooo, F-all-youuuuu!* It was sharp and ugly and eerily human, like a startling cry for help. One rooster would set off the whole island, and it would go around and around all night long—a true coconut wireless. With nearly a quarter million chickens on the island, it was a plague of noise, garbage-picking, rudeness, and poop. Feathered relics from the dinosaur age screeching, *We survived the asteroid, this place is ours!* Which is funny, because they're the least likely to *survive* anything—a dog, a cat, crossing the road. Yet here they were, wild and free and everywhere, running the joint.

"Sorry," I said. "I can't hear you over those assholes."

"I'm just surprised that you want to surf the Cove," Josh said.

"You said I was ready." I shifted my tank-style nightie over my rump. The stretchy cotton had made its way up my belly, exposing little worth mentioning, just my favorite satin blue underwear and my only excuse to do laundry more than once a month. Because, despite me having way, way, way too many clothes, I had only two prized pairs of hip riders that didn't bunch up my crack. I'd take granny-gonch and panty lines any day over up-the-ass undies. Besides, Josh liked me however he could get me—boxers, grannies, period panties, whatever—with one caveat: I be willing. Lately, not so much. We were a statistically sound, sex-once-every-week-or-two couple, with seemingly little time for poetry.

"I guess I did, just not on a big day, okay?" Josh stood and stretched on his side of the room, the window side, his face puffy and hair fluffed like he'd just stepped out of a wind tunnel. He looked a bit like his dad, a happy pirate, caring less and less for haircuts or a shave. "There's supposed to be a swell hitting today."

"Don't worry," I said from the bathroom, toothbrush hanging loosely from my fingers, slurping up minty drool, "you won't get me out there on anything with size. I heard today would be small to medium and fun. The swell's not hitting until tonight."

"Heard from who?" Josh asked, surprised that I had intel before he did. He was the all-things weather/surf/storm/swell guy, checking Surfline and Windy on the regular.

"That nice longboarder dude with the cheesy moustache." I spat into the sink, catching the bottom strands of my hair with toothpaste foam.

Josh nodded. "He's good. He's young, but he'd know."

Once the brown water had cleared from the island's worst ever, horrible-terrible rainstorm, I began the work of becoming a surfer. It was a dream I'd had since the day I tandem-surfed in Malibu for a shoot with *Inside Edition* twenty-some years ago. Only it didn't feel like a dream, more of an ache, like learning how to swim or ride a bike.

But surfing is not for everyone. It's rough and especially brutal if you're any good. Good surfers in heavy-duty waves get held under for a minute at a time, sometimes longer, tumbled onto sharp reef, tossed like a rag doll. The thrust of a big wave could be the equivalent of a few tons. That's a lot of pressure hitting the body if you wipe out or don't duck dive properly. Imagine big wave surfers with their float vests and rescue sleds, where hundreds of tons of pressure from waves the size of Everest are pummeling them as they gasp and scratch for air in endless foam, like a spin cycle the size of a football stadium.

In the past few months, my hold-unders were probably five or six seconds, laughable almost, but to me it felt like forever. I'd been karate chopped by my nine-foot-long board so many times I was ready to call it in. Once in the shoulder, leaving me unable to lift anything for days, and once on the thigh, leaving a giant hematoma with yellow-blue-green swirls that looked like a miniature planet Earth.

People think the waves in Hawaii are perfect. This is where the sport began! But there's nothing between us and the mainland, so there's lots of chop, storms, and junk waves amidst the big glassy swells that the experts flock to. Since I was no expert, I learned in the junk.

Paddling out during a wind swell—which was most of my sessions on the east side where the trade winds blow—was like riding a bull. Each wave flipped my body and my board, ripping it out of my hands as I struggled, yanking on the leash, with me careful not to wrap a finger or a limb for fear of having it ripped off. I'd heave the board under my torso to get back on, over and over again, arms limp like Jell-O—and I hadn't even made it out to the break.

Add summer and fall high temperatures to a brisk breeze, and we had a Pocho party. "Pocho" stands for Portuguese man-of-war, a nasty little blue jellyfish. Tiny translucent buggers with a long sticky tail, armed with poisonous barbs that wrap around limbs or neck or face, and sting like you've been sliced with a razor blade in the salt water. Once I flailed so hard trying to get the tail off my arm, Josh thought I was drowning.

I wondered why I craved such punishment. In the beginning there was little payoff—up and riding maybe two waves a session, short and quick, white water engulfing and throttling me from my board, salt water up my nose and throat, sand packed into my gusset and under my eyelids, scratching my retinas, attitude from other surfers who worried I'd crash into them, as they jockeyed for the perfect takeoff spot like wolves zeroing in on a kill—all of it.

Learning to surf was a metaphor for life. I scratched and tore for everything I'd ever gotten; surfing was more of that, and it made me feel at home. It gave me an identity when, in the last year, I'd lost mine, somewhere on that long arching flight over the big blue sea.

"Should we wake the kids?" Josh asked.

"Let them sleep a little longer. They were up late on the games," I said, breasts bare, yanking my new one-piece over my hips. A rare find because it had a bottom, not a big one, half a bottom—nearly impossible to find at a time when most girls were wearing full ass-chaps (something I'd never subject my boys to).

As it was, Tyde recoiled when he saw girls from school in thong bikinis. They were everywhere, big buns, little buns, pink buns, chocolate buns. A bizarre trend to anyone my age, or from Canada; having my ass hanging out was quite literally my worst nightmare.

"Why do they wear those?" Tyde would ask, his face contorted.

"Social media," I'd say, thanking God we'd held off buying him an iPhone all these years.

But fourteen was approaching and I wondered how that brilliant, yet frightening, rectangular device would change him. There was a time, long ago, I swore I'd never own one. Thanks to smartphones and computers, my sons were growing up in a brave new world, only maybe not so brave.

"Oh, sexy." Josh pressed his hips into mine. "We're alone, the house is quiet, maybe we should . . ."

I turned to squeeze his chest and kiss him on the cheek. "Not now, honey, let's get to the break before it gets too crowded."

He smiled as he often did. Rejected, but not painfully so.

How was I to balance any sort of sex life with the kids barging in, or the monthly visit from Aunt Flow coming faster and harder than ever before (which meant menopause was around the next corner or two), or the constant tidying up of the house, the lanai, the driveway, the farm, or the launching of my Pineapple Retreat *kinda sorta* business that was to make up for my former *real* career of six-day workweeks and serious clout. It was a rare day I wanted to wake up and charge anything, let alone surf. I had to jump!

Instead—this. The shame of being incomplete. A wife who couldn't give her husband the carnal loving he deserved.

"Tonight. Promise," I said with a wink, knowing he'd probably crash on the couch watching World Surf League with Tyde.

After a fifteen-minute drive, we parked and carried our boards down the beach and toward the pier to begin a long paddle out to the break. It was a crowded October day. I'd overheard someone in the parking lot call it "Sharktober." It sent a chill up my spine. It was the same time of year Bethany

Hamilton lost her arm years ago, in the same bay, to a tiger shark.

"Great whites aren't the issue here," I'd heard someone say, "it's the tigers."

Fierce beasts they were, with females reaching up to fifteen feet. Local marine biologists spoke of them fondly. "They're the clean-up crew. They do the job of chomping up dead or dying animals on the reef. If they wanted to eat humans, there'd be a tragedy every day."

This did not mean that tigers couldn't make mistakes. Sharks have notoriously bad vision. Like a puppy dog, they bite first to test.

"Don't worry," Josh said. "Just don't give off fear chemicals. Sharks smell fear a mile away, literally, a mile away."

Lips firmly closed, I focused on a slow breath in and out of my nose, making long, even strokes with my arms, attempting to imitate Josh's easy style. He was practically a fish. I wondered if that was what attracted me to him seventeen or so years ago.

Before we married, Josh would talk about surfing with such passion. Like a painter with a fresh canvas, curving the fingers of his right hand into a C, while the second and third fingers of his left hand scooped in and out like a miniature surfer flitting between air and water, up, down, and through the barrel. It was magical.

A turtle bobbed in front of me and I took it as an omen that scavenging sharks were elsewhere. The giant hawksbill then dipped beneath me as I settled on top of my board, careful to have paddled past where the larger sets would break. Anything closer inside put me at risk of getting pummeled by a large set wave. The trade-off was that I was sitting with the best of the best—the guys and a few girls, waiting for the outside waves to catch. People on the inside were usually the lesser surfers, picking off smaller waves, where I should have been. But I didn't trust my paddling strength or wave-reading capability and worried I wouldn't be able to paddle out of the way quick enough.

This was a no-mess-around break. Even on the small days, it attracted every type of surfer: feisty short boarders who whipped giant rooster tails; hardy long boarders who'd cross-step to the nose to hang all ten toes off; tough guys with high-performance Guns, faster than a rocket; and wily barrel-riding bodyboarders.

Beyond being intimidated, there was an incredible lot of talent on this island, and my greatest fear was getting in their way. Enforcers, as they were called, came in any size, color, and age. They were the kind of person who constantly jockeyed into place for the next wave, serious, almost menacing, playing on people's nerves, territorial with a *who-the-F-are-you* expression to anyone new, loud talkers, calling friends onto waves as though there was no one else around. I knew to steer clear of them.

Thirty minutes had passed and I hadn't paddled for a wave. This was unlike me, but I was plagued with insecurity.

What if I wipe out? What if I miss it and my board slams some alpha in the face? What if I'm caught on the inside and get dragged into the river mouth in the white wash . . .

Josh paddled up to me. He'd caught two good waves and looked pleased. "Paddle out to Pinnacle Rock with me. There are less people there and the wave's a better shape, easier to get into with the way the swell is hitting."

"I'm fine here," I said, sounding pissy.

"Come on, where's that feistiness from earlier?" He smiled broadly, his hair wet and curling into waves, pecs bloated from the paddle, making him look hunkier than usual. "Seriously, you can do this. It's not that big today. Follow me."

"Okay," I said quietly. I hated sitting there like a newb.

Having been an expert skier my entire adult life, it was hard to be the worst at something. With surfing, there was no hiding it. People were watching, waiting, and judging. There was little else to do except maybe meditate, and people only meditated when it was small. The vibe was, *Don't wipe out and F up my wave, or there'll be hell to pay.* So, I paddled behind Josh hoping to get a confidence boost and maybe go for one or two.

The waves really weren't that big, a solid medium, but they were good. As in a perfect shape, a slope just so such that the takeoff wasn't too steep, the pocket of the wave forgiving, the ride long and smooth and not too fast. I propped myself near a good takeoff spot and waited for a set while Josh sat slightly inside, given he was on a short board and required less paddle time.

There were two men beside me. I knew to be mindful that they were probably local crew and deserved to be treated as such. After mastering paddling and timing of the wave (which took years), the hardest part was managing the crowd. If I had my way, every break would be empty except me and my boys.

One, two, three—then six, seven, eight waves went by me. I was in the perfect spot, but I didn't go for it because of the two guys sitting near me. They were deeper, with the right-of-way. One of them, possibly Hawaiian, was good, catching a lot of waves, circling back and forth. His friend, a white guy about my age with an inch of zinc on his nose and cheeks, was lame by comparison. He'd paddle for some but didn't catch any that I saw. Such that when the next set came, even though he had the right-of-way, I assumed he would let yet another wave go by and decided to go for it, paddling my guts out.

Yes, yes, I've got it, I'm in, I screamed in my head. *I can't believe it. I'm in!*

It was my first wave out at The Cove, and it was glorious.

Then—*Shit, shit, he's right behind me, I caught his wave. Fuck. Should I kick out?*

Then—*Good God, this is fun! Holy shit, it feels good! On top of the world, Ma! He doesn't seem to mind. I haven't wiped out. We can ride together and share. Party wave!*

Then—*What the?*

Kersplash! Wa-bang!

I dropped. Plunged. Tumbled and rolled. White water all around me.

When I finally got my head to the surface, another wave crashed on top of me. I took a deep breath and dove deep as I could, hitting the rock the place was named for. Just a scratch. Seconds later, I came up choking for air. The set was done and I was safe, leash taut, my board waiting beside me, ready to be ridden again. I was elated, scared, and thrilled, but mostly, I was proud.

I paddled back up the channel toward my spot and readied for another, when—

"What the fuck you do?" The brown-skinned guy from earlier paddled up to me. I hadn't seen him coming. "You snaked my friend. Who the fuck you think you are?"

"Nobody. Nothing. I'm sorry. Is he hurt?" I knew the answer.

"You cut him off! Who the fuck you think you are?"

"I'm sorry. I didn't see him. I promise," I lied, regretting every second of that most exhilarating, best-of-my-life wave. "I'm really sorry. But did I hurt him?" I asked, out of breath, my face flushing crimson, craning my neck to make eye contact with zinc face, who I knew was not hurt. "Did I wipe you out?" I said with regret. "I'm so sorry, are you okay?"

Waah poor baby! WTAF is going on here with these men?

"No matter," said the enforcer. "You catch every wave. Who you think you are?"

"I caught one wave, actually, that was my first and only."

"Where you from? You think you can take off on any wave you want. Cut people off. Where you from?"

"Here."

"No." He shook his head in disgust. "You're not from here. Go home."

"I said I'm sorry. Really. It was a mistake. I don't know what else to say. I'm just so sorry that happened. I made a mistake."

"You think this is your break? Come fucking do whatever you want?"

"No. I don't. I told you, I'm sorry. I won't do it again." I was breathing heavily, and everyone was staring, and I felt like I was on a stage, naked, boobs out, butt out, ass glowing and people chucking rotten mangoes at my head. "I don't know what else to say—it's done! I'm sorry. There's nothing I can do now. No one's hurt. We're all okay, so please back off."

But he continued, in my face, like he might pull my hair or punch me, flinging out the same stupid comments and questions for a whole ten horrendous minutes. It was like I was ten years old again, and my dad just died, and the whole school was staring at me in the halls and at recess for months and months, making a wide berth like I was a giant frothing boil that would explode any second and smother them in goo.

Does he have a wife? Children? What would they think of this? He's got to be fifty. Same with zinc face. WTF? How are two grown-ass men okay doing this to a lone woman? And how are all these people okay with this? Watching me. Staring. Maybe enjoying it. Cowards! Wait—how is Josh okay with this? Where's Josh?

I sat there red-faced, fingers trembling, weak all over but unwilling to budge or let them see me cry. Eventually, they paddled away. All the surfers within earshot stared at me except my husband. Where was he? Had he seen this? Was he too busy catching waves?

Anger bubbled up my throat as I decided it was *his* fault. Yes, *his*. Not mine for snaking the wave that I was perfectly positioned for, that me and zinc face could have happily shared; not the bully's, who'd berated me so viciously; rather, my husband's, my protector, my buffalo at the apex of the herd during a bitter winter snowstorm. Intentional or not, I'd been left in the cold to wither.

CHAPTER 9.3

The '70s

Pink was my favorite color and my mother made sure I was surrounded by it. I had a pink four-poster bed that I shared with my sister until I was seven or eight, when Robin moved to the basement, into the bedroom that Grandpa and Dad had built for her. My carpet was pink shag, the living room red shag, Mom and Dad's carpet purple, and my brothers' blue.

The walls of my room were bright girly pink with one covered in a dusty rose doll print. My Barbie dolls wore pink, and though I didn't own much pink myself, in grade 6 I had a pair of pink Adidas shoes and a pink silk disco jacket that made me feel like a movie star. I'd dream about roller-skating in that outfit on *American Bandstand* with the big kids—only I'd be skinny and have Farrah hair and Jordache jeans with rainbows stitched on the pockets.

To me, pink wasn't about femininity; it was about pleasure. Pink made me smile from the inside out, like ice cream. What little girl didn't bust out an ear-to-ear grin when offered a strawberry sundae or pink bubble gum or a fuchsia-colored dress. These were the great pleasures of life, at least to me.

"Pink, pink, you stink!" my siblings used to tease me. They'd call me a baby, or princess, and tell me to grow up and stop being *so spoiled.* This smacked against my young logic. I never felt like a princess nor did I act like one.

Cartwheels nonstop on the grass or on the wooden balance beam Grandpa built at the end of the garden, each new trick landing me hands and knees in the dirt, slivers in my fingers, bugs in my hair, mosquito bites on my arms. Though I did love my Barbie collection, and the wardrobe I'd amassed for her, that hardly made me a princess. My Black Barbie, Cara, was besties with original Barbie; and cheap Barbie, Lana, whose legs didn't bend, who cost me two dollars of birthday money at Kmart, was always the mean one. Sometimes I felt sorry for her. But someone had to be the villain and her cheap plastic limbs had sealed her fate. Plus, she was an awful shade of creamy white and very hard to dress. One time I cranked her neck so hard to kiss Ken her head popped off. Good thing Barbie hadn't seen; she'd have done it herself.

There wasn't a summer where my knees weren't scabbed over from wiping out on my sister's 10-speed, or I wasn't scratched from flinging off the school's merry-go-round at breakneck speed. Being a princess couldn't have been further from the truth. Plus, I only ever got half of what I wanted for Christmas. Unlike my bestie Tracy who got Baby Alive and a Cabbage Patch doll, and a stocking stuffed with twenty chocolate Santas wrapped in bright red tinfoil, to my two mandarin oranges and five sugar candies sticking to the fuzz of my stocking. Now *she* was spoiled.

This teasing from my siblings crescendoed around the same time that I began to really loathe going to church. Plus, there were two other contributing factors. It's like the planets were aligning, only not in a good way.

First, my parents said they were *scared* to go to church because they felt like *hypocrites*. They had to play in their band on Friday and Saturday nights, and the fourth commandment clearly states: "Remember the Sabbath day to keep it holy"

(Exodus 20:8). Our pastor had told them, "Don't even worry about it. The church is full of hypocrites." Somehow, it still kept them away.

Second, Mom had bought me a pair of black canvas shoes from Kmart. They looked like slippers. The other girls at church (whose dads *didn't* drop them off at 10:05, running in the door late, with their brother by their side or, if he had hockey, alone) would prance into class in their patent leather baby dolls, looking cute as buttons, while I tucked my feet beneath me to hide.

My aunt Lynne said my shoes were made in China, and nobody should buy anything from China because it's cheap and they're communists, and something about all of our manufacturing headed there. Which confused me, except the part about being cheap. I already knew that because I saw them in the eight-dollar bin at Kmart, and I'd never seen shoes for eight dollars before. I also knew I sounded ungrateful because my parents loved me and my church shoes shouldn't have mattered.

Meanwhile, my mom had really nice shoes. She wore them to play the piano and teach school. When she left the house, I'd try them on and twist my ankles, because the seventies were all about platform shoes.

One day, the older girls in sabbath school pointed at my canvas shoes and giggled. It was winter, which meant the shoes were slippery and snow melted clear through the canvas to my stockings. The picture of Jesus on the wall looked at me with kindness. But I wondered how he allowed such mockery. And why was I the only kid in my entire neighborhood going to church on a Saturday? My parents didn't go, I had no friends there, and all I wanted was to sit in my jammies in front of the TV and laugh at Bugs Bunny and Elmer Fudd, wrist deep in a bowl of Fruit Loops.

Every time I wished for this my face flushed red with guilt. I knew God heard me and would not be pleased that I'd rather watch cartoons than worship. It didn't help that I had my Ken doll accidentally cheating on Barbie with Lana—so much drama—and they were always kissing and wanting to lie down and hump. It made me wonder if I'd ever make it to Heaven.

There was a time when church was not so horrible for me, back when the whole family would go together. My father was a deacon, and he would help people find seats for the eleven o'clock service when families would congregate after sabbath school. This was usually pretty boring, but Grandma helped by letting me rifle through her purse for Doublemint gum, and play with her pens and crumpled Kleenexes, while nearby ladies shushed me and told me to sit still.

Mom had bought me a crisp white coat with Marimekko-style green flowers and giant buttons. I can't remember what I wore underneath, but I do remember the crotch of my cream-colored stockings hanging halfway down my thighs, such that I was always pulling them damn things up my hips, to no avail. No matter, I loved that coat so much I could have been naked underneath and I wouldn't have cared, even at church.

I was four years old and extra excited to go to church that particular day, because the sooner we got there, the sooner it was over, the sooner I would be at A&W drive-in for a teen burger and a pack of onion rings that I'd share with my brother in the back of our station wagon. Dad had promised. Eight o'clock in the morning and I was already salivating for lunch.

However, I didn't feel right. When I went to the toilet, nothing came out, except a drop, and it scorched me like acid.

It felt like my bladder was overflowing, I had to pee so badly. But nothing would come, and it burned.

I screamed and cupped my *nunu* (my and Tracy's code word for pee-pee), which only made it hurt more. Mom ran into the bathroom and asked if I had been wiping from front to back or back to front. *What the heck?* My nunu was ablaze and she wanted to know which way I wiped? I cried, barely able to speak. Then, weirdness of weird, my siblings started acting extra nice to me. "Are you okay, Shanni?" I knew I had to be dying.

Next thing I recalled, I was on a hospital gurney surrounded by nurses and a silver-haired man with round wire-rimmed glasses in a lab coat. He held up a needle, a whole foot long, and asked the nurses to support my limbs. Doctor code for *pin her down!*

"This will only hurt for a second, sweetie." He chuckled maniacally and stuck that needle clear up the pinhole at the end of my nunu and into my bladder as I thrashed in pain, shocked that my mother allowed this.

"It won't hurt," she had said twenty minutes earlier.

"You promise, Mom? You swear on the Bible?" I begged.

"Yes, Shanni, I promise. Trust the doctor."

That's how it went, straight from the mare's mouth, minutes before my arrival to a medieval torture chamber called a hospital, minutes before the doctor decided to filet me like a forty-pound tuna, flipping and flopping, begging for my life.

"Lord help me, pleeeeeeeeease!" I screamed. "I promise to be good. I promise to not just want to go to church so I can eat A&W."

Excruciating was an understatement. I don't remember the rest. Except that I'd never trust doctors again. Or nurses. Or anyone at a hospital. If I had my way, I'd never enter a hospital again in my entire life.

Hours later I woke up at home, got out of bed, and went to the bathroom. Lo and behold, like magic, the pee flowed. My nunu was working again. This, after I thought I was a goner, my body just filling with urine until it was so full that I'd burst and die. I was so pleased I could barely contain myself. Though it still hurt a little, which made me fearful again—

"Mooooooooooommy!" I yelled from the bathroom.

It could come back as quickly as *it* had arrived. Whatever *it* was, nobody had told me. My body flooded with adrenaline.

"What now?" Mom burst through the door having run as quickly as she could from wherever she was. Her eyes looked hollow and round, her mouth stiff and serious.

"How could you!" I started. "You promised it wouldn't hurt, you promised, you said they wouldn't hurt me and they hurt me so bad, Mom. You didn't protect me. You lied to me, you lied, you lied, you lied . . ."

According to outside witnesses (my sister eavesdropping from the hallway), I spent the next thirty minutes pacing the bathroom, which was black with a pink shag rug (which I loved) and looked a bit like a tiny disco. Legend has it, I wore a groove right down to the floorboards that day, marching back and forth, waving my finger.

Mom said to Dad later that evening, "What manner of child is this? A four-year-old bawling me out for a whole half an hour. I was in shock, Jim, bemused. This little soul, so self-assured, so . . . Wow. I just had to let her keep going. It was unbelievable."

Mom took my berating like a champ. Not one single *how could I have known* or *no one said anything about a needle* or *I told you never to wipe back to front!* Nope, she simply apologized, over and over, then took me for strawberry ice cream.

I learned a few things that day. One, God certainly knows how to make a point. Two, I'd never trust doctors again. Three, my mom was the nicest mom ever because I could sass her and still get ice cream.

CHAPTER 10

What's the best way to fix your family and fill each other with unconditional love?

a) Hire a therapist for the kids because *they're* the problem. Pray the kids show up because it's $200 for forty-five minutes and she's counting.
b) Hire a therapist for the adults because, oops, you're the problem. Pray your insurance covers it because you're going to need the ten-session package.
c) Save the money and call a family meeting. Fight over who's in charge. Watch the meeting collapse into a power grab. Then bust out the credit card—you're going to need that therapist after all.
d) Adopt a dog. They're a hundred bucks at the Humane Society and you'll be saving a life. Though, over time, you'll wonder who saved who.

CHAPTER 10.1

Ayahuasca Journey

September 2021

They say the gateway of the Shaman's power is his mouth where all the magical practices pass: singing, chanting, sucking and blowing. . . . The sickness that is being healed often travels through the Shaman and it is thus important that he or she knows how to master these energies.[10]

Guillermo's eyes cast toward me but not on me, more like the space between us, out there, beyond that thin band of waves on the electromagnetic spectrum that we humans can sense, while from his mouth arose the sound of the jungle, over and over like a drum.

Resistance was futile. It only hurt more. Thoughts delivered at light speed. Memories colliding in layers that came so fast it bent my mind. Scenes of life stacked like corpses, layer after layer, the rings of a five-hundred-year-old tree. If this had happened in my day-to-day, I would have gone crazy. But I had no choice but to be totally present to the visions.

---

[10] *Grandmother Ayahuasca* by Christian Funder © 2021. Reprinted by permission of Inner Traditions International and Bear & Company. www.Innertraditions.com

"*Om-gom-godda-bodda . . . om-gom-godda-bodda . . .*"

I began to see images from ancient Aztec art, intricate carvings and maps bubbling up on Guillermo's skin. Then I'd focus on his mouth and the sound to keep me from spinning out, trying not to be self-conscious, thinking only of healing.

My head bobbed with the rhythm . . . *Is he saying, Om, gom, God and Buddha? Is he calling God? Maybe Guillermo is calling on our one and only? Yes, that's it. He believes in God. Hey, Grandma, it's okay, Guillermo is one of us, a light warrior too!*

This had to be the truth. There was no other way. I had to trust. I repeated the chant in my head, *Om, gom, God and Buddha*, and felt the vibration of the words deep in my chest, the sacred energy of the word *God* hitting me in a low rumble like a sheepskin mallet on an Indian hoop drum, soothing my heart.

Surrender, I heard a voice say. *Everyone deserves healing. Even you.*

By nature of proximity to Guillermo and the energy between us, the patterns began to straighten and organize. The cosmic dust seemed to settle around me. For the first time that night, I felt a sense of calm.

"Move up," Sarah said, nudging me forward on the mat.

"More?" I said, my outward expression slow and sticky.

"Get closer to Maestro." She nudged me again. "He needs to reach you."

She's bossy, I thought, wanting to laugh about it, or cry. Because that's what judgment does, makes you feel good about yourself, superior and proud; then just as you trust it, it slices you down to the bone to swim in a pool of disgust. It's the teeter-totter of the mind—we're good and we're bad; we're free and we're afraid; we love and we hate. Always sliding toward one end or the other, rarely balanced in the middle where peace lives.

In truth, Sarah wasn't anything to me. She was *she* whether I was there to judge her or not. Guillermo would chant whether I was there or not. It wasn't personal. The world would keep spinning. People would keep peopling. Our judgments are just a program we run, a mask that keeps us from truth. We need it but can't rely on it. As it was, in that moment, I still felt unable to trust anything.

You're beautiful, I wanted to say out loud to Sarah but couldn't. Instead, I mustered what little strength I had to crawl toward Guillermo like a limp cat who'd lost an alley fight, no clue what was in store for me or why he'd need to *reach* me.

"*Om-gom-godda-budda . . . om-gom-godda-budda . . . om-gom-godda-budda . . .*" he chanted, looking at my eyes and into my soul, through me and past me all at once.

The vibration swirled about like miniature jolts of electricity. Each breath brought me composure as my cells filled with life force. I stiffened and sat taller the way a freshly watered plant grew with moisture. My previous desperate thoughts of what a nothing I was began to melt like snowflakes on an autumn lake, as sound energy echoed from Earth.

Only Earth wasn't Earth anymore. She was Gaia, spirit body, pure energy, and this connection, this channel, flowed direct to me through this odd but brilliant little man. Strict, yearlong mono diets of medicinal herbs and plants from the Amazon—the most prolific of gardens and our one true Eden—had trained his body to replicate her energy through vibration and intention, creating a symbiotic channel where Guillermo had become, quite literally, part jungle, part Mother Nature herself.

After hours of gore and ugly, I had come to see that maybe I could handle it. That I, too, was capable of processing the harshest realities of this existence with the help of the plants,

Maestro and his song, also Sarah and Steven, and the two men who wandered the tent with their little red flashlights, looking for whoever needed them most.

I loved that they would kneel and sing at the end of our mats, then place their hands on their hearts and pray for God to guide us and pull us from our fears. This was a tribe of spiritual healers walking the warrior path. And maybe, just maybe, I was becoming a warrior too.

CHAPTER 10.2

Hurricanes

August 2018

"Stop it, stop!" Tyde pulled the sheets over his head, giggling and red-faced.

"Oh no, here she comes. She's going to get us!" I flipped onto my stomach to let Josh and Canyen take the tongue pummeling from our newest addition, a sweet pup we picked up the week before at the Kauai Humane Society. We named her Saffron, Saffy for short.

"Help, it's Hurricane Lick!" Josh tickled Canyen to add to the chaos. "She's going to get you! The hurricane is touching down."

In a few days, Saffy had brought us more laughs, more silly, more cuddling magic then we'd had in months. It was now routine to start weekend days on the master bed, snuggling while she licked our faces with fervor, like we were great big delicious lollipops.

She was everything we'd hoped for in a dog. Fifteen pounds of terrier and something else: wild like a jackal, cuddly like a kitty, with a wiry mohawk and eyes lined black like Cleopatra. She was also fast as lightning and so pretty and wise. Our sweet little *cadoggal.*

The way Saffy looked at me was like nothing I'd ever experienced—not from Josh, not my mother, my children, well maybe my children when they were babies—as though Saffy knew my heart, as though we'd met before.

The lady at the Humane Society said, "I think she's your *familiar*."

Though I didn't know what that meant, it sounded true. *Yes, sure, my familiar.* I later learned that a *familiar* is not just a special pet; it's a spiritual being that connects with its human in mystical ways. *Sounds perfect. I accept.*

"I've got to get moving," said Josh, slipping out of bed and already in front of his closet in his underwear, fingering through his growing Hawaiian shirt collection while adjusting his package with the other hand. "Keep your eye on the weather. That hurricane could make a sharp right turn any moment and hit us."

No sooner had the sun made its long-awaited summer debut, with its mighty rays and peaking temperatures that would dry up the island (and our orchard), than a hurricane was headed our way, force four. From floods to typhoons, in less than a year of our arrival, we'd survived a near-nuke, incessant rain, a flood, and God help us, a hurricane to come.

Strangely, I wasn't worried. I never bought the whole *bad things come in threes.*

Her name was Hurricane Lane, and she was a few days away. The air was swollen, dripping with wet anticipation. Josh had readied the plywood, left behind from the original owner-builder of the house, to nail to windows and doorframes. During a neighborhood hurricane prep meeting, I sat riddled with worry about our too many windows and all glass doors. Then a neighbor told me not to worry, we had the most hurricane-proof house on the street. Ours was a single-story, multisided, ranch-style home with a thirty-foot roof pitch and hurricane tie-downs on every single corner, built with hurricanes top of mind.

"You want coffee?" Josh yelled from the kitchen, while the crackle of the grinder buzzed through the house.

"You mean your morning booze?" I answered sarcastically.

Josh made the strongest coffee ever. At that level, it was officially a drug. I entered the kitchen in my baby-doll pj's.

"You know me, tea first. And, hon?" I pointed to the air conditioner with longing. "Could we please, do we have to be so . . ."—I struggled to think of the least offensive words—"*budget* all the time?"

"You know how expensive running that thing is?" Josh protested, twisting the lid on his to-go mug and collecting his papers to get out the door for work.

"I know, but how about just today in this wicked heat?" I pulled my top away from my chest and peered at the sweat beads dripping between my breasts.

Josh hesitated. "You know that big commission I got two days ago?" He asked, brow crinkled in frustration. "They retracted."

"What?" My heart sank. Josh needed this. Six months on the job and he'd barely made minimum wage, no thanks to deals folding at the last minute. "They can't do that."

"They can," he said. "They have a week to cancel the contract." He leaned in to kiss me on the cheek. "Have a good day. See you around three."

Good God, he's resilient, I thought as he walked away, giving the dog a squeeze. *Such a hard worker. Unlike me, I'm becoming such a sad sack.*

In the year since we'd arrived, I'd failed at so much. First, my twice-a-week gig as a yoga teacher. Almost no one came. After parting ways, the studio owner told me she thought I was going to bring my own students. This made me laugh because I had taken the job to meet people and get clients.

Second, my Pineapple Retreats: a two-hundred-dollar day of yoga and meditation in my tree house (built for this purpose), plus an orchard tour, grounding in the red dirt of the pineapple field, a citrus foot scrub, mini nutrition consult, and raw food lunch, all of which I offered through the Airbnb app, along with the one and only hotel on the entire island whose concierge was willing to promote me.

Every two weeks, the hotel brought me small groups in their passenger van. This was nice. However, during the few months since we'd begun, these groups had morphed into more of a french-fry-burger crowd. So my retreats devolved into twenty-five-dollar farm tours where tourists gorged on our fruit and took selfies with the lychee tree and baby pineapples.

Third, I had received exactly zero calls from the Vancouver production companies that had once loved me. Sure, some of them knew I'd moved to Kauai and started a nutrition business, but they could have at least called to check in. *Oh, how the mighty fall.*

I was officially tanking. I'd stopped making my YouTube health videos, despite a decent following and thousands of views. And I no longer offered my outrageously cheap ten x ten-minute health consults for a hundred dollars as that was just dumb. So, against my will, and at not even fifty years old, I'd been forced into premature retirement.

My phone rang as Josh walked out the door. I didn't answer. It was Daniella. Something about another plant medicine retreat coming soon, and did I want to go? "You loved the last one so much—please come, darling. It was so good for you."

Saffy licked my ankles. Amazingly, she already seemed able to read my thoughts. I deleted Daniella's voicemail and decided to check emails.

Brazil Openly Threatens Genocide of Indigenous Amazonians.
15,000 Scientists Send SOS for Earth.
Species Going Extinct at 1,000 Times the Natural Rate.
307 Mass Shootings in America This Year.
California Experiences Most Deadly Wildfires in History.
Scientists Work to Dim the Sun.
Third Straight Year of Declining Life Expectancy.

Delete. Delete. Delete.

"This movie sucks," I said to Josh, foraging the last bits of yummy off the Fudgsicle stick with my tongue, deep in the seat cushions of our comfiest couch ever. "Want to watch something else?"

"It's getting late," Josh said, flipping the TV off. "And I have to work early."

"What's wrong with Hollywood?" I pressed to the edge of the cushions to get up while pulling at my shorts that had glued to my legs. "These days they can't make a movie without a raunchy sex scene or heads getting blown off in the first five minutes. How debased do they think we are?"

"It's pretty sad." Josh got up then pointed to the loft at the center of our living room and whispered. "One of us has to go up there and shut that down."

The boys had been on the PlayStation since six o'clock. It was going on eleven. Josh and I had taken turns calling them to get ready for bed, to no avail. Neither of us were up for a fight. Especially Josh, with his full days at the office then home to clear farm shrapnel or grind down a tree stump.

"How can they stand it up there that long?" I looked at Josh. "It's so bloody hot." I pulled my hair off my neck and tied it in a knot at the top of my head, then started the dishes.

"Maybe it's the calm before the storm."

"It's never not windy here." I looked out the kitchen window, the full moon casting shadows from our giant monkeypod tree like a pretty silver spotlight. "Should I be worried?"

"Let's look at the storm tracker." Josh grabbed his phone from the table and swiped the screen for a careful look at the map. "Shit."

"What?"

"It's been upgraded to a category five!"

"No! How close is it?"

"Plodding the same track from Baja." Josh squinted his eyes and swiped at the screen to enlarge it. "It could still miss us."

"Oh, man, we better pray for a miracle."

"Let's see if the wind picks up overnight."

Thump! Smash! Crash!

"What the heck?" I turned my glance upward.

From Tyde's bedroom loft streamed cries of fury. Two wild beasts in a brawl.

Ka-thump!

One of them hit the floor hard. Josh and I flew up the stairs.

"He's wrecking my headset!" Tyde screamed with his arms wrapped around his brother in a headlock. "I bought it with my own money!"

"He never lets me play!" Canyen screamed back, digging his nails into Tyde's forearms and kicking his legs. "I never get time!"

"You've both had more than enough time!" Josh boomed, driving his hands and elbows between the boys as they knotted into one vile organism. "To bed!"

"Dammit!" I added to the fray. "These violent games make you two act crazy!"

Josh managed to grab Canyen while I pulled at Tyde's torso with all my might. Both boys had tears streaming down their swollen, ruddy faces.

"Josh, take Canyen to his room." I quickly stood between the boys. "I've got Tyde!"

"I'm gonna kill him!" Tyde swore as I grabbed his arms to restrain him. "Fuck!"

"Stop it!" I yelled. "And watch your mouth!"

"He always swears, Mom, always!" Canyen shrieked. "You're the worst brother in the world. I hate you!" Tears dripped from his chin as Josh pulled him out of the room.

I looked at Tyde, then looked at the PS4 and shook my head in disgust. I grabbed the controllers. "You guys are grounded."

After a few minutes, the cyclone dissipated. The house was quiet. Tyde got to brushing his teeth, while Josh helped Canyen get ready for bed in the opposite corner of the house. My heartbeat slowly returned to normal, but I couldn't erase my frown.

Saffy perched her furry little body on my feet, looking cute as ever, as I prepared a lavender tea in the kitchen. *Thank God for you, sweet little thing, no clue how crazy we are, huh? Are you sure you want to live with us?* I smiled at her sadly.

From the corner of my eye, I saw Tyde tiptoe toward Canyen's room.

"No!" I whispered. "Leave him alone."

"It's okay, Mom," Tyde said. "I just want to say I'm sorry."

"Seriously. Don't!"

He knew better. And I knew better. I'd seen it before. Tyde would creep into Canyen's room and apologize with an undertone of sarcasm. Canyen would detect said tone, unready to forgive, and a second, bigger and scarier fight would ensue.

Tyde ignored me. Reluctantly, I let it go, quietly sipping my tea and hoping this time would be different. Two minutes later—

Thump, wallop, whack!

"Tyde, get out! Get the hell out!" Josh yelled hoarsely.

"I can't do this anymore," I said to Saffy, placing my hands on my ears.

Doors slammed. Walls crunched. Tyde came barreling down the hallway at full tilt and into the living room, Josh sprinting behind him.

Slam! Josh tackled Tyde to the ground.

"What the fuck?" I gasped.

Indeed, the ballistic missile had arrived after all, detonating in my living room.

"Stop!" I shrieked. "Please! Everyone!"

Canyen stood in the hallway cupping his face in his hands, crying, while I stood opposite, shaking and breathless. Between us, Tyde was pinned to the ground under Josh, whose face was the color of a radish.

I hated all of us. But especially, I hated that machine—the square box filled with zeros and ones, vulgarity and violence. How had we allowed this demon in our house? First-person shooter games made by evil geniuses with 160 IQs and the emotional intelligence of a fruit fly, programming our children for bloodshed. I cringed at the dysfunction.

Welcome to the twenty-first century: children called to fantastical screens that showcase worlds so extraordinary that anything in the real world—fingers in the dirt, climbing a tree, building a fort, kicking a hacky sack, playing kick the can (let alone reading a book)—paled in comparison. Not all kids, and mine often went to the beach to surf, rope-swing, and climb trees, but come evening, their precious would call.

Josh and I did our best to teach our boys about the poisons of the world. We fed them good food, ate dinners together, tried to talk about important things, held off on all the various screens and devices as long as we could. Sometimes it even felt like it was paying off. Just last week, Tyde's teacher called to say how all the kids were on their iPhones at lunch except Tyde, who sat and had a heart-to-heart chat with her instead.

"What a great kid!" she gushed. "Good job, Mom. He told me you're not getting him a phone until he turns fourteen."

I was proud, for a minute. Then lamented that this was what qualified as *great* these days. I wanted to say: *Yes, he is a good kid. But society's bar is set pretty low, and we go to blows for it on a regular basis.*

"Get off me!" Tyde screamed.

"Say you're sorry!" Josh spat.

"Stop!" I slid between them and felt my guts spilling onto the floor.

How has this gone so wrong for us? This isn't the good life, the simple life; this is the bullshit life! Fuck it—

"We're moving back to Canada!" I yelled.

Josh lifted his head in shock. "What did you say?"

"This isn't working!" I shrieked, my voice hoarse from yelling. "I've tried to tell you, but you're so fricking distracted with your stupid time-shares!"

Josh was still on top of Tyde with a death grip on his wrists. Nobody moved.

"You never said anything about moving back." Josh glared at me.

"I've tried to tell you. Canyen's miserable—"

"Canyen has Keanu!"

"One person isn't enough. Not for him or for me. This place is making us crazy! Look at us!" I slammed my arms at my side. "Our boys need their friends. And a good school! We have no family here. Look, just look." I pointed to the wreckage. "They fight constantly. They play video games instead of board games. We're not off-grid! We're not farmers. We're not special!"

"That's because I do all the work! No one helps! I have no say! *You* don't help at all!"

"I don't belong here!" I shouted, unable to catch my breath, like a true ha'ole, a breathless, soulless, lifeless outsider.

"We could. We would! If you guys ever got outside to be a part of this!"

"You need to help, you two!" I glared at my boys, as though this would take the strain off me and the Pandora's box I'd just blasted open. Had I never really embraced our farm? Really? Guilt rose in my belly.

"You do nothing on the farm!" Josh roared at Tyde, still holding his shoulders in a vice. "We have to yank you, kicking and screaming."

"Not true!" Tyde wailed into Josh's face, mustering all the strength of his adolescent body in a warrior cry. "I surf! I help on the farm. I worked an hour today!"

"I drag you, and then you're right back inside on the goddamn PS4!" Josh spat.

The truth was, Tyde spent ten minutes in the garden, then came inside for a drink, then another ten outside, then wandered the house back and forth, barely breaking a sweat. I thought of myself as a teenager: fights with my brother, him punching his fist through the wall; fights with my mom, her slamming the cupboard door so hard it blew off the hinges; wanting so badly to be a grown-up, but not really, needing firm boundaries and protection too, pushing and pushing to make my mom prove how much she loved me.

Somehow, we pushers make peace with ourselves just short of landing in juvie. Is this part of a universal resentment we all have toward growing up? If so, I get it.

"Stop! He's a goddamn child, Josh!" I yelled. "He's already going to school in a tent on the grass on a fucking farm, with fold-out tables, and it still costs $650 a month! This is a joke. No junior high or high school on the whole North Shore? Ridiculous! Trying to get kids to do farm work is hell—any work! You weren't lining up to clean the house when you were thirteen." I huffed. "The farm is *your* thing! Yours! You wanted it. Not me!"

"So, the answer is to leave?" Josh fumed, releasing Tyde and rising from the floor to confront me. "Canada! Months with no sunshine. Cold, wet, awful! Kids inside all winter on devices. Nothing else to do!"

"We ski! We visit family! Tyde has his friends there, in the flesh, not on a game system!" I spewed.

As sure as that hurricane to the south was swirling and twirling and threatening to hit land, we were swept into the storm, a boiling cauldron of half-truths, miscommunications, and needs not met. What a joke to think sweet Saffy could have saved us. Nothing could.

"I can't get a job here. I'm a glorified housewife. I'm nothing. I'm trapped!"

Nearly two hundred years ago, Queen Liliuokalani heroically attempted to restore her Hawaiian monarchy that was, in the eyes of time, already dead. For this, she was forced into house arrest in Oahu, in her own home, on her own land. There, she wrote plucky songs and drew pictures. Nice songs, sure, but the woman was meant to rule—she was a queen! And I wanted a tiny version of that. At the very least, I knew I had a calling beyond housewife on a pineapple farm. Canada was my motherland. It was special to me, to Canyen, to all of us, all but Josh, it seemed. We ruled Lions Bay in our own small way. We were sovereign there. Maybe hearts do have a geographical home beyond the body.

"So, this is just about you?" Josh fired.

"No! It's about us, family, friends, belonging, a good education! If we stay, our only good option is to send the kids to private school, that's two thousand dollars a month per kid. By the time they graduate, it'll be hundreds of thousands of dollars for something that's free back home! We'll be broke in no time!"

My throat felt raw. I had no one here—no one who cared about us the way family could, or friends who'd known us for years. It was me at age ten all over again: a dead dad, a mom who worked too much, a move away from grandparents and all that was familiar, and no one to hold my hand.

"I can't breathe." I grabbed my belly, sweating and pumped with cortisol.

She did this! It's her fault. Mama Kauai! I'm suffocated by her gnarled roots, fat wet soil, sweltering air, and jungle jungle everywhere.

"Fuck it. Go. All of you!" Josh heaved. "I'll stay alone! It's done."

He'd been pushed to his edge. My timing was the shits. Plus, I was a liar, as duplicitous as the rest. I had promised Canyen we would go: *our little secret.* And that, plus this fight, plus another move, could ruin us.

Josh shook his head furiously. "I worked too hard for this. No one fucking cares. And you—" He stopped short, opening his arms wide like Moses parting the Red Sea, then stormed out of the room in disgust.

What stopped him? I thought for sure the D-word was next.

The boys scattered into their rooms while I stood alone, tissues balled up in my sweaty palms, heart pounding like I'd fought a fifty-foot dragon, and wholly unable to cry.

Saffy looked at me from under the table with her chin on her paws, her chocolate-brown eyes wide and gazing curiously into mine.

"You up, sister?" I held my phone to my ear. It was 6:30 a.m., and it was Daniella.

"I'll be there in five," she trilled. "I've got lilikoi kombucha!"

It was the morning after the fight and the sun was shining, oblivious to the wrecking ball that had just wiped out my family. Daniella and I were to go to a Purium conference at the Hyatt in Poipu. I wanted to cancel, but I was part of her downline—plus, I had promised. Which meant, hell or high water, I would go.

No one was up but me, which was probably for the best. I quietly grabbed my tea, my greens, my coffee, and a notebook, and slipped out the door without a word. All I could think of was how miserable I felt. How broken we were and how we had to fix it. Then I wondered if *this time* it was possible.

The drive to Poipu was over an hour, so despite my not wanting to speak, spits and spurts of last night's drama came out in clumps, a meaty hair ball tossed up from the cat. It made my stomach twist to think of it. Tyde's face flushed red, his tears coursing, us leaving, moving home, Josh threatening to stay.

Oddly, she responded with trifles: "Mercury is in retrograde . . . Your kids are awesome . . . Try Purium CBD oil or Chill spray, that will help for sure . . ." Which wasn't like her. Clearly she hadn't understood the severity of it all.

I shut up and looked out the window, regretting having said anything.

Five hours later, at the other end of the island, I sat frustrated and bored listening to multi-level-marketing megastars present their rags-to-riches stories about how they lost twenty pounds drinking beetroot smoothies, and how Purium transformed their lives, and how easy it was to get to Diamond status—*just find your why*—thinking them all liars and wondering what the hell I was doing there. When out of the blue, I got a call from Josh.

He was mowing the back of the property after work, when he went in the house for a water break to find two police cruisers sitting in the driveway, and two policemen standing in front of the boys, giving them an earful. Presently, the police were inside our home, sitting at the kitchen table, filing a report.

What—the—fuck?

For the second time in twenty-four hours, and about the twentieth time in a year, my heart leapt into my throat and my insides twisted into a sickening black knot. This time, it wasn't about a hurricane (that had just—as in one hour earlier—redirected away from us), or a nuclear bomb about to blow up the island, or a flash flood that would cause a billion dollars of damage, or even me and Josh and our busted marriage. This time, it was a *domestic disturbance*. This time, it was my children.

CHAPTER 10.3

1988

This was the year I nearly died. It was a *near* near-death experience, an NNDE (yes, I just made that up). It was an almost.

I know, *almost* only counts in horseshoes and hand grenades. In this case, having an NNDE especially sucked because I had all the fresh horror of dying: the suffocation, the torment of drowning, and the unbearable fear of losing my life. I had come so close, but got none of the glory of actually crossing over and stepping into the light, the presence of angels and feelings of ecstasy, bliss, and such.

Maybe that was a good thing. People don't want to come back from that—it's so damn good up there. And when they do, you can't shut them up.

"Archangel Michael told me I have a critical purpose back on Earth. Which is why he, Grandpa, and Billy (remember little Billy, got himself electrocuted?) sent me back through the tunnel. Yeah, it hurt, squeezing back into this mangled skin suit, not to mention those awful fluorescent lights above the hospital bed, inconceivable after a blissful immersion into the ineffable light and love of God! But, you know, orders from the boss, 'Go back, spread the good word. It's not your time.' So here I am. Out of my way, minions!"

Cue nervous chuckle. Because those people knew if they ever kicked the bucket again, it would be for good. At least I had that going for me. Plus, they don't have ice cream up there.

Earth was the best ticket in the galaxy, maybe the universe. The aliens knew it—the Greys, Pleiadeans, Reptiloids—that's why they're always hovering around watching, beaming us up to check out our meat suits, wondering what it's like to feel love and hate, sorrow and joy, not to mention the incredible beauty of this place—waterfalls, mountains, glaciers, deserts, flowers, evergreens, big fat hippos, and ridiculous peacocks. They want a piece of this, but they can't have it because their meat suits don't work like ours. Some of them don't even have sex organs or nostrils, and they can't eat lasagna or cake, or sing, or write sonnets, because they communicate telepathically, which is cool, but also slightly dangerous. Do we really want our friends and enemies knowing what we think of them?

So, yah, Earth is where it's at, third dimension, solid matter, material world and so on. And I'd like to stay as long as I can—*please and thank you.*

The day I nearly died I was in Jackson Hole on a ski trip. It had snowed twenty days in a row. The powder so deep it was waist-high on the green runs. The maintenance crew couldn't keep up, so nothing was groomed except a few runs at the bottom.

At nineteen years old, I fancied myself a bit of a hotshot, a card-carrying member of the Southern Alberta Freestyle Ski Team. I had just healed from a serious back injury where I compressed a disk and fractured a vertebra on a trampoline, screwing around and not using a spotting belt. The upside being that I wasn't paralyzed and could still walk. Aside from a fancy new C-curve in my spine, and being half an inch shorter, I was back on the sticks and ready to carve.

Kurt, a new friend and ski racer, led the way out of bounds. The racer/freestyler dynamic at that time was not a healthy one. They thought we were free-dogging kooks, and we thought they were snobby pricks with no imagination. So, I had something to prove.

"Follow me," Kurt said mockingly. "Don't be a chickenshit hot-dogger."

"Haha, Kurt." I dug my poles in to take off behind him, but the snow was so deep I had to press through with my legs. "Right behind ya." *Sort of.*

Kurt traversed until he came to a rope marked OUT OF BOUNDS.

"How about here?" he suggested, ducking under the rope onto a steep slope dotted with trees.

"Why here?" I asked in surprise, huffing and puffing from the slog over and fogging up my goggles. "The whole mountain is a powder bowl. We don't need to go out of bounds."

"Don't be lame. We need the steep or we can't move in this shit," he said with too much confidence. "Plus, the trees will help us see. Don't want vertigo in this pea soup."

"Fine, let's go," I said, feeling wholly uncertain as I turned my skinny bump skis (aka not the standard-issue wide-plank powder rig required for heavy snow) perpendicular to the slope.

After teetering back and forth a few times, my skis began to slip. Eventually, and thanks to the intense vertical, I found a flow. Meanwhile, Kurt bounced side to side, floating through the deep powder like a snowshoe hare, a far better powder skier than I.

In no time, he was thirty, forty feet ahead of me. I felt in over my head yet lumbered along, attempting to balance speed with staying upright and sitting back-seat in my skis (though necessary in this powder, a no-no for a free-dogger who's all about dynamic centering). Falling in powder this deep would be a disaster, and losing a ski or pole would mean it was lost forever.

My jaw became sore from gritting my teeth, while a layer of mist and ice permanently covered my goggles, making it nearly impossible to see with the flat light and nonstop flurries from the giant cloud that had swallowed the mountain. But I persisted, attempting to mimic Kurt. He looked to be dancing; it was so easy for him. I just wanted to catch up.

Suddenly, I shifted too far forward on my skis and lost my balance. Next thing I knew, I'd launched headfirst toward a tree like Superman, literally shooting forward in flight, eight feet in the air, then hit the snow like a missile, diving through the fluff like it was water.

I was sure I looked hilarious, like a ski cartoon upside-down with my legs protruding and my face and torso fully submerged. Yet I was confident I could shimmy or dig myself out by hand. But when I went to move, my arms were stuck in place, molded into the snow above my head, the weight of my body above me. I kicked, then kicked again. The more I kicked, the deeper I slipped, the more the snow packed around me. That's when I got scared.

"*Help!*" I screamed as loud as I could, thrashing and shimmying. "*Heeeeeeeeeeelp!*"

No one could hear me. The weight of my body pulled me where the snow was no longer white, into the well of the tree. All I could see were tiny blue crystals. My ears were muffled and stuffed with snow. I couldn't swallow and it was getting harder and harder to breathe.

"*Heeeeeeeeeeeelp!*" I screamed again into the wall of snow, terrified I would die.

Like a rope around my neck, it hit me, headlines from the past few years: the boy the ski patrols found dead at four thirty in the afternoon, headfirst in a snowbank at Nakiska; the teens who died in an off-piste avalanche at Fortress after a week long snow dump that closed the hill; the girl found stuck, dead in a tree well at Sunshine Village. These were my home mountains in the Rockies. Every year, someone perished. It was suddenly very possible that I would be next!

I'm going to die here. Kurt is way too far ahead of me to hear me, or climb back up and dig me out. And there's no one else here. We're out of bounds in a blizzard!

With a front row seat, the movie of my life began, a warp speed review of the mistakes, accidents, endings, deaths, and how they'd all pulled me under like this. Fathoms deep into an ocean where light no longer penetrates, where bizarre glow-in-the-dark fish with rainbow-hued bodies and light bulbs dangling from antennae glided by like floating skeletons, reminding me that life exists in the void, but only as long as there's breath . . . and mine was running out.

The minutes ticked by. I sank deeper, past the bioluminescent fish, and long past the deep-sea cliffs where giant octopuses hid.

"*Heeeeeeeellllllllp!*" I yelled again into my snow-filled sarcophagus, praying for divine intervention, screaming and kicking, and kicking some more, ironically unable to move.

The snow packed harder around me until I'd cemented into place, head-down and up to my ankles. Now, the only part of me protruding was my skis—also the only thing preventing me from full submersion, such that no one would have found me until spring. My entire body was packed in the snow like I'd been rolled in an avalanche. I needed a miracle.

Please God, something, anything, I beg you, don't let me die. I began to cry.

Suffocation was imminent. I was out of tries.

Breath no longer came and there was nothing I could do to save myself. My hands, arms, and now my legs were locked in the void that every skier is warned of—the dreaded tree well. It sucks you in like quicksand.

I pictured my obituary: *"Nering died doing the sport she loved. A tragicomic end in the Tetons, smothered by five hundred inches of snow. Poor thing, gone too soon — but hey, at least it was a record year."*

It was in that silence that I found a small space to forgive myself and say goodbye. *Okay, God, let's see if it really is better on the other side.* And, with no other choice, I surrendered.

Since I was ten, Grandma promised I would see my dad in Heaven. In my darkest moments, I would picture him surrounded by a golden orb of light in a cloud in the sky. It gave me solace, and it was the only reason I was willing to give up that day, buried in a trench of snow: the hope of seeing my dad again, quite possibly in a few short minutes.

Then I thought of my mom. She would be devastated. I was her angel. It's why she called me Celeste. Even when I was a brat (which apparently was often), she would say, "You're my angel, just what I needed when I didn't know I needed you."

Grandma would tell the story of how Mom cried inconsolably when she found out she was pregnant with me. Already with three kids under the age of six, she got pregnant in spite of being on the pill. Mom ran down the alley for Grandma's house, embarrassed, feeling like a baby factory, on kid number four when she'd only wanted two. Even the two she'd wanted weren't planned, or came too soon, or something. Like many women of her era, she wanted to first make her mark in her career and have it all just like Gloria Steinem and the Enjoli perfume commercial had promised.

Instead, Mom had to do everything all at once with a husband so immature and hotheaded that she felt thwarted at every turn. At age twenty-one, she hadn't finished her university teaching practicum when she became pregnant with my sister. How many marriages began that way? And wasn't it supposed to be fun! Instead, my mom got babies, toddlers, kids of her own and kids at school, running her band, climbing the ladder, managing a house, dancing backward and in heels.

My grandma said, "Don't fret, Marguerite. This one will be your little angel, always by your side."

Grandma knew. She always knew. The wise woman next door.

Then Mom lost her husband ten years after my birth, just when he'd become her rock, her protector, an excellent provider and a wonderful dad. Just as they'd found their rhythm. Just as life had stitched so neatly together, it all fell apart with his death.

I'm so sorry Mom, I thought, my body buried in the snow. *For being too much, and all the times I've been a jerk—the brawls between Troy and I, as you stood there and screamed for us to stop. How hellish that must've been. I'm sorry I made Troy so mad that he punched a hole in the wall. I'm sorry I made you so mad that you broke the cupboard door. I'm sorry for saying I hate you; it couldn't have been further from the truth. You've worked so hard for us kids and have been through so much and shone through it all. There is only love in my heart for you and my family forever . . .*

And with that, I released one last meager breath.

Snow crunched. Bindings clicked. Voices spoke.

Dad, is that you? White light, am I here? Am I home with the angels?

In that last breath, I heard them. It was the three ski patrols that I'd passed at the top of the lift. They'd had their eyes on me and Kurt. *Hallelujah!* They followed us and were digging me out, clicking my skis off, and yelling to each other—

"Move, move, move! Quick! Get her skis off. We don't have much time!"

After a flurry of action, words, and shovels digging madly around me, I was surrounded by golden light, earthly light, and air, fresh mountain air, and valiant men cradling me as a mother would, speaking to me in hushed tones, with no admonishment, no *you stupid girl*, only the harmony of humans caring for each other, caring to save a life.

"It's okay, girl, we got you," the ski patrol said tenderly. "You're going to be okay."

I gasped in relief then began to cry uncontrollably. It came in shakes, shivers, and waves, my body releasing the panic from my blood and tissues.

Maybe it was a *near-death* experience after all. I got the bright light, the angels (albeit earthly), and a glimpse at that thing that binds us all.

Well played, God, I said silently, *well played.*

CHAPTER 11

What do you do when your ten- and thirteen-year-old kids are beating the hell out of each other over video games?

a) Send the kids to juvie. It's time.
b) Send yourself to an ashram where you contemplate how *you've* contributed to this spiral of dysfunction.
c) Grab yourself a two-six of whiskey. Pour that liquid fire down your throat and watch your troubles dissolve. All will be well (until the next morning).
d) Call your mother and tell her to *get her ass over here* because the family needs inter-generational help, as in the village, as in elders, as in Grandma! It's officially beyond your little unit to solve things now. Parents were never meant to do this alone.

CHAPTER 11.1

Ayahuasca Journey

September 2021

This seemingly magical dimension, this doorway to the mystery, is anchored in the plants that live in our world. Plants don't tell you that you are lost or a heretic if you don't believe in certain religions. They provide an access to the sacred for the individual to go see for oneself. [11]

Finally, I was on the other side. Not on my terms but hers, the plant, the Mother Vine. She took me to Hell. Would she show me Heaven, immerse me in pure love and light energy?

Maestro was doing his best to help . . .

Once before I'd felt something like this, driving home from Colorado, age twenty-two, in my yellow Camaro that my mom helped me buy. It was the end of summer. I'd just finished an internship at a Denver TV station, living at my aunt and uncle's house, and was due back at college in September. Weeks earlier, I'd sent a talk show pitch to the man in charge of Calgary's public cable station and had just heard news that

---

[11] *Grandmother Ayahuasca* by Christian Funder © 2021. Reprinted by permission of Inner Traditions International and Bear & Company. www.Innertraditions.com

it was green-lit. Yahoo! My first TV show of my own making, and I hadn't even graduated! Inside my head rang the phrase *do what others are unwilling to do.* This was my mantra.

On this day, I was in the Wyoming section of my eighteen-hour drive home. The highway was a curvy single lane with nothing but prairie backed by mountains for hundreds of miles. There were hardly any cars and the sun basked low on the horizon, ready to set behind the foothills. As I flipped my visor down to block the sun's harsh rays, I was blinded.

The entire windshield flared with white light reflecting in every direction. I could not see, yet I kept my foot on the pedal, ninety miles an hour, feeling strangely invincible. The brilliant white light entered me like a laser beam, piercing my heart. I saw my future flash before me.

Actually, I didn't so much see it as feel it in every cell. The path before me felt perfect and whole. There was nothing to fix. It was all unfolding as it should. My failings, my mistakes, my sorrow, my shame—from losing my dad and grandma and the feelings of unworthiness that came with it, to snapping my back on a trampoline, to quitting my dream of becoming an Olympic freestyle skier, to the abortion two months earlier—it was all forgiven, all part of the plan, all necessary for me to fulfill my purpose as a unique fractal of God.

If there had been a mirror, I'm certain I was glowing. Divinity had enveloped me. Maybe this was how it felt to be an angel. I had so much to give. If I could just hold on to this feeling of the sun blasting my heart wide open.

I sipped and savored the golden white rays as part life force, part primal energy from God, praying this superhuman state would last forever. But, as quickly as it arrived, the sun set behind a mountain and the illumination and feelings of divine connection set with it. Back in rolled the familiar, *I like,*

I hate, programmed into me since day one. I was still strong, still hearty, but not so super.

Thirty years later, sitting on Maestro's mat, I had that feeling again. Only different, because it took all night to get there. It was like someone took the lid off my brain to reveal what humans missed in normal sensory perception: that thin band of infrared and sound waves that our eyes register and ears record, and that thin band of consciousness that is our normal waking state.

I never understood when scientists said we only use 5–10 percent of our brain; now it made sense. Our prefrontal cortex protects us from all that is out there. Otherwise, we'd explode! Without the brain's brilliant filter, we wouldn't have a clue what to do with all that information. We would literally blow our own minds every single day.

I'm listening, Abuela Ayahuasca. I saw the dark, now show me the light. Show me what I need to see, teach me what I need to learn, awaken me to the truth.

"*Om-gom-godda-budda, om-gom-godda-budda, om-gom-godda-budda . . .*" the steady thump of Maestro's song filled the air.

Bits and pieces of me—shards that had split away long ago, fragments that had scattered throughout the cosmos during my worst sorrows—slowly returned, splicing themselves together like film clips.

Each beat pumped me fresh with healing plant-spirit energy.

Each inhale traveled my bloodstream to collect my fears.

Each exhale released them, strengthening my arms like marble columns to hold me.

I finally exited that desolate loop of despair.

No fanfare, no explosions, just ashes flitting in the wind.

CHAPTER 11.2

Blood Moon

September 2018

Bzz. Bzz. Bzz.

My phone vibrated from the charger cable in the corner of the bedroom like it was alive. A message from Daniella. It wasn't even eight o'clock. I'd had a bad sleep.

The twenty or so wild chickens that called our lychee tree home screeched all night long, no breaks, just *er-er-roo,* over and over. I'd never get used to it. A quarter-million lived on the island with no natural predators. Saffy did her small part. The day we brought her home, an unsuspecting rooster crossed her path. In a flash, she snapped its neck and sprinted for the hills. We were both proud and terrified of our sweet new dog.

"Darling," Daniella's voice sing-songed from my messages, carrying a red wine timbre and velvet cloak of syllables. "Aguirre will be back on the island next week for his fall retreat. Please come. It will be so great!"

Delete.

My best bet was to make a trip to Lihue to buy a bundle of sage to smudge the house, then Josh, then the kids, then me. My second option was to convince a doctor to prescribe a motherload of valium. I did neither. I got to work.

When the mania wasn't commanding my headspace, I worked on my retreats: pounding the pavement, approaching new hotels, posting on social media, finally, actually busy, carrying on like a proper entrepreneur.

Things seemed to be coming together just as we were falling apart. Josh got a big commission for a contract that did *not* fall through. Canyen had more homework in a month than he'd had in a year and was actually getting it done. And Tyde kept up his good grades at his backyard hippie school, but still spent too much time online with his best friend from back home. He would fib and say he was doing homework, only to be caught, headphones on, yelling at the screen, "Kill him, Liam. Shit! Get him!"

It was no surprise that the police incident was caused by my sweet beloved boys. They had yet another blowout over whose turn it was to play the PS4. Given Josh was on the back of the property, he hadn't heard the commotion. Though it sounded like hellfire broiling from the core of the earth, no knives were drawn, or shots fired, there was just a lot of slamming doors, screeching kids, and running around like little maniacs.

For the neighbor, it must have been especially loud because the boys took it outside to the carport, versus the bedroom, and threatened to kill each other—which Josh and I knew to be just words. To complicate it further, it wasn't our neighbor who called, it was the farmhand who lived in an illegal shack that fell practically on our property line. This guy had already annoyed us with late-night drum circles and green-wood fires that wafted the worst smoke through our kitchen windows. In fact, we had thought about calling the cops on him, but that wasn't our style. Anyway, he beat us to the punch.

The police had scolded the kids for a minute, then wrote up a report, "in case it happened again." No big deal. The end. Believe me, Kauai police had better things to do than reprimand my children. This island was bustling with drunk drivers, meth heads, thieves, cult leaders, and the occasional serial killer who thought Kauai a great place to disappear from society.

None of that stopped the humiliation. It left me rattled. Because I knew we had real problems, divorce-sized problems. Josh's voice echoed in my head: *three biggest life stressors: death, a move, and divorce.* Everything was coming to a head, a festering boil. I wondered when it would blow, like Kilauea Volcano blow, engulfing the place in flames and destroying half the island. Anything to relieve the pressure that mounted each day.

Aside from taking away the PS4 indefinitely (read: two weeks) and holding a family meeting conveniently timed with dinner, where we all acted civilized for a whole thirty minutes, we were business as usual. We buried it. Life was too busy and we were too distracted and it all felt very mainland/rat race/antithesis of these mystical islands.

However, most often at night, I could think of little else. Neurotically replaying our quarrels, searching for answers to the problem of us and turning up with nothing. Lying beside Josh, his warm body next to mine, yet feeling alone in our nest.

A week later, while weeding the driveway and trying to appease my conscience by listening to a Tara Brach podcast on anger and transformation (and finding it surprisingly helpful), I got another call from Daniella.

"Shannon, darling, can you talk?"

"Uh, I mean, I have five minutes. I have an appointment," I lied.

I didn't want to talk. Lately, I rarely felt like talking to anyone, but especially not cheerful lovely Daniella, despite her being one of my favorite people.

"You okay, sweetie?"

"Fine. Yes. Busy. Retreats are filling up and I'm doing regular tastings now. It's a lot of prep and stuff. I've got to keep this place spic-and-span."

"Oh, wow, congratulations, how exciting," she fizzed from the back of her throat, sounding legitimately happy for me.

Barf. I didn't deserve congratulations on running a quasi-functional business; I deserved a *what the hell took you so long?* Besides, I was barely breaking even, not exactly an accomplishment.

"Did you get my message?" she asked. "Aguirre's retreat? Can you come? He's here tonight. You'll love it, honey. Yes?"

"Sorry, Daniella," I clipped.

No part of Aguirre's medicinal plant retreat felt right to me. Not the timing, the people, or the evanescent miracle plant I would ingest.

"I'm busy and so is Josh. He'd have to do the kids alone plus work time-shares."

"But sweetie, have you asked? Maybe if he understands—"

"Daniella, this isn't a *Josh* thing," I lied; it totally was. "The bottom of our mower rusted out. It's going to cost eight grand to replace. I need the grounds mowed for retreats." I snarled a bit, then pulled back. "I need to be here for the kids. It's been rough lately."

Shit! Why'd I say that?

"Rough? Oh, what happened, dear?" Daniella gushed. "You okay? Should we pray?"

"Nothing. Just the usual, kids fighting, too much time on the games. It's different raising boys. Your daughter is sweet and easy comparatively. I'm knee-deep in boy crap."

"I'm sorry. I understand. Feel better." She hung up.

Six hours later, I was back outside sorting piles of recycling at the side of the house while Tyde whizzed by me on his skateboard. I was planning to take the boys to the beach to surf, or walk the dog. And I was still hoping Josh would acknowledge my plea to move back to Canada, which neither of us had dared mention since our fight.

Josh had had another rough day with the gold-chainers. An older couple from Kansas seemed a slam dunk, but after a day of courtship and buckets of POG, they bailed. Josh had reached his daily bullshit limit and was walking his penguin walk: short, stiff, angry steps with his toes turned out that said *don't mess with me*, as he gathered extra-large pails of tangelos for a vendor who'd sell them at the market for three times our price.

"Mom! It's for you." Canyen ran to me with my phone.

"Ah shit," I said out loud. I hated it when the kids answered my phone. Canyen had grabbed it from the shoe rack, a waste of space because my kids were shoeless vagabonds who rarely changed their clothes and I was pretty sure Canyen hadn't showered in a week.

"Hello?" I tried to hide my annoyance at the interruption.

"Hi, honey, it's me again," Daniella said, her butterscotch tone extra creamy.

Oh my God! Seriously, woman?

"Hey," I said crisply. "What's up, Daniella?"

"Just to say, I'm at the retreat and it's five minutes from your house on the ocean. It's so beautiful. Come! You should see the giant rose quartz that lights up. It glows! Tonight is full moon, blood moon. It's going to be epic."

This girl should be in time-shares—she's relentless!

I felt the cortisol rising in my body, as sweat from my face glued my phone to my cheek, conjuring an image of Salvador

Dali's melting clocks in the desert, like we'd liquefied together, me, my phone, flesh, metal, plastic, earlobe, all oozing down my neck.

"Look, Daniella, this is getting—"

"Listen, darling, I can get you in free." She spoke over me. "We need help in the kitchen. You can do dishes after midnight. But first, do the medicine. Come. You need it."

What I wanted to say was, *Are you for fucking real? And dishes, really?* But I was civilized (ish), so what came out was, "Why do you want me there so badly?"

"Honey, I love you," she said in her Peruvian drawl, her intentions as pure as the spotted doves that I watched every morning from the window. "And you need it."

Then, just like the Grinch whose heart grew three sizes thanks to those pointy-eared Whos from Whoville and their *wa-hoo wa-hoo* ballad of love and forgiveness, I began to melt. Someone wanted to hold my hand. Daniella had extended a lifeline in a way no one ever had. And, though I thought it was too late for me, her timing was weirdly bang-on.

"Text me the address."

I didn't ask Josh for approval. I didn't wait to see if the kids would be okay, or if this would upset Josh, or make *me* out to be even more indulgent and screwy than I already felt. I simply surrendered and said okay.

A tinge of dread filled my belly as I ran to my bedroom to change clothes and dab on some lip gloss. I grabbed my phone, my wallet, my scarf, and scurried down the gravel road in my Mini with the checker-flag mirrors.

September 2018 - Midnight

Dance and sometimes you dance alone. No more hatred left. Not when I'm mean to my kids or my husband, and especially no more mean to me. We are here to heal, here to forgive. We arrived broken and now we heal.

Match your heartbeat to nature. You're a good human and you're a bad human and you don't need to want anymore. Don't let the demons win. They will try. They are angry.

I saw angels and babies and demons in the sky tonight. That's all there is! Babies in the womb. We are all so innocent! And we react and life hurts and we hurt the people we love most. Then we drink alcohol to forget. But plant medicine is the answer. It forces you to hate yourself for your self-crimes, then love yourself because that is all that's left.

And I found all that in a special piece of chocolate, laced with mushrooms and ayahuasca, sitting alone on the cold tile because I gave my blanket to the woman who saved me from me and forced me to come here. She wouldn't take no! And she had to keep talking. Then I told her she was perfect and to sit down and shut up and watch the clouds float by.

I have nothing to prove, not to anyone, not the people I thought could make or break me, because I got what I asked for tonight. I said I don't want to want anymore and I got it. I don't care about empires or success. I just want my family and Josh to forgive me and love me, as I do them to the beautiful dancing moon and back.

Got my validation and I got it from the moon! All copper beautiful, promising to have my back just how I am, horrible mother, horrible person, beautiful mother, beautiful person. Full forgiveness, acceptance of Josh. New chapter begins today.

Everyone hurts. Never compare demons. I'm beautiful. I'm

ugly. I'm all things and no things. Thank you, special chocolate, for knowing what I need and not making it painful. Even though I wanted out of my body for hours, I came back and lived as a child of the moon watching the show in the night sky . . .

"Darling, you okay?" I felt a gentle tap on my shoulder as I awoke from my haze, staring spellbound at the moon.

"Clear as ever. Do they need me? Is it time I do dishes?"

"Anytime." Daniella placed her hand on my back, oozing nurturing safety.

"Did you have a good journey?"

"I saw it all. Answers. In the sky. It was incredible."

"Amazing," she said warmly. "And you *feel* okay?" Daniella peered into my eyes, really trying to read me.

I placed my hand on my heart. "I'm complete, dear friend. Honestly, I need nothing."

"Wow, full circle in one night." Daniella stroked my hair like my grandmother might have done, many years ago. "Girl, you're a quick study."

"Is this what it's like to have no ego?"

"I think so," she said, nodding, her face glowing like she was some sort of angel.

"I love you, I love everyone," I sighed. "I'll do dishes now."

We hugged. Then I pulled away with one final thought: "This feeling will go away, won't it?"

Her eyes became serious. "That's why you must find time to remember, to integrate and remember this feeling. Breathe it into your heart every day."

The moon lit the path to the house like a tractor beam from a spaceship. So brilliant and warm. I thought of the Bible lessons my grandma taught me and how the blood moon signified that we were in the era of the apocalypse, a time when old ways must come to an end. Was this my own personal apocalypse? Had part of me died this night?

For sure, something had escaped my brain and body as I writhed alone on the lawn chair for what felt like all time and no time, forever and a minute. It was a deep ache that twisted the gunk from my tissues the way Grandma used to wring out a wet cloth with her strong kitchen hands. I wiggled like a butterfly bursting from a cocoon. I'd never before felt such meaning, or purpose, with nothing else required.

As I washed dishes quietly in the kitchen, I felt the experience pour through my body the way rain showers a forest, hitting every branch and leaf, each clump of moss, lichen, and fungi, until the entire forest swells with life, nourished and satiated with love. Best of all, I wasn't leaving the experience with a to-do list, or goals, or resolutions, just the journey and the task of remembering.

CHAPTER 11.3

October 2001

"Why are we pulling over?" I asked the driver, who looked all of twelve.

"Just following the team," he replied with a drawl.

The team in the passenger van ahead consisted of a cameraman, a soundman, a camera-assist, a production assistant, and a driver. My van contained an associate producer, myself, and the cast: five men from Alaska and five women from LA, coupled up in the back seats, probably groping each other, happy to have the cameras off of them for a change. Nevertheless, I sat vigilant in the front, eavesdropping for *story* that could be used in my interviews.

"Who wants out?" I slid open the van door, then stepped onto a patch of Alaskan velvet grass that lined the side of the highway, then looked up in awe. "Wowee."

It was after midnight on Alaska's Kenai Peninsula in October. The aurora borealis blazed overhead, putting on a show. Only, rather than the usual blue-green magnificence, the sky had turned an otherworldly red. Electron clouds danced in crimson currents, swirling and colliding in the magnetosphere, while the cast and crew of our quaint reality show, *Bachelorettes in Alaska*, stood in the ditch in a semicircle, oohing and aahing in wonder.

"I didn't know the northern lights could be red," I said, as a frosty breath cloud escaped my mouth. "I've seen pictures of purple but never this."

"It's been years since I've seen it myself," our young driver responded, a local boy who grew up hunting elk.

"So stunning," I replied, my eyes now focusing past my driver to a certain member of the crew behind him.

While I was blown away by the sky, I was equally blown away by a certain guy. Tall and fit, with cinnamon-colored hair, sweet blue eyes, and a handsome smile. He and another guy were on their knees, setting the camera to night mode to capture the incredible visuals. As though feeling my eyes on the back of his head, he turned to catch me, then winked.

I quickly dropped my gaze, feeling silly, then looked up again at the sky like the others, making sure not to look his way again. It was hard. He was damn cute.

We were one month into shooting, and this handsome soundman and I had only been crewed together a few times. Each time, we had been too busy to talk one-on-one. There were always so many people around. So, we settled for flirty glances (his) and blushing and butterflies (mine).

On my days off, I had been secretly hanging out with the host of the show. He was striking, and though I felt he wasn't my best match, we had fun together. I also had the impression Mr. Soundman was taken. Someone told me that he had hooked up with the curly-haired brunette in accounting. Which didn't add up because every time we had lunch or dinner in the mess hall, he would stare at me and grin and cross his arms across his chest as though to say *you're mine*. Meanwhile, I'd be caught dumping a second helping of fries on my plate, or doubling down on dessert, wishing no one had seen that.

The day after the northern lights, I woke up to a message: "Do you want to go for a hike? I know a good spot."

Mr. Soundman had checked the call sheet to see that we both had a day off. A shiver of deceit made its way up my spine. *What about the host? I can't date two men at once on the same show!* My mind wavered. But saying no would have meant blowing my one and only chance with him. A guy like that would not be the type to take sloppy seconds.

I couldn't remember the last time I'd had a date, let alone two guys vying for my attention. But we were fresh off the horror of 9/11, the first reality show to be green-lit just two weeks later, and it was like we'd been given another chance at being good humans. Top that off with being flown to film in the pristine outback of Alaska, and pretty much the whole crew felt we'd won the TV contractor lottery. Everyone was openhearted and social, with parties most nights in one of the set decorator's rooms. He had turned it into a disco and even built a bar with leftover wood from set construction. It was a behind-the-scenes lovefest.

Plus, odds were in my favor. The ratio of men to women on the crew was about six-to-one, and in Alaska, ten-to-one. This was the very reason producers had shipped five women up from LA in the first place. Surely these ladies could find a real man here. Maybe I could too. Though, quite honestly, I was there to work. I had made my peace.

Ten months earlier, having felt my clock ticking in a somewhat pronounced way, and feeling rather dramatic, I made a pact with God that if a man of husband potential did not surface soon, I'd accept that I wasn't meant to be married or have children. It was New Year's and I was visiting a producer friend at her parents' home in Martha's Vineyard. At the stroke of midnight, on the back of a cocktail napkin, she and I listed all the things we wanted from life, whether with a man or without.

High on my list was security; I wanted to own a proper home. At age thirty-two, it was time for me to put down roots. Next, if there was going to be a husband, he had to be entirely un-full of himself, unlike the pretty-faced wannabes who clawed their way to LA in hopes of a big break (including my recent master manipulator ex). Honesty was another nonnegotiable (again, hats off to my ex for helping me place that top five on my list). I also wanted adventure, to climb mountains, go spelunking, snowboard the Alps, sail to Fiji, dive the Great Barrier Reef, and more. Lastly, I wanted success. Ambition had come baked into me. Life's just more fun with the fixings.

"I figured you weren't originally from LA," Mr. Soundman said as we stepped onto the lookout, the snow packing beneath our boots with each step, sinking us to our ankles.

"How'd you know?" I preened, batting my eyelashes.

"First, your gloves." He pulled my hand to his as I quickly snapped it back.

"Stop!" I giggled.

"No, I like it." He pulled my hand again to inspect it closer. "I've never met a girl who duct-taped the fingers of her gloves."

"They're my favorite and they're still good, minus a few rips and tears." I flitted my hands at his face. "And look, there's a built-in goggle wiper. Pretty cool, eh?"

"*Eh?* There's that Canadian accent," he said with a smile. "That explains all the gear and why you'd want to keep these *awesome* gloves." He laughed, making fun of me.

It wasn't my fault I was thrifty. Pragmatism coursed through my veins. I grew up with a grandma handing me banana sandwiches on the same Styrofoam trays that her ground beef came on, cleaned of course. That way if I misplaced it, it was no loss. This was the same grandma who, on Halloween, gave trick-or-treaters fresh carrots from her root cellar and Kraft marshmallows from a bag. My brother's best friend was pissed and chucked the carrot at Grandpa's car. Which I did not appreciate one bit. Grandma also packed away a hope chest for me filled with real silver flatware, electric frying pans, and beautifully embroidered Hungarian linens, tucked away somewhere in my Santa Monica apartment at that very moment.

"Thank you," I said sarcastically, still giggling as he tugged me toward him, wrapping both arms around my puffy coat like I was a giant pillow.

"You're not like most girls, are you?" He looked at me intently, his powder-blue eyes gleaming from the reflection off the snow.

"What do you mean?" I knew exactly what he meant.

Most girls didn't lose their father at such a pivotal age. *Most* girls didn't have a virtuoso for a mother, off playing most of the time, no plans to remarry. *Most* girls didn't quit a cherry TV anchor/reporter job, sell their brand-new 4Runner, and take off to study at the New York Film Academy, only to return home broke, tail between their legs. Half the things I pursued were bold failures. The other half took me places I'd never dreamed of, like this . . .

"I'm not sure. You're just . . ." He looked up to think. "Different. Cute. I saw you pick up someone's trash on the glacier the other day."

"I hate litterbugs. Especially here. Look at this place." I swung my arm out to the expanse of silver trees and a half-frozen river decorated with frosty white boulders and a set of deer tracks.

"I know, there's nothing like being in nature and I figure you must ski or snowboard because you have the gear, and you're probably good at it, judging by your body. I mean, I'm not *judging* your body, well, I'm appreciating . . ." He chuckled. "You look strong."

I chuckled too. "Uh-huh, go on."

He brushed away a wisp of hair that was sticking to my cheek, then gently ran his finger along my lip. "And I just really want to . . ."—he hesitated—"kiss you, Shannon."

"Permission granted," I whispered, unable to contain the swarm of monarchs in my stomach. "Mr. Josh."

It was in that very moment I had a vision, or maybe a déjà vu, of he and I together, like forever together, married, with babies. I'd never done that before! *What kind of desperado thinks about marriage on a first date?* But I was thirty-two, and he was the first guy who reminded me of both of my brothers, and what I imagined my father had become for my mother in his last decade of life: hardworking, earnest, playful, kind.

Josh paused for another look, as though memorizing my features, then gently pressed his lips to mine . . . our very first kiss.

CHAPTER 12

How do you convince your overworked husband that if he wants to save your marriage, he needs to take a psychedelic plant medicine journey with thirty strangers in a villa on a cliff?

a) Drop him off. Pretend it's a low-stakes poker game. Cross your fingers he stays.
b) Be honest. You'll either be hailed a hero or spurned a madwoman.
c) Give him an ultimatum: "Go or else!" Pray it works because you have no clue what *or else* is and no means to back it up.
d) You don't. Best to just drop out and join the local Hare Krishna chapter instead. Those folks are fun.

CHAPTER 12.1

Ayahuasca Journey
September 2021

Until you make the unconscious conscious, it will direct your life and you will call it fate.

—Carl Jung

I was floating, I was dreaming, I was dead, I was alive. I was pulsing with the heartbeat of Gaia, flesh and blood, energy, sound, peace, vibration, earth, sky, water, fire; all things, no things, and everything at once.

Sitting before Maestro, one word flickered from the depths of my mind, from wherever spirit rests and we plug into Source. It glowed like a marquee: *Strength.*

Again the feeling of something inside me uncoiling, rising up my spine from root to belly, through chest and throat and out the top of my head, twirling into the ether. Taking the pain and creating a channel of love. Behind the vapor, past the smoke of the coil, *she* had been born—a cat, a lion, lying alongside the great felines of the sub-Sahara, then crouching beneath a tree in dense jungle where vines looped around branches and swung to the floor like heavy ropes, her coat turning black, her eyes yellow, and I felt her fur line my body like armor.

Maestro was breathing into me the spirit of the jaguar, the spirit of ultimate strength. Without moving an inch, I found myself scouring the wet grass of the tent on all fours, as though protecting my people, ready to rip those freshly purged demons to shreds.

Make no mistake, the room was full of them. Maestro's magic song, the *icaros*, was doing the very real work of clearing the space. With each violent purge came malevolence dislodged from the tissues of the cursed, and with each trauma we couldn't or wouldn't release, we held that curse somewhere deep in the marrow of our bones.

Maybe curse was the wrong word. Didn't matter. Without Maestro there to clear the void, we'd continue to be bound by chaos, stuck in loops of suffering and cruelty toward ourselves, toward others, toward Earth. Without Abuela and the angels to guide us on the journey, we might not return from despair, and we certainly would not recognize our role in it.

That's what we don't realize: We spend half our life disparaging. We're in despair even when we think we're not. Abuela showed this to me, dropping me into my most loathsome thoughts, feelings, and realities, then forcing me to live there for hours. Only after a thorough purging of my sorrows was she finally able to guide me home.

Never doubt your strength, I heard her say. *It's your job to help others find theirs.*

I began to smile. My body swayed the way the red ginger outside the kitchen window flickered in the wind. I felt light and free enough that I might float.

Maybe this was my superpower all along, right under my nose—to be strong, steadfast in ways others could not, and to be compassionate, fiercely so. I had now seen the horrors up close. Humanity deserves our care. This was the gift granted from all my hurts and abandonments, as well as the love and successes too. This was the gift of reliving it through Abuela—an alchemical gift from shamans of old, born of the woody Amazonian vine and precious chacruna leaves.

"*Om-gom-godda-budda, om-gom . . .*" Guillermo's voice cracked, the first glitch I'd heard from him all night. He cleared his throat, then kept right on the steady beat of the chant.

It was in this moment that I realized that he was a *man.* Not a spirit or a mountain or a mythological giant toad, but a very remarkable man, as human as I was. A shaman who, guided by the plant, could connect to the Great Spirit beyond, take our sorrows, fears, and the fractured bits of the good people who came for the medicine, and pull it back to Earth, to us, where Gaia and her progeny knew what to do. Binding us to the mycelium in her soil, up through roots and vines that pulsed with her heartbeat, where plant and medicine combine with man, woman, flesh, vein, artery, and bone; and where the shaman faithfully transmutes it into healing like the tick-tock of a clock, drumming it into us and into our spirit to make us whole again.

But we must be willing. We must participate. We must be open. We must agree.

Like a vacuum, I pulled huge whiffs of air into my lungs then pressed it out. In, then out. In, then out. Like nature herself pulsing great gusts across valleys and mountains and over the sea, an enigmatic force that connects us to all who walk this earth, all who did and all who will.

CHAPTER 12.2

Sea Salt

September 2018

It was four o'clock in the morning, and my pupils were the size of saucers. I'd just arrived home from my evening with Daniella, the magic chocolate and doing dishes. Josh was stirring, which meant he'd probably want sex, which I didn't feel like. My heart was juicy and full and I only needed to feel and to share, so I could *remember*. Then I wanted to sleep so I could function the next day, get the kids to school, as usual, only different this time, fully present.

Instead of waking crabby kids who were overstimulated and under-rested, I'd wake little light beings and nudge them toward their potential. Nothing drastic, just a slight shift on the dial—a couple degrees—toward love, toward leaning into their potential, toward their expansiveness. *Oh, what that could do for their perfect little hearts.*

"Honey, you need to go tomorrow," I urged Josh, our bodies tangled together after lovemaking, believing the plant medicine could wash away our troubles.

"I can't," he replied.

"It's the last night they'll be here. Daniella wants me back, but I told her you would go instead." I snuggled deeper into his chest cavity, less bothered than usual by his prickly chest hairs scratching my nose. "You need to experience this."

"It's your thing, Shannon." He stroked my cheek. "Sorry, but it's not for me."

"No!" I sat up, trying to keep my cool, clinging to my hope that we could fix things through the medicine. "I'm telling you, it's a rebirth. Aguirre's plant medicine is a conduit—a lifetime of information downloaded in one night—and he is a very skilled psycho-pharmacologist. He gives you a capsule or a chocolate or a small cup of tea and it's like a gentle spirit comes to heal your soul."

"Sounds cool." He kissed the top of my head. "Maybe another time."

He didn't get it.

"Josh—" I tried not to beg. "The pain we have, the stress and conflict, it's hurting us and our kids. It's visceral. It lives in our tissues." I tapped my chest. "You get to feel it leave your body, because that's where it lives. The plant leeches it from your bones and moves it to the sky . . ."

Josh listened. He wasn't shutting me up. This was good.

"I finally see a way out of our patterns. We poison ourselves with our neuroses. I see my role in our cycle of drama. It's a mirror. Our kids are mirrors and it's not pretty. I take full responsibility. That fight, moving back to Canada—I'm sorry I wasn't honest. Without truth, without love, we lose. Look at me." I lifted my head to connect eye to eye. "We need this."

He sighed and shifted onto his side, signaling he was ready for sleep. "Okay. We'll talk tomorrow. I've got an early meeting. Love you."

I kissed his shoulder, my body beaming like the moon, part of its cosmic structure—fully in acceptance of all that is. *The wind. Is. The rain. Is. The sun. Is. Fire. Is. The land. Is. No duality. Just a perpetual state of yes to all, yes to love.*

Twelve hours later, at four in the afternoon, Josh still was not home from work.

Why won't he return my messages? He's late. He'll miss Aguirre's opening sermon!

The kids were back from school and I was busy washing their smelly vinyl lunch bags while they watched *SpongeBob* and snuggled the dog. I tried Josh's phone for the fourth time when he finally picked up.

"Where are you?" I stepped outside to pace, not wanting the kids to hear.

"In my truck."

"You'll be late. You're normally home by now."

"I'm not going, Shan. I'm cooked." He let out a groan. "We had this couple from Arizona wavering all day, an eighty-thousand-dollar sale. We got to the end of the paperwork and their credit was rejected!"

Stupid couple, stupid credit, screwing up my big plans!

"I'm so sorry."

"I'm not in the mood. Plus, I work tomorrow."

"Josh, I didn't want to go either. Daniella made me go. It was the last thing I wanted and—oh my God—it was the best thing."

"Sorry, hon, not going."

My heart beat faster as blood jolted to my extremities and seemingly out my fingers and toes. The weight of my world hung on his decision.

"Listen to me," I said, reaching for a deep breath to halt the adrenaline surge, searching for that peaceful place from the night before. "Josh, I'm going to say this once: It's an ultimatum."

"Seriously, Shan?"

"You need to do this."

Silence.

"For Tyde and Canyen, but also for us." Breath. "Do it for *you.*" Tires rolling along asphalt. A lawn mower buzzing in the distance. "This medicine has come into our life for a reason. Daniella—a reason. I *need* you to do this. It's like fifty therapy sessions in one night."

More silence. My heart pumped like the cylinders in his truck. For a solitary moment, maybe the earth stopped.

Did I lose him? Is this a bad connection? Is he going through the Kalihiwai bridge dip? Where's the protest? He never makes it easy. He's rejected self-help his entire life. I grew up with Tony Robbins and Brian Tracy and Wayne Dyer. Why would Josh start now? Can't he feel me? Can't he see it works? Can't he see how badly he needs to connect to Spirit and heal his wounds? Who doesn't want to heal? Fuuuuuuuck!

"Shan, you there?"

On the edge of my seat. "Yes."

"Okay," I heard him exhale.

"Okay, what?"

"Okay, I'll go." Huge exhale. "But I'm going to miss work tomorrow."

"Good."

CHAPTER 12.3

That evening, 3:30 a.m.

Dear Mom,

Sleep eludes me. I know you know what that's like. Dead of the night, roaming the house. I'm still in a haze from the plant medicine. Ayahuasca and mushrooms in a chocolate. I'm told it's gentler that way, lighter, friendlier, less darkness compared to the tea. Not exactly the Amazon, but not bad for a prairie girl.

Can you believe it? Can you believe I tried it?

Now I talk to centipedes. Flicked on the light in the TV room and a centipede, huge, eight inches long, fell from a puck light, just missed my face. I'd scream but I'm too calm.

Can we be too calm?

She squirmed into a crack to hide. I thought to catch her so she wouldn't crawl into Canyen's bed and sting him in the middle of the night. It's like an alien sticking two sharp but supple needles deep into the flesh. *Jooooop!* Insert venom and release.

Three times, I've been stung, sticking my hand in dark places: a palm frond, cracks in the couch. Lisa told me that a friend of hers was stung in the vagina while sleeping (she sleeps naked, poor thing). We laughed our guts out.

Did you ever have a friend like Lisa?

Centipedes hate light. They run from it. Darkness is their safe place. We need the dark as we need the light. Otherwise, the light would blind us and how would we know our shadow?

One does not become enlightened by imagining figures of light but by making the darkness conscious. Maybe centipedes invented Carl Jung.

It's lonely in the middle of the night. The air feels ripe with secrets.

Where are you?

You've been gone so much that I no longer expect you to be home after ten years playing on cruise ships, sailing the seven seas, experiencing so much, your whole career a fortuitous whirlwind. Lucky you. They said they wouldn't hire you once you hit seventy.

What will you do if you can't entertain? Did you get what you wanted from your career?

I didn't. I thought my future was so bright I had to wear shades. I was wrong.

You were missed those years. Away from all of us. I should have been used to it. My boys were little then. They're less little now. I regretted not having you around.

Is that mine to regret or yours?

The best light is the light of the moon. A soft light that bathes us in forgiveness and hope, not bright sun interrogation and do, do, do. Moonlight says: *Forgive yourself. Forgive that girl for wanting so much. And you may as well forgive everyone else too.*

Did you want too much too?

Stupid question. I wanted the life of a talk-show host, a celebrity or a superhero, or the most fabulous person on Instagram. But it's not real. *Wants* can wreck a life. Half our desires aren't even ours, rather fabrications by media, marketers, liars, and dreamers . . . like me, clawing tooth and nail to prove myself.

I couldn't escape her, not even on the most isolated archipelago in the world! My want of validation was so heavy it garroted me like a noose. *Make me whole!* A chase, a recipe for rupture, and rupture we did.

Did you see this coming?

You're always too nice to tell me when I'm acting stupid. Sooner or later, the truth arrives like a head-on collision. Implosion brings failure. Failure brings opportunity. Rebuild and reset. That's the good news. Here's the bad.

For a while, I did nothing. Faked it. Held it together while I fell apart. All real support unaware or unavailable, then left behind in Canada. I just couldn't piece this transoceanic move into something useful, until now. Until I experienced the magical plant and a night of doing dishes.

Dishes—ha! I saw *the light* while doing dishes!

Can you believe it, Mom?

It's a perfect metaphor for being of service. No need to be acknowledged, it's too small for that. Just smile quietly and be the mother. Simple.

I realize how resentful I'd become about being *in service*. I used to wash dishes and my head-speak would run wild: *I hate how Josh and the kids never put their dishes away . . . I hate that they don't clean up . . . I hate that they never push their chairs in . . .* Hate's a low-vibe word. Hate may be the anti-Christ. *I know, dramatic much?* But it's the opposite of everything Christ stood for.

Did I learn that from the television or a teacher or you? Did I make it up? What came from who came from where? And where do I give back the lies?

Truth is hard to find when we're thinking about ourselves. Petty shit that adds up to nothing but a loop of annoyance, judgment, disillusion. It pulled my vibe so low I could have crawled. Too good for servant work, thinking I was wasting my talent and time.

Bullshit. Ambition keeps us from joy and appreciating the acts that make a good life. *Service to others is the rent you pay for your room here on Earth.* Muhammad Ali said that.

Surrender. Drudgery can be love too. The key is action. Service. Do.

Did you see this? Am I just slow?

You always knew how to serve. The gifted musician, performer on a stage, adored by strangers. I don't know what that's like.

What happens when the audience goes home?

My first journey didn't stick. It washed away with the flood that wiped out the island. Mama Kauai wept and she made me weep too. I wanted to be far away from this sad place. I yearned for home. I yearned for you—my mother!

Am I too old to need my mother?

I was already a mom and a wife, and I had to do the best I possibly could with my own children and husband. I quickly forgot about the burst of truth that hit me for six hours where my heart lit aflame and cracked open to show me what real love felt like. Magical. Unconditional. A mother's love. Like yours.

There were awakenings, at night, moon energy, feminine, subconscious. The moon is a force here. It illuminates the sky like a call to warriors with coded messages sprinkled through the stars. Black of night, I'd wake up aching with love for my boys and Josh and the mess that our broken hearts had made. The worst was weeks ago. Josh and I shaking and screaming a primal scream. Angry with the world. Things out of our control. That box, a wicked box of discord.

It wasn't our fault—was it? It's not anyone's fault, really.

I saw my ugly in his ugly, and his ugly saw mine. I wanted to hide, but not before I protected the boys. We couldn't continue like that. The kids wouldn't change. They don't know how. Not yet. They challenge, they forget, they push. It's their job.

We pushed so hard, we pushed so high, we pushed the moon clear from the sky . . .

It is *we*, the parents, who adjust. Prior to plant medicine, nothing worked. My not-so-divine masculine on autopilot, pushing, which meant there was no room for her, the feminine, creativity and love. I thought I could guide the universe in how to unfold for me, instead of trusting the universe to guide me in how to unfold for it.

Have you ever pushed so hard it hurt? Never mind, I know.

I didn't want to tell anyone my sorrows. Too ashamed. Also, I didn't want to feel frivolous, unworldly love from a magical plant. It felt indulgent. I felt judged. I forgot what it was like. I forgot to remember that plants are intelligent. They sing, talk, feel, and teach! They illuminate and command us to rise. None of this crumpling into a ball, feeling sorry and scared. *Face your demons, warrior-girl!* So, I did, thanks to Daniella.

Did you ever have an angel like Daniella?

Now, it's my job to hold space for the people I love, including you, but especially Josh and the boys. And it's okay that it's my job. I am mother. I am woman. I am nurturer and holding space is key.

That never meant much to me before—*holding space*. There's nothing passive about it. Rather, it's a state of willing love to someone through quiet presence so they can be who they are. Stop speaking and listen and hold them there. Allow them to be all the things: sad, mad, happy, frustrated, pathetic . . . Say yes to it all. Let them know that it's okay to be fully and completely human: good, bad, ugly, and divine.

Do you agree? Would you ever want to try plant medicine with me?

Doesn't matter. I feel complete no matter what anyone thinks. I'm not ashamed. *Outside validation no longer required.* This will fade, they say. Then I need to remember. That's all.

Mom, I'm sorry for the things you know, the things you don't know, the things I thought I knew, and for not always considering your journey and your hardships. I love you. Forgive me. Thank you for everything.

Forever, your dear daughter,

Shannon

CHAPTER 13

What do you do when you discover your heart's been broken and scattered into so many pieces, across so many galaxies, star clusters, and dimensions, and you only want to glue it back together?

a) Remember
b) Remember
c) Remember
d) All of the above

CHAPTER 13.1

Ayahuasca Journey
September 2021

When you understand your nature, you shine with your own light, like the sun. And like the sun, which is the only thing that does not cast a shadow, you no longer project your dark sides and the unhealed parts of your psyche onto others.[12]

Nearly finished with me, Maestro took a large sip of ceremonial rose water, gurgled and swirled it through his tongue and teeth, then cupped my jaw with both hands and blew into my face, two inches away, like a strong dry gale blasting my skin.

He whistled and swished, *shoooooeeeeeee*, clipping the *e* as though to seal it. Once, twice, three times, it sounded like the air compressors my grandpa used on his gravel trucks.

Our heads nearly touched. I saw him clearly now. This was not just a man but a relic, the edge of Everest, or a pyramid, a crystal light worker with the wisdom of the infinite inside him. I couldn't tell where he ended and the cosmos began. The lines on his face were like those of the Amazon, rifts and valleys, earth folding over earth. Hundreds of millions of years

[12] Alberto Villoldo, *The Heart of the Shaman: Stories and Practices of the Luminous Warrior* (Hay House, 2019), 12.

of evolution shrunken into this mysterious assembly of molecules, his eyes wide like black holes of possibility, billions of years of evolution tucked into that face.

Shooooooeeee.

Gaia blew her healing breezes through my body like a mighty wind off an ancient desert, the air heavy with the medicine of all the plants Guillermo had ever consumed. They entered me to work their magic and piece me back together. It was a smoky dense tonic, and I will never—as long as I live—forget what it felt like.

A thousand years of the Amazon was breathed into my spirit and corporeal frame that day. All to say, *You are not separate. You were never separate. All you had to do was trust.*

In that moment, I realized that we are the sum of all that came before us. Our birth delivers the blueprint of our existence inside a perfect human soul, the highest expression of God. And all this didn't just course through my mind in neon patterns and rainbow visions; it coursed through my body. Beyond the visits to astral planes and dimensions, this was an experience of feeling into my self in a way that only the plant medicine could do, deep into that part of me that was earth and cosmos too.

Did I feel what ayahuasca feels? Perhaps. Or did ayahuasca feel what I felt? A deep awareness that arrived in chills, sweats, prickles, shakes, tears, sobs, yawns, but no puking or pooping. Then long-buried emotion, gripping and tearing the cords of my heart, each pulse of knowing springing from that infinite intelligence at the center of it all.

"You're done." Sarah placed her hand on my shoulder and helped me rise to my feet.

"Thank you." I bowed with my hands in prayer to Maestro, who now sat still and silent as a rock, eyes fixed forward.

He didn't see what I saw. His was the invisible world around us.

Curling up on my mat with my mustard-colored sheet, I was a different person than the one who'd fallen on the edge of Guillermo's mat many minutes earlier. Cliché as it may have sounded, it was a rebirth. Now, like the spores of a dandelion lost to the wind, pulled from the edge of a riverbank, I felt my fractured bits return to me and stick to my heart like sap on a tree, restoring me to wholeness.

My hands floated above me to play with the air. I felt light, angelic, maybe I was glowing. I imagined Josh and I rolling together in space-time like shiny magnets, teetering on the edge of the cosmos in play, as if there was no one but us in the whole wide universe.

"Dear husband, I love you so much. You're the only one I want to share this with," I whispered to the soft night air.

Then, just as a seed would burst from the husk, a great golden cord shot from my belly button, a place the Vedas call *surya jal*, the solar plexus, the body's power center, my cosmic fire, my strength, my stamina, my will. Way up it soared into the sky, past the stars, and for a time, maybe a minute, or an hour, or maybe time didn't matter at all, I felt myself as a sliver of God, grafted and returning to the whole. Through this, maybe God's fractured bits were returning home to Him too.

CHAPTER 13.2

Salt Water

September 2018

It was 7 a.m. and Josh still wasn't back from the Daniella/Aguirre retreat on the cliff with the giant rose quartz crystal and the enchanted chocolates shaped like chubby little hearts. The kids would be awake soon. I needed to be sure my husband was okay.

The night before, I'd come home at four in the morning, so I wondered if something bad had happened. Maybe he wandered away from the retreat, deep into the jungle, never to return. That was always my biggest fear, abandonment: being alone on a farm on the tip of a volcanic mountain range in the middle of the ocean—without him.

"Hi," Josh said, sliding through the door to our bedroom like a ghost.

"Are you okay?" I sat up with a start. "You scared me. Tell me you're okay."

Josh slumped onto the bed, fully dressed, then dropped his head into his hands and began to cry.

"Josh." I stroked his head. "Josh?" I began to panic. "Are you okay?"

"It was good." He stared hard at me, as though he could see straight to my soul, his cheeks stained with tears, his eyes the color of celestite, radiating an ethereal crystal blue. "Really good. Really good people, good medicine. You were right."

I hugged him. "I love that you did this for us. I love you."

"I love you, Shan." And he hugged me harder than ever before.

Josh had tears in his eyes for a week, sorrow for traumas he'd buried so deeply he didn't even realize they were there. I saw the masks of anger, frustration, and misunderstanding begin to melt away. But I suspected this was just the beginning. We would need more work, more medicine, more integration, and more prayer.

He had taken the kanna and nothing else, nothing psychoactive, just loads and loads of CBD. This one therapeutic plant, along with Aguirre's sacred set and setting, was potent enough to crack open his heart and drudge up the pain of his childhood. Wounds I didn't know he carried, even after fifteen years of marriage and countless conversations about life and parents and friends and family, the painful relationship he had with his father, the hurt and dysfunction, which Josh was finally able to assemble and recognize the cycle with his own children. And though he was infinitely more present in our boys' lives than his father was in his, there were layers of anger and sadness so deep from traumas passed down alongside the same genes that gave him his blue eyes.

It's what we humans do: bestow our miseries, then pretend they're not real to protect our egos. We build fortresses around our hearts and bury the pain, only to have it follow us wherever we go to surface in tirades, cruelty, and darkness. Then we justify our actions through blame and victimhood. Meanwhile, the problem remains and continues to flare, until we stuff our hands deep into our guts and pull out the shrapnel from every last bomb that has ever exploded in our lives.

Our job, our only job, is to face our wounds head-on, then rebuild, create a life *of* purpose, *on* purpose, *with* purpose. And to forgive. Always to forgive. A meaningful life will always be one of love and connection, versus fear and separation.

That's what Josh did. He found compassion within himself so he could step into the sacred circle of meaningful life. That's what *we* did. We opened old wounds—scars, stories, blood, and bone—and let the light pour in. We faced that blinding light head-on, not to escape the pain but to meet it at its source. And there, in a brine of salty tears, the healing began, exactly where the breaking once was.

Josh never entered his time-share office again. He didn't even say goodbye.

CHAPTER 13.3

October 2019 – One year later

Up. Down. Arrived.

"Where am I?" I kicked at the sheets, confused. The feather duvet swirled around my body as though I was underwater, getting pummeled by a wave.

It's dark. It's gray. I'm ten years old and drowning . . . "Help!" I sat up with a start, then laughed at myself. *It's just a dream. I'm safe. I'm not ten, I'm fifty. Fifty? Yikes!*

"Hey Ma, Mama, Mom, Mommy, Mother!" Tyde called from the hallway with humor in his voice, then burst through the door into the bedroom.

However, it was not my Kauai door with the glass pane, dusty rose curtain, and ocean breeze slamming it shut. It was the extra-wide, sliding shoji door of my Lions Bay bedroom. Windows and doors were shut tight due to an autumn chill in the air. And there were no waves to yank me under for many miles, just the tempered water of the Howe Sound and a mattress so hard it felt like straw.

"Do we have today off school?" Tyde asked, flopping onto the foot of the bed.

We were home, old-home, Canada home. Josh and I had arrived a month ago, almost two years to the day that we had sold everything and departed for Kauai on a grand adventure to find ourselves. Every time I thought about it, I got a lump in the back of my throat the size of a bufo (slang for cane toad). It hurt, mostly because time layers memories like a delicious club sandwich and I could taste what we'd left behind in Kauai with each and every bite.

But we had to keep up optics. Mainland life was about that, acting like you planned it all along. *Dear Friends, we didn't fail at Kauai. We just missed you so much we came back!* Posting pictures on Instagram taken precisely at that moment of harmony and bliss, then chucking the camera in a drawer when the family takes a headfirst plunge into the swamp.

If there was one thing I'd learned, it was that life was a journey of successes and failures and the bumps in between. Why hide it? Each of us on a roller coaster, though maybe not the *same* one, ours was the Twisted Colossus, the force of gravity so great that half the time our entrails were in our eyeballs.

"It's a professional day," I said, unwinding the sheets that had tangled my torso into a whippy dip cone. "Time for some fun!" I swiped my hair away, then straightened my nightie to hide any loose bits.

At age fourteen, Tyde was easily grossed out by his parents. To state the obvious, a grown woman's body looked nothing like a teen girl's body, especially those on social media, wiry and firm, or over-the-top cartoonish voluptuous.

"Good!" He leaned toward Saffy to kiss her tiny mohawk. "She's so cute. I love her so much. Hey, Mom," he said, pulling at the duvet to snuggle under the covers with me. "Can I ask you a question?"

"Of course."

"How old were you when you lost your virginity?"

I choked up a laugh. "Excuse me?"

"You and Dad never talk to me about these things." He smiled a wry grin.

"Baloney!" I gave him a shove. "You, my son, have selective hearing."

Tyde played with Saffy's ears and jingled her tags that still had our Kauai phone number and address. I felt a pang of regret: the agony of being stuck between two places, both of which had brought out the best and worst in us. And Kauai did something else—she brought out a part of me I never knew existed, a side I most needed to see.

"If you won't do it, I'll have to be Canyen's puberty guide," Tyde teased.

"No way," Canyen grumbled from beneath Josh's pillow. He had wriggled over to the view side of the bed, groggy from a restless night of sleep.

For the last month, Canyen had been slipping into our bed around four in the morning, making for spotty sleeps for Josh and I. He'd roll sideways then upside down, then kick us, then kick the dog. The back and forth over the ocean had taken a small but stressful toll on his tender psyche. Thankfully, he was able to pick up where he left off at school. His elementary school went to grade 7, so he had the comfort of returning to the same class, same principal, same playground, and most importantly, the same friends.

Moving back had been easier than moving away. Josh and I sent the boys home a few weeks early in time to start the school year. They stayed with close friends while we packed our things and found an affordable groundskeeper and decent renters for the farm.

In typical *me* fashion, I couldn't just pack the house like a normal person. I had to make a *deal* with the renters that in exchange for half a month's rent, I would do their ten-day colonics package. So, while spending fourteen-hour days packing all our worldly possessions into boxes, yet again, then into a container, I also spent ninety minutes a day on a colonics board, over the toilet, with a steady current of ozonated water flushing my insides. Suffice to say, the whites of my eyes were glowing like moonbeams and I could not pinch an inch anywhere, except the inside of my thighs, and that wasn't budging without a suction.

It was all kind of weird. Weird in a good way—mystical, groovy, what-the-heck-is-even-happening weird. Just when Kauai was finally clicking—a solid crew of friends, me surfing my longboard without totally embarrassing myself, the sweet spot of meaning and momentum—we up and left. With the same wild force we'd left Canada two years earlier. We did it for the kids. For the schools. For free health care. For the relative sanity of Canada. And, okay, for me.

We had our troubles at the border but that was expected. Shipping my Mini home was the worst of decisions with five trips to the border for paperwork and rubber stamps, plus thousands of dollars in upgrades. *Thank you, Transport Canada!* But some days, if I squinted hard enough while driving the Sea to Sky Highway north, I could see the pink and peach rays of a tropical sunset behind the lush green mountains of Bali Hai.

And even with a second round of packing and container ships, border guards, and customs officers, what was most remarkable was that Josh and I never came close to an eruption. No Madame Pele, no hurricanes, no deluges. We griped a little but laughed together more. Maybe, just maybe, I had gotten what I needed from my precious Mama K.

"What's this about?" Josh strolled out of the bathroom with a towel tucked around his waist, no longer any sign of a tan, his hair slicked back from the shower exposing a view to a deepening widow's peak.

"Looks like Tyde needs the birds and the bees talk again," I teased, reaching my hand up to Josh's as he leaned over to kiss my forehead.

"No!" Canyen commanded, nestling deeper into the covers. "Tyde's a weirdo."

"One day, Canyen, you'll be googly in love just like your brother," I said while finger-combing Tyde's hair to the side, happy to be laughing instead of locked in the usual mom-versus-teenager tug-of-war. "So, what's her name, Tyde?"

I went to squeeze him but he rolled away too quickly with the dog cradled in his arms, his gangly limbs and elbows flailing about. He'd grown at least six inches in six months and was beginning to act more and more like a young man.

Now in grade 9, Tyde seemed to be Mr. Popularity thanks to his streaky blond surfer hair and cool stories from the tropical outback. He was almost six feet tall and bursting with life force, and I was happy to see an assortment of new, and the best of his old, in-the-flesh friends doing real-life stuff, rather than glued to a screen. In his affable way, Tyde would tell us who's smoking pot, having sex, skipping school, addicted to Snapchat (all of them), or vaping bubble gum–flavored chemicals.

"How come this is the first I'm hearing about this?" Josh said, slipping into the closet to get dressed.

"Dad, when are we going to Kauai?" Tyde asked, changing the subject. "I need to surf or I'll lose my progress."

Josh and I had cooked up a loose schedule of back and forth to Kauai. The kids would go to school *for free* in West Van until they graduated, and we'd spend summers and holidays in Kauai, adding up to three or four months of the year. Fingers crossed it would work.

"November break," Josh answered, "for ten days. If, only if, you're caught up with your assignments."

"All right, boys, time to get ready." I pounced to my feet. "We're taking you mountain biking in Squamish. We've got to meet Uncle Marc and the cousins at noon."

"Okay." Tyde rolled over Canyen and off the edge of the bed to land on the carpet, then looked up at me with doughy eyes. "Seriously, Mom, how old were you when you lost your virginity?"

"I'll tell you if you tell me about this girl," I whispered.

"No," he laughed, now wrestling my sock out of Saffy's determined grip. "Maybe."

"Listen," I said as I slid open the curtains to reveal a pristine but familiar view of water and islands in the distance and a giant cedar poking out of our deck.

It was so pretty that I wondered how we ever moved away from here in the first place, then imagined all the lemons ripening on the trees in Kauai, dropping to the ground, ready to be juiced into my lemon-ginger-honey concoction that I sold at the side of the road with the kids. The entire farm would be exploding with fruit right now: avocados, pineapples, tangelos . . . I then wondered how we ever moved away from Kauai.

"Here's the thing." I turned to lock eyes with Tyde, trying to avoid the spiral of regret about to ensnare me. Thoughts of what *could have been* would only pull me from the present and have me mentally flopping like a fish on a line. "First, be in a relationship—like, committed. Go slow. You've got your whole life to be a grown-up. Second, be in love. That's nonnegotiable. Third, sex makes babies, so use protection. And also? You're too young. So stop it."

"I know, Mom, don't worry. I'm just curious," he said, peering at me the way he did when he was small, crisp blue eyes wise beyond their years. "Love you."

"To the moon."

Nothing in Kauai came easy for us, despite Josh's hunger for the *simple life*. The island was all about copiousness of everything: life and death, harmony and conflict, rain and mud, ocean and wind, sun and sorrow, moon and wave after wave after wave . . . And she erupted through my entire family, making sure we felt all the feels and a little of the crazy.

Every day, I loved her more for her lessons. Mama Kauai gave me the tools to dive deep past the flotsam and jetsam, under the waves and below the seabed. I knew better how to connect with my husband and kids, even if I didn't always do it. I knew not to wash their fuzzy blankets when they smelled of cheese puffs and the dog, and to hug their sweet floppy heads every chance I got, because someday I'd miss it, probably too much. I knew to let things go and smell the roses and the cherry blossoms, and appreciate the songbird cranking out a tune, even and especially at six in the morning when I wanted to load a spaceship for Venus for a little peace and quiet. I knew that home is in the heart and that was never really the question. The question was always, *Where is my heart?*

For now, it rests high on a hillside on a giant rock swept by rain, snow, and the wild northern wind. But I could still hear her, with her thunder and lightning bolts and long-held secrets, whispering to me at night. She tells me she's waiting on the other side.

BOOK CLUB QUESTIONS

This book was written from the bones of a true journey—one that asked everything of me and gave me back more than I imagined. These questions are offered to deepen your reflection and spark honest conversation. My hope is that they invite you to reflect, connect, and remember what matters most to you.

Chapter 1 – When a Good Life Isn't Enough

1. Shannon uproots her entire life in search of "something more." Have you ever felt the same urge, and if so, what did you do with it?
2. What does Shannon's nervous energy before her first ayahuasca ceremony reveal about the human desire for healing versus control?
3. The family's arrival in Kauai is described with a mix of beauty and tension. What were your impressions of the move? Would you have made the same leap?
4. In the flashback to Shannon's childhood, what seeds do you see being planted for her future search for healing?

Chapter 2 – When the World Flips

1. Shannon begins bargaining with God as the ayahuasca journey intensifies. How do you respond to fear—with resistance, prayer, surrender?

2. The family's first night in their new home is full of disappointment and chaos. What does this reveal about expectation versus reality?
3. How does grief show up in Shannon's origin story—especially around her father's death—and how does that shape her adult self?
4. In this chapter, what does "home" mean—physically, emotionally, and spiritually?

Chapter 3 – Dream or Detour?

1. Shannon's medicine journey begins to expose personal flaws and hypocrisies. How do you think plant medicine mirrors our inner selves?
2. The dream of paradise turns into a confusing reality. What does this reveal about the gap between fantasy and embodiment?
3. How do the early experiences in Kauai reflect the classic "dark night of the soul" in transformational journeys?
4. In the college flashback, Shannon seeks independence in an unfamiliar place—how does this story parallel her present-day move to Kauai?

Chapter 4 – Maggots, Micromanagers, and Meaninglessness

1. In the depths of her ceremony, Shannon enters a loop of birth and death. How do you interpret this symbolic cycle? Have you ever felt trapped in a similar loop?
2. When Shannon monologues during an unexpected visit with Tyde's new friend's mom, what deeper emotions might have been surfacing?

3. The chapter includes a moment of caregiving with Josh's mother who remains controlling even in illness. What lessons around boundaries, compassion, or family obligation arise for you?
4. This chapter leans heavily into discomfort—insects, sickness, awkward social dynamics. What role does discomfort play in transformation?

Chapter 5 – What Would You Save from the Fire?

1. Shannon describes a haunting vision during her ceremony, feeling herself as one of the parasites. What do you think this metaphor is trying to reveal about shadow?
2. The arrival of their shipping container causes more chaos than joy. What does this scene say about material possessions and their relationship to emotional baggage?
3. The trip to Hungary with her mother reveals deep tension in Shannon's marriage. How do you interpret the collision of cultural roots and current identity?
4. When everything feels like it's burning down—metaphorically or otherwise—what is the one thing *you* would save?

Chapter 6 – Ballistic Missiles and Biblical Warnings

1. The emergency missile alert moment forces Shannon into a real-time reckoning. How does the possibility of

death recalibrate her priorities and fears?

2. In ceremony, Shannon is pushed to her absolute limits. What's the difference between spiritual surrender and spiritual panic?
3. Her grandmother warned her against "dark spirits." How does Shannon reconcile her grandmother's faith-based warnings with her plant medicine experience?
4. This chapter brings in the legacy of female elders—grandmother, mother, Shannon. What is the role of ancestry in this stage of her journey?

Chapter 7 – What the Children Know

1. Shannon is confronted by her careless use of language and energy. How do the words we speak shape our spiritual and emotional reality?
2. The family's physical environment has shifted from "paradise" to persistent rain and illness. What does the weather symbolize here?
3. When Canyen says he "picked Mommy from the clouds," how did that moment land with you? Do you believe children carry spiritual memory or wisdom?

Chapter 8 – Sassafras and the Storm

1. In this chapter, Shannon reaches a profound emotional breakthrough with the help of another plant medicine, sassafras. What role do emotional "openers" (plant or otherwise) play in healing?
2. Female friendship becomes a lifeline here. What do these sacred sisterhood moments reveal about what

women offer each other in midlife?

3. The hundred-year flood is both literal and symbolic. What did the deluge wash away for Shannon—and what did it reveal?
4. Shannon makes a silent promise to her son that may be impossible to keep. Have you ever made a promise out of love that challenged your truth?

Chapter 9 – Half the Family Wants to Leave

1. The surfing scene reveals disappointment in a moment of hope. What does Shannon's reaction to the bully and Josh's silence reveal about old wounds in partnership?
2. In the hospital flashback, young Shanni scolds her mother with piercing honesty. How do children reflect our emotional states in surprising or uncomfortable ways?
3. This chapter begins to expose the rift forming in the family. Have you ever experienced a time when a dream or risk fractured your household's unity?

Chapter 10 – Therapy, Dogs, and Tree Wells

1. Shannon begins to doubt whether her plant medicine work is divine or dangerous. How do we discern the difference between healing and harm on spiritual paths?
2. The new family dog offers hope for connection. What role do animals play in helping us regulate, reconnect, or soften?
3. Shannon's near-death experience in a tree well becomes a metaphor for risk and rebirth. Have you had a brush

with danger that later revealed hidden strength?

Chapter 11 – Screens, Chocolate, and the Warrior Path

1. The family's tension over screen time mirrors modern struggles. What's your relationship with technology, and how does it impact emotional or spiritual balance?
2. Shannon's first ayahuasca journey comes in the form of a gentle chocolate shaped like a heart. How does this experience compare to the overarching story of her drinking the more potent ayahuasca tea from the Amazon?
3. Have you ever experienced a moment of divine light embodiment? What does "the warrior path" mean to you, and how do we walk it in daily life?

Chapter 12 – A Villa, an Ultimatum, and a Letter to Mom

1. Shannon insists that Josh attend his first plant medicine retreat. Where is the line between a loving nudge and a spiritual ultimatum—have you ever crossed it?
2. In her expanded state, Shannon receives the jaguar spirit and experiences deep feminine power. What animals or archetypes do you associate with your own strength?
3. The transformation Shannon experiences with Daniella is mirrored by her hope that Josh will understand. How do we navigate when partners grow at different speeds?
4. Shannon writes a vulnerable letter to her mother. What would you say in a letter to a parent—spoken or

unspoken—that could open your heart or theirs?

Chapter 13 – The Heart Remembers

1. In her final ceremony, Shannon sees Maestro not as a man but as the very fabric of the universe. How do you interpret this vision? Have you ever glimpsed a moment of divine unity?
2. Josh's emotional opening marks a huge turning point. How does this shared healing experience shift their marriage?
3. Shannon describes her heart as scattered across galaxies, then slowly remembered. What pieces of your own heart are you still calling home?
4. The final scene reveals that Shannon and the kids have once again crossed the ocean in search of a dream. What does "home" mean now—and how has it changed?

Sneak peek at *The Mother Vine* sequel

September 2021. Back on the pineapple farm . . .

The sun fills my pores like beams of golden honey. My skin blooms a dusty rose, while earth-colored freckles form beneath. Is this it? Is this how I tan now, like a spotty old lady? Not the Coppertone caramel of my youth? I don't feel old. Anyway, I suppose it's not just about getting bronzed; it's about life-giving photons that ride on waves of infrared, sinking past skin, through sinew, to bone, firing up the mitochondria, those tiny fireflies in our cells that carry our spark. Life is so yummy. How I've missed this—the temperate breath of Kauai. Stepping onto spongey grass thick as shag carpet, cradling our orchard in a velvet hush of green. Lying here now, it tickles my legs and stomach. And who knows how many venomous centipedes dig in the dark dirt beneath me, daring to poke at the slab of tender flesh above them.

I spoke softly, repeating the words I'd just written in my journal, then rolled to my back to expose my powder-pink belly to the sun. This was the beginning of my quest to take the *nervous* out of my nervous system, to override and expand past that steady drip of cortisol that I'd become accustomed to.

Palm fronds rustled in the breeze while the buzz of Josh on the Weedwacker sliced the stillness like skate blades on a frozen pond. It was like we had never left. I took a deep breath in through my nose, then closed my eyes and held it.

Yellow and white starbursts lit the back of my eyelids as flickering sunrays poked through cloud after cloud—a most impressive light show. It had been too long since I'd laid in the sun, eyes shut on the grass, nothing to pull me this way or that. I finally blew out a blustery exhale feeling more peaceful than I had in the entire two years we had just spent in Canada.

"Mom, where are you?" Tyde called from the house.

I ignored him. Just for a minute. All I'd wanted was a single hour of no one needing me.

Plus, I was processing. There had been a lot of that lately, processing events and feelings in an out-of-body sort of way. It felt as though I might no longer be material, rather a swirl of energy, barely encased, the wind picking away at my frame, dissolving it to the ether the way dandelion pappi escape to the sky.

"Mom, Canyen and I are going surfing with Jowen!" Tyde yelled.

"Oh, Canyen too?" I squinted, forming a visor on my brow with my hand.

My kids had a way of dropping me right back into my body, no matter where my mind had been. Since we'd left Kauai for Canada, the world seemed to have turned inside out. I'd always thought things were a bit mad here, but having never lived on any other planet (that I knew of), I lacked the comparison. I chalked it up to the usual culprits: greed, war, and the Peter Principle (a classic from my mom's bookshelf)—incompetence and gluttony locked in a slow, grinding dance of destruction.

I hadn't grasped just how deeply those grisly tentacles had threaded themselves into every layer of life. How blind we'd been. And to think, the whole thing sparked by a noxious microscopic protein, slipping silently into our collective bloodstream . . . and just as stealthily, into our collective psyche.

The fear, the grief, the unraveling, all bound to polar ends of ignorance and awakening.

"He'll probably just rope swing," Tyde said with sarcasm. "But I'll try to get him to surf. The waves are good right now."

"Will you be home for dinner?" I listened for the sound of his voice, which bent and swirled around the corners of the house, in and out of range. "Should I make enough for your friends?"

"Probably," he said, his tone becoming more distant, colliding with the sound of truck doors slamming and young male voices.

I flopped back into position. "Now, where was I?" I said to myself, content roasting like a hot dog under a heat lamp, back to my body as a slur of molecules.

Ahh, yes, deep breath. I was somewhere between the center of the earth and the moon, no longer solid, just energy, atoms—actually, smaller than atoms, electrons, biophotons, strings!

I was feeling particularly smart for having paid only twenty-five dollars for a holotropic breathwork course and getting my every penny's worth. It was all the rage online and probably only a matter of minutes before everyone on Kauai was doing it. Here where all things cosmic/new age/spiritual birthed their way into the zeitgeist.

This shit actually works! I can't believe I feel euphoric from just breathing really hard, and fast, so fast my fingers clamped into lobster claws. Now that was strange.

The concept was to breathe rapidly for twenty minutes through the mouth (*for twenty whole minutes, in-out-in-out-in-out*). According to the two psychiatrists who founded it in the seventies, this quick, open-mouth breathing technique would shift the balance of oxygen to carbon dioxide in the bloodstream. As CO2 dropped, the brain would release feel-good chemicals that led to strange sensations and vivid images, possibly uncovering lost memories and pent-up emotions. Which explained me tearing up ten minutes earlier for no apparent reason.

"Breath is the bridge between the seen and unseen. It's the mystery force that animates life," said the man in the video. He also said most people take their breath for granted, lumping it in with the basic technology of being human—like hunger, thirst, sleep. Rubbish. Breath is far more sacred than that.

Everyone knows the rule of threes: Thirty days without food, three days without water, three minutes without air, equals death. Usually. Humans always defy the rules. We're so much greater than biological robots—complex-yet-figure-out-able material beings (says science)—that's just half the story. The other half is a wonderful mystery. I was all about the mystery because that's where truth lives. And, like most of my recent pursuits, deeper investigation (and a few rabbit holes) could only inch me closer to answering all the questions I had for God.

When I finally sat up properly, as told to do by the nice man on the video with a scarf the size of a twin sheet twisted around his neck, heaviness returned. My heart beat rapidly, pulsing through my chest and into my ankles and thumbs. *Great, back to being a slab of hot meat again.* I only wanted to be the gravity-free orb I was a few moments ago. Maybe forever. The troubles of the world didn't matter there.

"We're living in end times." Grandma's voice boomed from the speakers of yesteryear, echoing stories from the Book of Revelation—seven plagues, fire, brimstone, wrath of God.

It was that kind of talk—plus an ill-timed dystopian Netflix drama (*Years and Years*—two thumbs down)—that sent me into my very first panic attack two days ago. That and a pot gummy. Combined with on-again, off-again government lockdowns, plus media telling people *we're all gonna die*, it took my full mental fortitude to override it. My hope was that my exotic new pursuits (holotropic breathwork and a special three-day ceremony coming up) would make week five of pandemic house arrest bearable. This or chew my arm off.

"Honey!" Josh made his way toward me from the banana patch where he'd begun chopping banana trees that had finished fruiting to make way for their rhizomes. "Tell me again, when does your mom arrive? And when is the retreat?"

"This weekend." I giggled. He was covered in dirt. "Mom arrives three days later."

"Already? I don't think I'm ready. And didn't you say we couldn't go together?"

Josh and I had signed up for a ceremony to drink ayahuasca—jungle-style, just as Amazonian tribes had done for thousands of years. Real deal. Bare earth, stars overhead, and a true-blue Peruvian shaman at the helm. This wasn't going to be anything like our gentle warm-up with Daniella a few years earlier, the sassafras, the kanna, the special chocolate. That was empathogenic plant medicine with a side of sparkle. Ayahuasca tea from the Amazon was something else entirely. The mother of medicines. No frills. No fluff. Just you, the brew, and the cosmos. No hand-holding. No talking. Definitely no snack breaks. And yes, there would be purging. Buckets of it. And visions. Like, *close-encounters-with-your-soul* visions.

With the global pandemic looming like a storm cloud over the people of planet Earth, the timing could not have been better. I needed a break, distraction, lightness, love, hope, anything other than doom and gloom. This felt necessary, ancient meets out-of-this-world healing. Aside from Daniella, no one

I knew had ever done a real ayahuasca ceremony. Most of my friends had never even heard of it. Plus, far as I could tell, there were only a few reliable ways to reach divine alignment, and I wanted to try all of them.

"I go Friday, you go Saturday, then Sunday we go together," I said with a hollow sort of confidence, hoping Josh wouldn't hear the wobble.

Every time fear crept in, I reminded myself: This was part of the plan. A cosmic breadcrumb trail. Josh and I were piecing together the puzzle of this world, and whatever might lie beyond it. After the litany of sanity-flipping global events, this felt not just bold but necessary.

"I'm not so sure, Shan." Josh shrugged, then wiped his brow with the back of his hand, dirty from chopping, whipping, and digging.

"Me neither." I laughed. "But we're doing it. *And* we need to start the diet soon, like tomorrow, or else."

"Or else what?"

"It could mess with the medicine."

"How so?" Josh looked at me, eyes wide.

"I don't know. Just no coffee, no tryptophan, that means no turkey, also no citrus, onions, and garlic, just eat really clean. Starting now." I scratched my legs, itchy from the grass.

"No coffee?" He looked at me like I'd just asked him to squirrel-suit into the middle of a lava-spewing volcano. "When were you going to tell me?"

"Today." I brushed the dirt off his chin, pretending I had it under control. When really, I had only just read the handbook that morning.

I'd been so lost in breathwork and housework and coursework and understanding-the-world work that I had completely lost track of time. *Shannon*, I said to myself admonishingly, *were you seriously planning to wing it? You don't wing an ayahuasca ceremony!*

"Don't worry." I tapped Josh's hand. "It's only for a few days. I'll feed you right."

He pressed his finger onto my stomach. "You're getting crisp," he said, then watched the blood pour back into his fingerprint.

"Stop it." I swiped his hand away. "Anyway, cross your fingers we make it through our first night." I coughed up a giggle from somewhere in my gut, then immediately regretted it.

"What do you mean 'cross your fingers'?" Josh flopped onto the grass beside me, looking anxious, while specks of dirt flung through the air.

"Nothing. We'll be okay." I inhaled deeply then flattened my body to stretch my arms above my head to stare at the clouds drifting by like sheep in a herd, hoping to be brave enough for the both of us.

He sighed and turned his gaze to his happy place—the fruit orchard he'd so carefully coaxed into perfection. "I don't know, Shan." His eyes scanned the trees while the breeze tugged at his collar, flapping it against his jaw until he caught it with calloused fingers that yardwork had worn raw. "I just hope there's still time to change my mind."

No! You mustn't. We need this, I thought but did not say. That particular neural groove—the *please-please-please gimme-gimme-gimme*—ran deep. It took every fiber in my stubborn blonde head to not bulldoze my way to a yes, to leave Josh to contemplate in silence, to let him think, to let him choose.

Truthfully, it wouldn't have been the worst thing if he didn't go. This was his path to walk. Anyway, the silence between us was nice. Better he listened to the wind than me . . .

ACKNOWLEDGMENTS

First, I want to thank my mother, Marguerite, for being both a character in these pages and a quiet force in my life. You've shown me strength, softness, and what it means to keep going. You've handled pressure with the poise of a seasoned mountain, and always placed beauty at the foundation of everything. Some say the universe was formed not only by love but also by beauty. You've taught me both so elegantly.

To my grandmother, Helen, whose memory still grounds me, thank you for being one of my earliest and most enduring teachers. Much of the seeker I've become traces back to you. Your wisdom lives in me like a thread woven through everything I do.

To my sister, Robin, thank you for being a source of fun and creativity in my early years. You treated me like your living doll, putting me in parades as one of your *Flowerettes*, teaching me baton and other lessons. Your devotion as sister, mother, grandmother, and auntie inspires.

To my brothers, Marc and Troy, thank you for shaping me with both grit and grace. You toughened me up in all the right ways, but you also showed me kindness when I needed it most. Writing this book let me flow back into those early days, when our family was whole and the world was small, and let me cherish them all over again.

To my dad, Jim, your light, your humor, and your steady, loving presence is woven throughout this book. Losing you shaped me in ways I've only just come to understand. The strength I had to grow, the resilience I had to find, these are the roots beneath everything I've become. In many ways, the path that led me to ayahuasca began with the pain of losing you. Thank you for the deep imprint of your love.

To the women and men of my extended family—thank you for the gatherings, the kinship, the stories, the resilience, and the love. You are the soil I grew from.

To the dear friend who introduced me to plant medicine (*you know who you are*), your nudge changed everything, and I honor that moment and the deep ripple it created in my life.

To my dear friends who read and offered thoughtful feedback on early drafts—Jodi Roth, Kylie Barker, Lisa Hicks—to those who've championed my writing over the years, holding space for late-night ramblings, creative doubt, and everything in between—Andree Fiorvich, Christy Leslie, Diana Nakka, Heather Cornell, Heather Hood, Jackie Bagley, Joanna Baxter, Joanna Wheeler, Karin Willard, Krystal Penrose, Leah Pagonis, Meighan Jury, Minoo Greenhall, Nicole Alagich, Pegge Erkeneff, Stara Luz Anana, Susan Teton, Tanya Cosgrave, Tanis Fritz, Theone Masoner, Wendy Vogrincic—to writing coach Laura Lentz whose creative fire inspired me in myriad ways—to Cea Person and Jane Morgan whose sharp minds and generous hearts helped shape this book into its clearest form—thank you from the bottom of my heart.

To those whose names may not appear here—friends near and far, online and otherwise, who offered kind words, thoughtful comments, or quiet encouragement through the years—please know, I felt you. Your support reminded me that my words mattered. Female friendships, especially during this midlife passage, are sacred, as we come together as mothers, sisters, and soul companions. You are part of this story too.

To my publisher, Brooke, thank you for your faith, your patience, and your eye for what matters. And to the team at She Writes Press and The Stable Book Group, thank you for shepherding this book into the world with professionalism and care.

To my boys, Tyde and Canyen, you are my greatest teachers. The mirror, the test, the gift. Thank you for growing with me, for letting me learn as I parented, and for showing me who I truly am. You were just boys in these pages; now you are young men, and remarkable ones at that. Steady, smart, and kind to the core. You will always be in my heart, and I in yours—quite literally, as science tells us I'll carry your cells in my body for the rest of my life. What a wonder. What a bond.

To my husband, Josh, you've been my steady ground through every wild wave. I know it's puzzled you, this urge I have to sit for hours and shape stories while life blooms outside our door, but you never made me wrong for needing it. More than that, you had the courage to join me in this journey, to meet the medicine and do the work alongside me. That takes strength. You're my rock, my protector, and my partner in becoming. I couldn't have found my voice without you.

Finally, to Mother Nature, thank you for the wisdom of the plants. What an extraordinary thought, that a plant might fulfill its destiny by living through us, helping us heal. That we, in return, offer it the gift of our breath, our story, our surrender. I bow to the intelligence of the natural world, for its medicine, its mystery, and its mercy.

And Mama Kauai—this land has held me, tested me, fed me, and grown me. She is fierce and fertile, raw and generous, loving and wild. For those who come with reverence, she gives in abundance. For those who don't, she teaches hard truths. I am endlessly grateful to be her guest, her student, and her daughter in spirit.

And to every reader holding this book, thank you. I hope something in these pages has opened something in you.

God bless.

Step into your next chapter with me.

If *The Mother Vine* stirred something in you—a longing to heal more deeply, to reconnect with your body, or to explore the sacred intelligence of plant medicine—I've created a space to help you continue that journey.

Visit **ShannonNering.com** to explore my work, join the Glo sisterhood and find healing protocols alongside my recorded **Glo Well Cleanses**, simple yet powerful programs designed to help you reset physically, emotionally, and energetically from wherever you are.

You'll also find my **Free Plant Medicine Dieta & Preparation Guide**—a gentle protocol to align your body and spirit before ceremony, or anytime you're ready for deeper clarity and connection.

Come walk this healing path with me.

It's not just a detox—it's a homecoming.

Loved the journey?

Kindly leave a review on Amazon or Goodreads so *The Mother Vine* can find new hands and hearts.

ABOUT THE AUTHOR

photo credit Shannon Nering

Shannon Nering is a former television producer, director, and on-air host whose two-and-a-half-decade career took her from newsrooms in Calgary to reality shows in Los Angeles and Vancouver. After years creating stories for the screen, she turned her lens toward the healing arts. A **Registered Holistic Nutritionist**, her work bridges the worlds of media, motherhood, and modern health transformation, drawing from advanced studies in consciousness and ongoing PhD research in natural medicine.

Through her wellness practice, **Glo Kauai**, and her online platform, **ShannonNering.com**, Shannon supports women through midlife vitality and transformation, leading seasonal detoxes and retreats from her home on the North Shore of Kauai.

Looking for your next great read?

We can help!

Visit www.shewritespress.com/next-read
or scan the QR code below for a list
of our recommended titles.

She Writes Press is an award-winning
independent publishing company founded to
serve women writers everywhere.